JOURNAL FOR THE STUDY OF THE OLD TESTAMENT
SUPPLEMENT SERIES
138

JSOT Press
Sheffield

The Right Rev. Professor Robert Davidson, Moderator of the General Assembly of
the Church of Scotland, 1990–91.

TEXT AS PRETEXT

Essays in Honour of
Robert Davidson

edited by
Robert P. Carroll

Journal for the Study of the Old Testament
Supplement Series 138

Copyright © 1992 Sheffield Academic Press

Published by JSOT Press
JSOT Press is an imprint of
Sheffield Academic Press Ltd
The University of Sheffield
343 Fulwood Road
Sheffield S10 3BP
England

Typeset by Sheffield Academic Press
and
Printed on acid-free paper in Great Britain
by Billing & Sons Ltd
Worcester

British Library Cataloguing in Publication Data

Carroll, Robert P.
    Text as Pretext: Essays in Honour of
    Robert Davidson.—(JSOT Supplement
    Series, ISSN 0309-0787; No. 138)
    I. Title II. Series
    221

    ISBN 1-85075-295-8

CONTENTS

This collection of essays in honour of Professor Robert Davidson attempts to celebrate a number of notable achievements of this outstanding Scottish churchman and scholar. It is published for the occasion of his sixty-fifth birthday (30 March 1992), but it also marks his retirement from full-time university teaching (30 September 1991) and nods in the direction of his having been the moderator of the General Assembly of the Church of Scotland (1990–91). With his retirement from the Chair of Old Testament Language and Literature in the University of Glasgow, an active university career teaching Bible for almost forty years comes to a close. Mosaic in length, Robert's teaching, unlike Moses' wilderness career, will not come to an end with his retirement but will continue, at a lesser level, to contribute to the life of the Department of Biblical Studies in the years to come. This volume, however, does mark his passing as a full-time University man and acknowledges the length and power of his contribution to teaching Bible in the four ancient universities of Scotland.

Born in Fife—I cannot hope to convey to those who do not know Scotland just what the word 'Fifer' signifies—he has been associated with each of the ancient universities. He studied at St Andrews (classics and then BD, with distinction in Old Testament), then taught in the Department of Biblical Studies (Faculty of Arts) in Aberdeen, before returning to St Andrews to teach there. Moving on to Edinburgh in 1967 he eventually succeeded John Mauchline in the Chair of Old Testament at Glasgow in 1972. Thus he has had the unique experience of teaching Bible in all four universities and in three of the Faculties of Divinity. His strength as a teacher of Hebrew Bible and Old Testament theology will be testified to by many, many students across the length and breadth of Scotland. As professor in the Faculty of Divinity he has also functioned as Head of Department, Dean of the Faculty and also has been the Principal of Trinity College. As conductor of the Trinity College Choir his tolerance has been saintlike. His churchmanship was recognized by the Church of

Scotland when it made him the Moderator of the General Assembly, an honour which poetically coincided with Glasgow's year of being European City of Culture (1990).

The guiding principle governing this collection of essays is the notion of the Bible as the generator of other texts and cultural productions. The contributions are drawn from Robert's wide range of colleagues and former students and focus on many different aspects of this generative force within the Bible itself and in materials related to it. The intertextuality of the Bible is the heart of the matter. In putting these essays together I must acknowledge the assistance of my colleague Alastair Hunter for contributing the bibliography of Robert's work and that of Margie Balden (secretary of the Department of Biblical Studies) for turning Christopher Evans's original manuscript into readable type for publication. I should also thank Christopher Evans for allowing me to publish here his 1985 Alexander Robertson Lecture as a contribution to this collection. All of us join in wishing Robert a happy retirement, while knowing that he will go on teaching and publishing, we hope, for many years to come.

Robert P. Carroll

ABBREVIATIONS

AB	Anchor Bible
BDB	F. Brown, S.R. Driver, and C.A. Briggs, *Hebrew and English Lexicon of the Old Testament*
BETL	Bibliotheca ephemeridum theologicarum lovaniensium
Bib	*Biblica*
BZ	*Biblische Zeitschrift*
BZAW	Beihefte zur *ZAW*
CBQ	*Catholic Biblical Quarterly*
CPJ	*Corpus Papyrorum Judaicarum*
Enc Jud	*Encyclopedia Judaica*
ExpTim	*Expository Times*
FOTL	Forms of Old Testament Literature
FRLANT	Forschungen zur Religion und Literatur des Alten und Neuen Testaments
GKC	*Gesenius' Hebrew Grammar*, ed. E. Kautzsch, trans. A.E. Cowley
GRBS	*Greek, Roman & Byzantine Studies*
Int	*Interpretation*
JBL	*Journal of Biblical Literature*
JJS	*Journal of Jewish Studies*
JNES	*Journal of Near Eastern Studies*
JSJ	*Journal for the Study of Judaism*
JSNTSup	*Journal for the Study of the New Testament*, Supplement Series
JSOT	*Journal for the Study of the Old Testament*
JSOTSup	*Journal for the Study of the Old Testament*, Supplement Series
JTS	*Journal of Theological Studies*
LSJ	Liddell–Scott–Jones, Greek–English Lexicon
NTD	Das Neue Testament Deutsch
NTS	*New Testament Studies*
OBO	Orbis biblicus et orientalis
OTL	Old Testament Library
RB	*Revue biblique*
RSR	*Religious Studies Review*
SBLDS	SBL Dissertation Series
SBS	Stuttgarter Bibelstudien
SJT	*Scottish Journal of Theology*
SNTS	Supplements to New Testament Studies

SNTSMS	Society for New Testament Studies Monograph Series
TWNT	G. Kittel and G. Friedrich (eds.), *Theologisches Wörterbuch zum Neuen Testament*
TynBul	*Tyndale Bulletin*
TZ	*Theologische Zeitschrift*
USQR	*Union Seminary Quarterly Review*
VT	*Vetus Testamentum*
WBC	Word Biblical Commentary
WUNT	Wissenschaftliche Untersuchungen zum Neuen Testament
ZAW	*Zeitschrift für die alttestamentliche Wissenschaft*
ZNW	*Zeitschrift für die neutestamentliche Wissenschaft*

LIST OF CONTRIBUTORS

A. Graeme Auld is Senior Lecturer in Hebrew and Old Testament Studies at New College, University of Edinburgh.

John M.G. Barclay is Lecturer in New Testament in the Department of Biblical Studies at the University of Glasgow.

Ernest Best was Professor of Divinity and Biblical Criticism (New Testament) in the Faculty of Divinity at the University of Glasgow (1974–82).

Robert P. Carroll is a Professor in the Department of Biblical Studies (Hebrew Bible) and currently Dean of the Faculty of Divinity at the University of Glasgow.

Robert B. Coote is Professor of Old Testament at San Francisco Theological Seminar, San Anselmo, California.

Paul E. Copeland is a postgraduate research student of Robert Davidson's, is between ministerial posts and currently lives in Kansas.

Christopher F. Evans is Emeritus Professor of New Testament at King's College, University of London.

J.C.L. Gibson is Professor and Head of Department in Hebrew and Old Testament Studies at New College, University of Edinburgh.

Alastair G. Hunter is Lecturer in the Department of Biblical Studies (Hebrew Bible) at the University of Glasgow.

William Johnstone is Professor of Hebrew and Semitic Languages in the University of Aberdeen.

Heather A. McKay is a postgraduate research student in the Department of Biblical Studies at Glasgow and currently teaches R.E. at a school in Doncaster, England.

Iain G. Matheson is a Church of Scotland minister in Prague, Czechoslovakia and a graduate in Theology from the Faculty of Divinity at Glasgow.

George G. Nicol is minister of St Peter's (Church of Scotland), Inverkeithing, Fife and a graduate in Biblical Studies from Glasgow University.

Hugh Pyper is a postgraduate research student in Hebrew Bible and also a part-time Tutorial Fellow in the Department of Biblical Studies, University of Glasgow.

John K. Riches is a Professor of Divinity and Biblical Criticism and Head of the Department of Biblical Studies in the University of Glasgow.

James A. Sanders is Professor of Intertestamental and Biblical Studies at the School of Theology at Claremont and Professor of Religion at Claremont Graduate School, California.

Douglas A. Templeton is Senior Lecturer in New Testament at New College, University of Edinburgh.

CAN A BIBLICAL THEOLOGY ALSO BE ACADEMIC OR ECUMENICAL?

A. Graeme Auld

> O wad some God the giftie gie us,
> Tae see oursel's as ithers see us!

If 'oursel's' are largely Christian academics and their educated reading public pondering Old Testament theology, then some God—and a
largely Jewish one—has been making strenuous efforts in the last
decade to provide such a mirror for their reflection.

In this paper I should like to describe and comment on six recently
published essays relating in one way or another to biblical theology.
Four of these are by Jewish scholars; the other two are by Christian
theologians responding to elements of this fresh Jewish discussion
which the 1980s have witnessed. It is a pleasure to dedicate these
remarks to Robert Davidson, one of my teachers and an honoured
colleague whose own writings have repeatedly and sensitively probed
some of the most 'Jewish' books of the Hebrew Bible.

Jon Levenson's piece, 'Why Jews Are Not Interested in Biblical
Theology', is a combative telling of some home truths by a Jew to his
Christian colleagues. Despite its title and many of its main points, this
article discloses the considerable interest of that one Jew in the subject
of biblical theology, although he claims it is essentially a Christian
concern, and in fact the academic descendant of anti-Jewish polemic.
Such a concern with, and even a need for, biblical and especially Old
Testament theology is one of the marks which distinguish Christianity
from Judaism. Judaism does not require such reflectiveness: its relationship with its biblical roots is more immediate, more historical,
more genealogical—Jews are natural and not adopted children.

Moshe Goshen-Gottstein's more irenic views were known to
Hebrew readers of the periodical *Tarbiz* long before they were
contributed in English to a volume in honour of Frank Moore Cross.
For him, the accident of biblical theology's origins in eighteenth-

century Protestant Christianity is less important. The subject, now that it is a part of the academic curriculum, is too important to leave to Christians, whatever its pedigree: Jews, though late-comers to the field, should now make their distinctive contribution.

Matitiahu Tsevat, carefully writing as an individual and not necessarily a representative Jew, seeks a definition of biblical theology independent of the labels Jewish and Christian. Theology for him is simply a part of philology. And the theology of the Old Testament is no more and no less than that part of the linguistic and literary study of the Old Testament which 'verges on the history of ideas' and which, more especially, discusses ideas of God.

Bernhard Anderson, offering a Christian response to Tsevat, is unhappy about such a 'rationalistic formulation of the theological task'. Tsevat's approach he finds more intellectualist and objective than is appropriate to God-talk.

A different Christian position is sketched by Rolf Rendtorff, who appears to share with Levenson, Goshen and Tsevat the view that greater objectivity is desirable than is generally manifest in [Christian] Old Testament theologies: we should not put *our* questions to the text, but look for *its* questions. We should be reading the text as a theological book, not seeking to distil or otherwise manufacture its essence. If it is such a theological book, we can expect to find the biblical authors' intentions in their work. We shall not require to distil its theological essence, or massage its contribution into theology.

My final essayist is Michael Fishbane who is concerned, as a Jewish biblical and literary critic, with 'the very notion of a sacred text for those of us who do not unreflectingly talk the language of religious tradition, or who cannot—and with whether this notion of a sacred text is at all retrievable at this historical hour'. His contribution is not ostensibly theological at all. And yet, if the notion of sacred text must be allowed to disappear for us to retain our intellectual integrity, then so too perhaps should biblical theology.

I

Levenson's essay had been prompted by the puzzlement of a Christian colleague at Levenson's own fumbling response to his enquiry as to which Jew had written the best biblical theology. Academic biblical studies is an international, ecumenical, inter-confessional, collaborative venture—yet not that part of biblical studies called biblical theology. Like Goshen-Gottstein he offers a useful review of the two-century-long story of a largely Protestant Christian concern that began with Gabler's much-quoted inaugural lecture at Altdorf.

For his opening exposition, he takes Dentan and Bright as typical North American Christian scholars. Both of them largely follow Gabler's definition of biblical theology over against systematic theology as 'what the sacred writers thought about divine matters'. As to the second distinction both attempt to make, that between Old Testament theology and the history of Israelite religion, he has greater doubts about their criteria. They claim that the diversity manifest in the religion does not prevent the portrayal of 'persistent principles' (Dentan) or 'an overarching unity' (Bright). Yet Levenson has no difficulty in documenting the selectivity implied in Bright's greater use of the short book of Amos, for example, over against the much longer book of Proverbs. Dentan's insistence that the theologian's 'concern should be the normative religion of the Old Testament' he blames as being at odds with his own commitment to the 'historical context' of each biblical book. He notes and is rather more content with the widespread Christian view endorsed by Goshen-Gottstein that 'biblical theology requires a measure of faith in its practitioners', not needed in historians of religion. It might seem that such a view limits ecumenical and almost precludes neutral academic study of biblical theology.

> How can a self-consciously Jewish biblical theologian take a personal stand on behalf of a text which he or she interprets against its rabbinic exegesis?. . . the 'personal stance' of a faithful contemporary Jew does not allow for the isolation of the Jewish Bible. . . from the larger tradition.

However, Levenson does allow that 'such an isolation is possible on historical grounds'. Here he seems to leave open the door to biblical theology as a historical discipline. Yet he immediately insists that unlike any other branch of biblical studies, biblical theology 'cannot lend itself to ecumenical, pluralistic collaboration. . . for the term "biblical" has a different reference for the Jew and the Christian'. It might be added that the reference differs among Christians too. As typical of what he cannot accept, he quotes Dentan's view that Old Testament theology is a preparatory exercise for New Testament study; and Porteous's judgment that 'Christ did not merely decode the Old Testament but fulfilled it'.

He then explains a second reason for the distance Jewish scholars have maintained from biblical theology: its 'intense anti-Semitism', its continuation of the ancient *adversus Judaeos* tradition. He finds that Eichrodt 'took the Pauline polemic against the commandments for historical fact'; while von Rad, gentler in spirit, predicated his theology 'on the disappearance of Old Testament tradition after the death of Jesus'. And he is worried that current liberation theology 'is rife with ignorant stereotypical depictions of the Judaism of Jesus' time. New life is being breathed into the old defamations.' He finds that these twentieth-century views essentially continue Wellhausen's 'questionable judgment that "Judaism" is cut off from its spring of vitality'. And he records Schechter's pungent response to the 'Higher Anti-Semitism of the critical historians which burns the soul though it leaves the body unhurt', and his call 'to think out our theology for ourselves'. Levenson blames this anti-Semitic aftertaste for the 'defensive, even reactionary posture among Jewish biblical scholars'. He notes that Kaufmann, responsible for the most substantial synthesis of ancient Israelite experience, 'was keenly aware of being a late-comer to the scene of biblical studies in a critical mode and, conse-quently, of having to clear out space in which to work'.

He develops his next point from the observation that Old Testament theology has been, until recent decades, pre-eminently a Protestant field of study. Yet he cannot forbear to claim that Reformation theol-ogy, and 'their unending Protestant quest for repristinization' had been adumbrated by the eighth-century founder of the Karaites in Babylon. As a better Jewish parallel to this Protestant dynamic he proposes some form of secular Zionism, where 'the urge to repris-tinize the Jewish people is intense'. However, 'most modern Jews are inclined to find their identity in Jewish history, not in Jewish theology'. He notes the anomaly that partnership between Jews and Christians in biblical studies 'is possible only on terms that cast the truth claims of both traditions into doubt'. Yet I observe that fair-minded and open ecumenical research must always work with such danger. The Christian reading of the Hebrew Bible 'draws much of its energy from the anxieties of the younger sibling'—and this observa-tion leads Levenson to his next topic.

'The impulse to systematize among Christians tends to find its outlet in theology. . . Among Jews, the impulse to systematize finds its outlet in law'. In terms of Kitigawa's distinction, Judaism is more like Asian religion—described in terms of practices—than like Christianity. Levenson endorses, at least as far as Judaism's haggadic dimension is concerned, Gerschom Scholem's view: 'not system but *commentary* is the legitimate form through which truth is approached'. He reviews the many candidates proposed in Christian handbooks for the 'centre' of Old Testament theology, and deplores the absence of humankind's duties from the list. Yet he does offer one rabbinic comparator to the Christian view that all the books announce the same message: the anonymous source in the Gemara which reports that

> forty-eight male and seven female prophets prophesied to Israel, and that they neither took away from nor added to that which is written in the Torah, with the exception of the reading of the Scroll [of Esther on Purim].

Of course, though he does not add this, the 'same message' in the case of the Gemara is the practical message which Torah teaches. However, Christians are much more prone to attempt uniform theology than Jews. They tend to use 'the Word' [*dabar*] as a comprehensive singular concept, while midrashic collections regularly introduce a new section by *dabar 'aher* ['another word/interpretation']. Similarly, what we call in English 'the Rabbinic Bible' is called in Hebrew *Miqra'ot Gedolot*, which really means 'great readings [or interpretations]'.

The essay concludes with a detailed critique of von Rad's 'elegant little study' of Gen. 15.6 entitled 'Faith Reckoned as Righteousness'. This blames von Rad for his keenness as Old Testament exegete to endorse the Pauline–Lutheran reading of that Genesis verse—and Levenson turns the critical knife with his observation that Luther was in fact more advanced than von Rad and most Christian Old Testament scholars, who believe 'one can be well-equipped for exegesis without knowledge of the medieval Jewish commentaries'.

Many of Levenson's observations are informative and his objections fair. However, his essay is descriptive rather than prescriptive. It explains a lack of past or present Jewish interest in the subject of biblical theology. But it does not preclude such interest in the future; in fact it even suggests some fresh items for the biblical theology agenda.

II

Moshe Goshen-Gottstein's 'Tanakh Theology: The Religion of the Old Testament and the Place of Jewish Biblical Theology' concerns the 'possibility and necessity of a hitherto nonexisting area of academic study'. He recognizes the fear that the achievements of academic non-denominational biblical study might be jeopardized by attention to a topic commonly associated with personal stances and partisan beliefs. To many Jews and Christians the very term 'theology' is questionable as the title of a discipline in an academic context. Since Gabler's lecture, the study of the religion of Israel and of the theology of the Old Testament have, however, developed as two overlapping yet distinct fields. These are a fact of the academic scene. And, while the practice of them shows they have not been successfully divorced from personal positions, Goshen holds that it is to the detriment of Tanakh study that Jews have been barely involved in Old Testament theology. He claims that, in the twentieth century, Old Testament theology has now become a subsection of biblical studies, rather than of theology. This assertion surprises me and requires some qualification; for the authors of the handbooks, while specialists in Old Testament studies as a whole, have always been located within faculties or departments of theology—never yet in departments of biblical studies within a faculty of Arts or Humanities.

Although Jewish or Christian are meaningless terms for describing aspects of mathematics, Goshen does find these adjectives meaningful within biblical studies. At the very least he will be reminding us here that the Bible has a different extent and shape within different communities. Yet Tanakh theology has not been a perceived option for Jews—notably not even for Kaufmann, although his magnum opus paid attention to a broad spectrum of biblical expertise. Can the name be side-stepped? May the legitimate subject be studied without using a title problematic for some practitioners? Most of the available Old Testament theologies, he claims, take their structure from New Testament categories, or from [Christian] systematic theology—and can be readily ignored. However, the quality of the two large-scale treatments—those of Eichrodt and von Rad—force them on to every biblical scholar's agenda, even though they too are not free of Christian polemic. Theologizing, he comments, is not inherently

Christian; yet the way it has actually developed in biblical studies has been a part of the Christian tradition of dealing with Scripture—and so it has been intuitively avoided by Jews. 'Theology is what theologians have been doing.' Stendahl's distinction between 'what it meant' and 'what it means' might offer a way forward—with the former given academic attention and the latter left to confessional exposition in different communities. Yet Goshen notes that this distinction was only suggested in part of a dictionary article, but never worked out in greater detail.

Rabbinic Judaism, by contrast to [Protestant] Christianity, has effectively cut itself off from further direct dependence on Scripture. Halakha and Tanakh have very little in common. Judaism has no prior history of trying to describe the content structure of any part of Tanakh in ways other than what tradition took it to mean. Yet, Goshen adds, it is Tanakh alone that serves as the common practical basis for Jews; and for no one else but Jews, Tanakh is the exclusive sacred canon. The second of these points we have already noted above. Does he mean by the first that not all Jews are in fact defined by adherence to Halakha, yet all have their roots in Tanakh? The 'theological' quest of 'what it meant' may be impossible to achieve, but is not improper to attempt. It is rather like the textual critic reconstructing an original text. Tanakh theology can be pictured as the job of a modern student of Tanakh religion, who does want to find a place in the edifice of present-day Judaism, but who also wants to reconstruct an earlier plan of that edifice. Goshen believes that a theology developed by someone who totally rejected the faith in question would probably go astray. A 'religious studies' line of enquiry would be inadequate, for descriptivism is a necessary but not a sufficient condition for the enterprise he has in mind.

In his concluding paragraphs, Goshen sketches his own preferred way forward. Most aspects of modern Bible research use methods developed in or shared with the humanities. Axiomatic presuppositions like the relationship between Old Testament and New are another matter; however, it is no wiser for an academic within the humanities to disqualify theology than for a natural scientist to deem history non-academic or non-scientific. Given then that [Christian] theology may be entitled to operate with its own axioms, a Jewish biblical or Tanakh theology would have to develop its own from a clear mainstream Jewish point of view. 'We must devise means to per-

ceive the structure clearly: what is central, basic, important, what is
the message repeated again and again—all over or in major parts of
Tanakh—and what is mentioned rarely, incidentally, unemphasized.'
He calls for a quantitative and qualitative sifting of the literal sense of
the whole text of the Tanakh [or Old Testament]. He expects that
'land' would play a larger and 'personal salvation' a smaller role than
in traditional Christian Old Testament theologies. And he offers a
sketch of the questions a Tanakh theologian might address when
studying the Sabbath.

His concluding remarks suggest that fifty years of Jewish academic
biblical studies may have been required to enable sufficient experience
and self-confidence to put the theological question, 'what is Tanakh all
about?' Goshen calls for 'a more realistic and deeply truthful atmosphere in the common work of Christians and Jews in the academic
study of biblical religion'.

III

Tsevat's Jewish view of Old Testament theology credits [or blames?]
argumentative Paul with the origins of Christian biblical theology and
its rather forced reading of the Hebrew Scriptures. He reckons that
the subject belongs to the origins and so to the essence of Christianity,
and not just recent Protestantism. Even though Paul's letters as a
whole may be too polemical to merit the designation 'theology', yet
'where the presentation is systematic, the entirety of [his]
thought. . . lacks nothing as a theology'. Tsevat, to be fair, does not
find Paul's hermeneutics any more forced than the interpretation of
his Jewish contemporaries: the difference is simply that they exercised
their ingenuity not on theology but on law. While they debated in
plenty on non-legal and more philosophical issues, no need was felt
for such discussions to lead to the resolution of contradictions. When
at the end of the first millennium there did develop among Jews a
greater measure of theoretical reflection, the impulse then was so
much from contemporary Aristotelian and Islamic systems that it was
not genuine Old Testament theology that was constructed.

Having offered an account of origins, Tsevat turns to his definition:
'to uncover and rationally to establish the commonality of [the] religious ideas' of the Old Testament. 'Theology may serve as a grid in
which isolated, incomplete, or vague phrases can be inserted and their

explanations found.' Despite the complexity and diversity of the Bible, the problems attending this sort of research do not materially differ from the issues faced by the scholar who has to generalize about Shakespeare, or even Romanticism. Discussing Stendahl's often quoted distinction between 'what it meant' and 'what it means', Tsevat protests that only the past is completely clear, at least 'within the confines which are placed on our knowledge' of it. The present is open and subject to rapid transformation, and regrettably 'the Bible is pressed into service to support every conceivable cause'.

> For goodness' sake, no interpretation of the Old Testament 'for our time!' Certainly we are influenced by the perception and the understanding of our time, but it should be our endeavour to lessen the results of the influence and not to enhance them.

Tsevat pleads for objective rather than Judaizing theology of the Old Testament. The subsequent classical literature of Judaism, Midrash and Talmud, absorb the Bible—but leave it unrecognizable: 'he who reads in Talmud and Midrash is rewarded with an image of the Old Testament which is entirely wrong, to be sure, but which is, in recompense, extraordinarily wondrous'. The research he envisages is quite open, and not predetermined by the stance of any faith. It must satisfy only 'the general demands of philology and the expectation of the Old Testament literature'. Of course such open study could not exclude Jews from claiming a particular relationship to this body of literature, for the Bible is speaking of the Jews all the time.

Because it is characteristic of modern times that the individual is standing alone before conflicting authorities, our essayist does not wish to assign relative rank to these two theological approaches, the Judaizing and the objective. 'The philologian-theologian, if you will, ought to explain the essence of either one, emphasize their responsive significances, and withdraw.'

IV

Anderson's contribution is specifically directed to Tsevat's article. He starts by questioning Tsevat's claim that Old Testament theology goes back within Christianity as far as Paul. This strictly could not be so. Paul had to deal with the intersection of two ages, the old and the new, with the co-existence of two communities, Jewish and Christian; but not yet with two bodies of canonical writings. That issue was put on the agenda a century later by Marcion. Anderson offers his own definition: 'To speak of "Old Testament" theology in Christian circles is to enquire into the relation between the two testaments that compose the Christian Bible'.

Commenting on his Jewish colleague's major hermeneutical principles, he agrees that Christianizing the Old Testament endangers its interpretation quite as much as Judaizing it. While the Old Testament enjoys only a quasi-independence from the new, it does have theological dimensions not [explicitly] present in the latter. Considering the other side of the same coin, Tsevat had called for a scholarly and objective reading of the ancient text. Anderson warns that this statement takes too little account of historical relativity, that 'knowledge is relative to the standpoint of the knower'. However, 'there surely is an *appropriate* reading of a text—one that is faithful to its genre and structure—and I think that is what Tsevat means when he says that the Old Testament theologian should be a "philologian".'

Anderson closes with three larger critical questions to Tsevat. His talk of rationally establishing the commonality of its religious ideas is too 'rationalistic'. God-related ideas require us

> to move beyond an intellectualist understanding into a consideration of how biblical language functions symbolically to express *relationships* between God and his people. . . It may be that one must be more of a poet than a philosopher to understand the religious language of the Old Testament.

Next, claiming all too briefly a contrast between studying either one of Shakespeare's plays or his whole corpus and studying either Amos or all of the Bible, he asks if it is possible to understand biblical books, which 'are essentially related to the story of a people', apart from their sociological and historical context. The 'word world' of literature may not be an adequate model for texts that emerge from and are directed to a social setting or historical context. Then Anderson as a Christian cannot simply appropriate Tsevat's

> choice between the theological claim of the Old Testament and the position of Talmud and Midrash. . . The relation between the theology of the Old Testament and that of the New is not a movement in one direction, which leads either toward supersession or a choice between two theological alternatives. . . If the New Testament challenges, corrects, and

supplements the Old Testament, then in turn the Old Testament can correct
and restrain the eschatological enthusiasm of the New.

Anderson's contributions do not seem to me to engage fully with
Tsevat. The Bible may be more poetical than philosophical in nature;
yet that does not preclude the philosopher from assessing the status of
some of its claims. A number of biblical books may be quite as literary as Shakespeare, while his work is hardly without social and historical context.

V

Rendtorff, like others of our essayists, opens by noting that 'biblical
theology' in its earliest, eighteenth-century, sense 'represented a
search for the overall theological meaning of the Bible—the New
Testament and the Old Testament—from a Christian religious perspective'. However, in the intervening two centuries, biblical studies
have become more closely related to various disciplines in the
humanities and less to traditional [Christian] theology. Then, while in
the decades since the Second World War the Hebrew Bible has been
studied in a newly inter-confessional and truly international venture,
theology is generally excluded from discussion in world congresses.
Rendtorff's interest is in just what difference it makes 'to the search
for a "biblical theology" that the first part of the Christian Bible is at
the same time, and was already earlier, the Jewish Bible'.

Although he is aware that there is new Jewish interest in biblical
theology, he insists that the Jewish origin of part of the Christian
Bible is an issue to be faced quite independently by Christian theology.
The classic answer, given in rather different forms, sees this Jewish
book as deficient and without a contribution to make on its own. A
second answer views the religion of the Old Testament phenomenologically, and often more neutrally, as a regional variant of ancient
Near Eastern religion: even when it is viewed as a peak of religious
development, lines are not explicitly traced to Christian religion.
Rendtorff seeks a third answer, refusing to 'assume that the Hebrew
Bible had no meaning at all before Christianity appeared'.

Rather than deciding which questions we should put to the text, he
asks that we 'look for the questions in the text itself', and 'read the
Hebrew Bible in its own form as a theological book'. We should
'expect to be able to find the biblical authors' intentions in their

work'. And he offers a concluding example from Genesis and Exodus, both of which tell of a creative start endangered by rebellion and reaffirmed in covenant.

I have considerable sympathy for Rendtorff's approach, not least this final point. We often detect patterning in the biblical books more clearly when we move behind familiar theological topics such as creation of the world and salvation from the hand of Pharaoh. However, he seems to give a number of hostages to fortune. 'Jewish' does not mean the same thing each time he uses the word. In a real sense the writers of the New Testament were quite as Jewish as those of the Old, while it also makes sense to say that pre-Christian Judaism was something different from that ongoing Judaism which was only part of the greater and more diverse family which had divided in response to Jesus of Nazareth. Then there appears some hermeneutical naivety in his opposition of looking and finding. Finally, his insistence that theology takes its departure from the final stage of the text is both ambiguous and too narrowing. It is ambiguous because there are several books where a 'final' form of the text is available to us in substantially different versions, just as the Jewish and Christian collections of sacred books are shaped in importantly different ways. There are far too many differences in the texts and their contexts for us to use 'final' [or 'canonical'] sensibly. It is also narrowing because, when we enter on this quest, we may find that sections within a biblical book, which had once had their own life, better stimulate theological reflection than the whole context in which we now encounter them.

VI

Although Fishbane's essay is not overtly theological, many of the issues he raises resonate with concerns already noted in this paper. I find very attractive his ability to articulate them clearly.

The basic problem he addresses is how the very 'notion of a sacred text [can] be encountered—given our present alienation from such matters and the fact that we come to this topic through a mix of modern notions regarding texts, their status, and the role of a reader?' His first move is 'to think [his] way back into older configurations of this topic in Jewish literature'. He hopes thereby 'to align [his] concern with pre-modern possibilities and to reshape [his] all-too-modern sensibilities through them'. Fishbane sketches in a few paragraphs of limpid clarity some implications of the transformation of 'the teachings and traditions of Israel' into 'a closed, written text', how 'the emergence of a fullblown exegetical system necessarily deepened the sacral possibilities of the received biblical corpus', how the formal boundaries between biblical books became broken down.

> New combinations of words and texts—hence, new meanings—were. . . endlessly possible. . . what the mystical esotericists did was to descend even further into the hidden mysteries of Scripture to that point where the essence of the Bible and the *deus revelatus* were One. Hereby the sacrality of the biblical text actually merged with the sacrality of the Godhead.

Judaism contributes to the history of religions 'its assertion that the divine reality makes itself humanly comprehensible through the structures of language'. 'The sacrality of Scripture lies in its emergence from the infinitely pregnant divine Logos. . . whatever can be humanly known of God is not fixed but only that which we can interpret about him through Scripture.'

Having sketched rabbinic Judaism's four levels of scriptural meaning [plain sense, hermeneutical development, symbolic structure, transcendent dimension], Fishbane's next move is to 'confront this historical achievement with a series of concerns which are very much part of the contemporary critical temper'. He notes that in modern criticism, too,

> the formal boundaries of a text and its interpretation are opened infinitely. There are no shared rules of interpretation, and no one interpretation fundamentally precludes any other. . . There is no will-to-meaning inherent in the text which awaits the patient interpreter. There is only the solitary will-to-power of the interpreter who regally reads and establishes meaning.

Yet that too is not the whole story; for, 'at another level, a whole series of evasions arises in order to outflank the relative voice of the interpreter and establish objective features of critical enquiry'. Concluding this section, he argues that

> the Bible does not address us in its entirety, but as a canon-within-a-canon—as a selected cluster of texts or fragments which live within us amid many other, non-biblical clusters. To put it bluntly. . . we value the love lyrics of the Song of Songs more than the deuteronomic laws of extermination; the images of spiritual inclusion more than the laws of national exclusion; and so on.

From this dialectical conjunction, he next offers a personal synthesis. One 'hermeneutical hope is in the indissoluble link between the divine and human *textus*—the divine *textus* being the texture of truth as it converges on itself, and the human *textus* being our rationalized versions of this divine texture in culture'. To Job he attributes the prophetic destruction of 'self-serving visions', including 'the deuteronomic rationalization of divine involvement with the world', 'for the sake of a more honest crossing from the divine *textus* to the human one'. His next attempt to salvage a concept of textual sacrality is to note 'the capacity of the Bible to incorporate multiple structures of reality. . . just as the Bible is characterized by prophetic instructions and critiques (which alternatively sponsor and shatter exclusive visions), the entire text may be regarded as a prophetic eruption in its own right'—one which enables us to achieve some critical distance from our human religious travail. 'The sacrality released hereby would not be the competitive sacrality of segregated symbols. Rather, this new Bible-sponsored sacrality would allow the awesome transcendence of the divine reality to chasten our constructions of order and sacrality.'

The integrity of Fishbane's essay and its relevance to our opening theological question is encapsulated in his closing exegetical reminder: ' "The voice of the Lord is in strength",' says Scripture (Ps. 29:4); and the rabbinic sages added—in the strength of each person's understanding.'

BIBLIOGRAPHY

Anderson, B.W.
    1986   Response to Matitiahu Tsevat, 'Theology of the Old Testament—A Jewish View'. *Horizons in Biblical Theology* 8: 51-59.

Fishbane, M.
    1989   The Notion of a Sacred Text. In *The Garments of Torah: Essays in Biblical Hermeneutics*, 121-33. Indiana Studies in Biblical Literature; Bloomington: Indiana University Press.

Goshen-Gottstein, M.H.
    1987   Tanakh Theology: The Religion of the Old Testament and the Place of Jewish Biblical Theology. In P.D. Miller, P.D. Hanson and S.D. McBride (eds.), *Ancient Israelite Religion: Essays in Honor of Frank Moore Cross*, 617-44. Philadelphia: Fortress Press.

Levenson, J.D.
    1987   Why Jews Are Not Interested in Biblical Theology. In J. Neusner, B.A.
               Levine and E.S. Frerichs (eds.), *Judaic Perspectives on Ancient Israel,*
               281-304. Philadelphia: Fortress Press.

Rendtorff, R.
    1989   Must 'Biblical Theology' be Christian Theology? *Bible Review* 4: 40-43.

Tsevat, M.
    1986   Theology of the Old Testament—A Jewish View. *Horizons in Biblical
               Theology* 8: 33-50.

When I was preparing this paper I was not yet aware that subsequent essays on related topics by Levenson and Rendtorff were part of a stimulating volume wholly dedicated to this subject:

Brooks, R., and J.J. Collins (eds.)
    1990   *Hebrew Bible or Old Testament. Studying the Bible in Judaism and
               Christianity.* Notre Dame, IN: University of Notre Dame Press.

John M.G. Barclay

The figure of Moses was, of necessity, central to most of the varied streams of Judaism around the turn of the Common Era. Not only was he accredited with the authorship of the five books which stood at the heart of the religion of most Jews; he also had the star role in the story they contained, at least from Exodus onwards. As leader, law-giver, miracle-worker and military hero, Moses had no possible rival; as the model of Jewish life, the ideal figure around which Jewish identity could be defined, he was the clear favourite.

The story of Moses as presented in the Bible has many obvious gaps; large periods of his life are passed over in silence. For instance, next to nothing is recorded about Moses between his rescue from the Nile by an Egyptian princess and his encounter with God at the burn-ing bush, although, on some reckonings, this period amounted to nearly 80 years! Moreover, many of the facts that are recorded made him less than the ideal figure Jews wanted him to be and were bound to cause some embarrassment. He was born from a marriage between a nephew and aunt, such as is forbidden according to his law (Exod. 6.20; Lev. 18.12), and then himself married two non-Israelites, Zipporah, the daughter of a Midianite priest (Exod. 2.21; 3.1), and an unnamed 'Cushite' (Num. 12.1; LXX 'Ethiopian'); that was hardly a good example to a community which frowned on exogamy! He appar-ently neglected to circumcise his own son (Exod. 4.24-26) and in his reluctance to take on the task assigned to him by God (Exod. 4.1-17) presents a picture of self-doubt and cowardice far removed from the hero-image required by Jewish piety! There is clearly a lot of 'explanation' to be done by loyal interpreters of this story.

I have chosen to focus attention in this essay on six brief verses, Exod. 2.10-15, which contain the only two recorded episodes in

Moses' early life in Egypt after his rescue from the Nile: his upbringing as the son of an Egyptian princess and his killing of an Egyptian.
Concerning his upbringing, the biblical text says only that he became
the son of Pharaoh's daughter (who named him Moses). Nothing is
recorded about his life in the Egyptian palace, but questions were
bound to arise: what sort of education did he get, how did he react to
the royal family and Egyptian culture, what signs did he show of his
later greatness? In relation to the other incident, the slaying of the
Egyptian, the text is alarmingly straightforward. Seeing an Egyptian
beating one of his fellow Hebrews, Moses kills the Egyptian and hides
his body in the sand; but the next day, while rebuking two fighting
Hebrews, he learns that the incident has become known, and, when it
is reported to Pharaoh, flees in fear for his life. Many awkward questions inevitably arise from this story: was Moses' act murder or
justifiable homicide and, if the latter, why the great secrecy in hiding
the body? Neither the Israelites, who here reject Moses' leadership,
nor Moses himself, who runs away in fear of Pharaoh, seem to come
out of the incident with great credit. How can the story be explained,
neutralized or made into an edifying example?

   We are fortunate to have many examples of Jewish interpretation of
these verses, including two from that offshoot from the Jewish tree,
early Christianity. In order to keep this discussion within bounds I
have chosen to restrict my survey to texts emanating from the Jewish
Diaspora in Egypt (in this case, the Septuagint translation, the extant
fragments of Artapanus, Ezekiel's play about the exodus and the
works of Philo) and two early Christian texts which found their way
into the New Testament (Acts and Hebrews). Other evidence could of
course be marshalled, especially from Josephus's *Antiquities* and the
rabbis; but, beyond sporadic references in footnotes, I could not
attempt to cover that territory without extending this essay well
beyond limits.

   The Egyptian texts are particularly interesting given that the incidents in these verses concern Moses' life in Egypt and were bound to
be significant to Egyptian Jews in their attempts to come to terms with
Egyptian and Graeco–Roman culture. At the same time, the New
Testament texts provide fascinating glimpses of the intense and
extremely diverse hermeneutical efforts of the early Christians. In
each case we will find how much the manipulation of the biblical text
reveals of the concerns and interests of the interpreter. I am delighted

to offer this work in honour of Robert Davidson, a most valued friend and esteemed colleague, whose insistence on asking awkward questions has been an inspiration and whose lectures on the history of interpretation of the Bible have challenged and fascinated generations of Glasgow students.

Interpretations from Egyptian Judaism

1. The Septuagint (LXX)

Any translation is, of course, an interpretation; but it also takes place under certain constraints whose rigidity depends on the character of the translator(s) and the expectations of the audience for whom the translation is intended. In the case of the LXX version of the Pentateuch, almost certainly completed in Alexandria in the third century BCE, it is clear that both the translators and the Jewish community wanted a translation generally faithful to the Hebrew original, although not in slavish fashion. In the stories of the early life of Moses, there are no major deviations from the Hebrew although the choice of vocabulary at some points and several minor additions may be of some significance.

In describing the baby Moses, the LXX uses the adjective ἀστεῖος (Hebrew טוב, Exod. 2.2), whose connotations could include not only outward beauty but also inner character ('elegant', 'refined'): as we shall see, this is a term highlighted both in Philo and in the New Testament. In the verses of immediate concern to us, it may be significant that, at the beginning of v. 10, in place of the straightforward 'when the child became big' (ויגדל הילד), LXX reads ἀδρυνθέντος δέ τοῦ παιδίου. The notion of maturity in ἀδρυνθέντος is probably not accidental (in v. 11 the translator is content to render the same Hebrew phrase with the more literal μέγας γενόμενος). It not only gives a more positive picture of Moses' growth (he did not just get big, he matured), but it also implies that he was a mature lad before he was handed over by his family to the Egyptian princess. Whereas the Hebrew is vague about the stage at which this transfer took place (when is a child 'big'?), the LXX suggests that he had already imbibed the educational training and religious atmosphere of a Jewish family before he ventured into the palace. The small shift of nuance here may reflect a concern to preserve the 'orthodoxy' of this Jewish hero.

Small changes elsewhere in these verses (like the addition of ἐχθές in v. 14) are stylistic rather than ideological, although the double insertion of 'the sons of Israel' after the references to Moses' brothers in v. 11 may serve to reinforce his identification with the Jewish nation. Finally, we may note that, in describing Moses' departure from Egypt, LXX chooses to translate ויברח in v. 15 by ἀνεχώρησεν. Is this an attempt to remove the ignominy of a flight (ἔφυγεν would be the more obvious translation)[1] by describing it in more polite terms as 'withdrawal'? Certainly, as we shall see, later Jews preferred a less embarrassing understanding of Moses' departure from Egypt.

2. *Artapanus*

We owe a great debt to the Hellenistic historian Alexander ('Polyhistor') for the snippets of Jewish historiography he preserved (later to be used by Eusebius). Among the most entertaining and intriguing of these are the three fragments of Artapanus, a figure otherwise wholly unknown to us, whose dates can be fixed no more exactly than between 250 and 100 BCE.[2] In the third and longest fragment, obviously much abbreviated by Alexander, Artapanus gives a highly romanticized version of the life of Moses, fascinating for the way it simultaneously exalts both Moses and Egyptian religion.

Although he knew the LXX text (there are several verbal echoes in his account of the plagues), Artapanus obviously felt free to alter and embellish the biblical text for the greater glory of its hero, Moses. He

---

1.   The Hebrew root ברח is usually translated in LXX by φεύγειν (27×) or ἀποδιδράσκειν (23×); only on 3 occasions is ἀναχωρεῖν used.

2.   The three fragments are found in Eusebius, *Praeparatio Evangelica* 9.18.1; 9.18.23.1-4; and 9.27.1-37. I will refer to the text by the number of the fragment followed by the section in the Eusebius text (i.e. 3.9 = Eusebius 9.27.9 etc.). The most recent edition of the Greek text is by C.R. Holladay, *Fragments from Hellenistic Jewish Authors*. I. *Historians* (Chico, CA: Scholars Press, 1983). There is also a valuable English translation and commentary by J.J. Collins in J.H. Charlesworth (ed.), *The Old Testament Pseudepigrapha*, II (London: Darton, Longman & Todd, 1985). On the date, between LXX Pentateuch and Alexander Polyhistor, see E. Schürer, G. Vermes, F. Millar, and M. Goodman, *The History of the Jewish People in the Age of Jesus Christ (175 B.C.–A.D. 135)*, III.1 (Edinburgh: T. & T. Clark, 1986), pp. 521-25, where a full bibliography can be found.

exploits to the full the silence of the text on Moses' career in the palace: this is a large time-gap which can easily be filled with stories of Moses' prowess and, in particular, of his benefits to Egyptian society and culture. In retelling the stories of Abraham and Joseph (fragments 1 and 2), Artapanus had made them out to be great cultural benefactors (giving Egypt such skills as astrology and measurement, and introducing political stability and justice). Moses, adopted by the Egyptian princess, could clearly do even more: among his inventions were ships, weaponry, stone-lifting machines and irrigation systems (vital for Egyptian agriculture) all of which made him dearly loved by the people and popular with the king (3.3-6). What is more surprising from this Jewish author, but is clearly of very great importance to him, is the catalogue of Moses' achievements in the sphere of Egyptian religion. Dividing the country into 36 nomes, he assigned to each a God, for instance, cats, dogs and ibises (3.4)! The veneration of the ibis is explained by its usefulness in destroying animals harmful to humankind (3.9), but this rationalistic explanation of ibis-worship is not meant to diminish its value but to explain its purpose in terms probably familiar to Graecized Egyptians.[1] Honoured by the Egyptian priests for these and other benefits, Moses is accorded divine honours and is known among them, says Artapanus, as Hermes (because of his skill in the interpretation—ἑρμηνεία—of sacred writings, 3.6). His rod is also a sacred object in every Egyptian temple (3.32).[2]

This picture of Moses is clearly motivated by a complex commitment both to Judaism and to Egyptian culture. We have evidence that Moses had a mixed reputation among Egyptians, some considering

---

1.   In my view, attempts to play down Artapanus's syncretism should be resisted. Older opinions that the author was not a Jew, or was a Jew adopting a pagan mask to present views he did not really believe, have rightly been abandoned. More recent attempts to read the text as if Artapanus was subtly distancing Moses from the worship of animal deities collapse in the light of 3.4 and 3.12. It would also be unwise to take his modified 'euhemeristic' explanation of ibis-worship as a sign of his scorn or disbelief: in this period rationalist explanations of religion usually functioned to support, not to undermine, its practice.

2.   I am attracted by C.R. Holladay's excellent suggestion (*THEIOS ANER in Hellenistic Judaism* [Missoula, MT: Scholars Press, 1977], p. 228 n. 178) that what Artapanus has in mind here is in fact a phallic symbol found in Isis temples (Diodorus Siculus 1.22.6-7)!

him 'remarkable, even divine' (Josephus, *Apion* 1.279), others deni-grating him as a leprous and impious impostor (Manetho's slanders are discussed and refuted by Josephus in the same context). Artapanus is determined to silence any criticism and to support any adulation, even to the extent of implying that in worshipping Hermes, Egyptians are in fact paying honour to Moses.[1] And in this panegyric of Moses, Artapanus clearly has in mind the status and reputation of Jews, Moses' compatriots (ὁμόφυλοι, 3.19). The glory of their hero, who is accredited with many of the exploits of the Egyptian hero Sesostris,[2] supports and justifies their continuing commitment to their religion. At the same time it is clear that, for Artapanus, Judaism and Egyptian religion are quite compatible. This polytheistic Jew feels very much at home in the Egyptian countryside (he probably lived outside Alexandria).[3] Moses in the palace of the king (Exod. 2.10) is for him a symbol of the integration of Jewish and Egyptian culture.

But Artapanus also knew the story of the assassination of an Egyptian and of Moses' flight to Midian (which he takes to mean Arabia). However, the biblical version, where Moses' commitment to his fellow Hebrews results in this dramatic rejection of Egypt, would hardly fit his purposes. He therefore combines this story with another, of unknown provenance but related to a tale used by Josephus,

1.   This association was no doubt aided by the equivalence of Hermes and the native Egyptian God Thot-Mosis; see G. Mussies, 'The Interpretatio Judaica of Thoth-Hermes', in M. Heerma van Voss *et al.* (eds.), *Studies in Egyptian Religion Dedicated to Professor Jan Zandee* (Leiden: Brill, 1982), pp. 89-120. I do not think it is necessary to posit, as many do, that Artapanus is responding to *literary* slanders of Moses. Manetho claimed that his attacks were drawn from popular accounts (Josephus, *Apion* 1.229), and Artapanus could be responding precisely to such widespread mythology.

2.   See especially Diodorus Siculus 1.53-58. On Artapanus's account as an example of Jewish romance in competition with Egyptian, see M. Braun, *History and Romance in Graeco-Oriental Literature* (Oxford: Basil Blackwell, 1938).

3.   Cf. P.M. Fraser, *Ptolemaic Alexandria* (Oxford: Clarendon Press, 1972), I, p. 706 and II, p. 985 n. 199. Fraser proposes Memphis as a possible location, but given the repeated and favourable references to Heliopolis, I would speculate the latter. The sense of being 'at home' in Egypt is indicated by the exclusively positive accounts of the experiences of Abraham and Joseph in Egypt and by the attempt to define the meaning of Ιουδαῖοι without reference to Ιουδαία (fragment 1).

concerning a military expedition to Ethiopia.[1] The king, Chenephres, envious of Moses' prowess (ἀρετή) plots to have him killed by sending him as general in command of an inadequate army against the Ethiopians. When Moses surprisingly returns triumphant (having even won the affection of his Ethiopian foes!), Chenephres with great difficulty persuades a friend, Chanethothes, to assassinate Moses and sends them off together on a task. Moses, however, is tipped off by one of the other conspirators, and by Aaron, and decides to flee. Chanethothes ambushes him on his way to Arabia, but Moses, in self-defence, rebuffs the attack and kills Chanethothes (3.7-18).

This story is almost certainly a radical reworking of that in Exodus 2, wholly remodelled to fit Artapanus's purposes. Moses makes no choice here to side with Hebrews against Egyptians; his departure is purely the result of the malicious and highly individual envy of the king.[2] His flight to Arabia begins before his violent encounter with Chanethothes; it is not motivated by fear or shame arising out of his slaying of an Egyptian. Finally, and crucially, he kills purely in self-defence; and there is all the difference in the world between homicide in self-defence and murder.[3] Artapanus has managed to use Exod. 2.10-15 to produce a faultless Moses, as fully integrated into Egyptian life and culture as Artapanus himself.[4]

3. *Ezekiel*

Among the other gems preserved by Alexander are several fragments of a Greek drama called *Exagoge* ('Exodus'), written by Ezekiel.

---

1. Cf. Josephus, *Ant.* 2.238-53 and T. Rajak, 'Moses in Ethiopia', *JJS* 29 (1978), pp. 111-22.

2. Cf. Josephus, *Ant.* 2.254-56; both Artapanus and Josephus omit all mention of the incident of the disputing Hebrews (Exod. 2.13-14).

3. Philo, *Leg. Gai.* 68; note the references to Roman law collected by E.M. Smallwood, *Philonis Alexandrini Legatio ad Gaium* (Leiden: Brill, 1970), *ad loc.*

4. No doubt many other Jews would have considered Artapanus's account scandalous, not only rigorous upholders of Jewish tradition like the author of 3 Maccabees but also comparatively 'liberal' figures like Philo and the authors of Ps.-Aristeas and Wisdom of Solomon: for their views on Egyptian 'animal-worship' (in reality, of course, worship of Gods with animal features) see, e.g., Philo, *Dec.* 76-80; Ps.-Aristeas 138; Wis. 11.15; 15.18-19. But it is unlikely that Artapanus's views were entirely unique: we may compare from an earlier period the syncretistic tendencies in the Elephantine papyri and the 'compromised' position of such people as Idellas, son of Sabathois, who tended sheep for the temple of Pan, *CPJ* 39.

Although attempts to pin down his date and provenance can never attain complete certainty, it is most likely that he was an Alexandrian Jew living in the late third or second centuries BCE.[1] The fragments are fascinating as the only example we have of a Jewish drama, almost certainly intended to be staged, and closely modelled on the style and structure of Greek tragedies.[2] That Ezekiel should write a play about the exodus, with Moses as its central hero and with numerous echoes of the LXX, is a sign of his loyalty to Judaism; that he should be able to master the form and vocabulary of Greek tragedy is a sign of his extensive education in Greek literature. He probably intended both Jews and non-Jews to watch his drama and to experience one way in which Jewish tradition and Greek culture could be made compatible.

The play opens with a prologue in Euripidean style: Moses recounts, in a lengthy monologue, the story of his birth and upbringing and the reasons for his flight from Egypt (the scene is at the well in Libya/Midian). In this narrative Ezekiel sticks fairly closely to the biblical story (later in the play there are several original features such as a merkavah-type vision given to Moses, and the appearance of the phoenix at the springs of Elim after the crossing of the Red Sea). Moses emphasizes the oppression of his race by the Egyptians and the cruelty of the king's decree to drown all Hebrew children. As we have already noted, Ezekiel is using Moses in this play to build bridges into Greek culture; thus, he can make connections with the typical disdain of Egyptian natives in the Greek cities and can afford to vent the full anti-Egyptian spleen of the Exodus text. Where Artapanus makes Moses an Egyptian hero, Ezekiel fashions him in the Greek mode.

In recounting the events of Exod. 2.10-15 (lines 32-58 of fragment 1), Ezekiel's Moses makes several very telling alterations. He remarks that, when his mother brought him to the princess's palace, she had already instructed him in 'my ancestral lineage and the gifts of God' (λέξασά μοι / γένος πατρῷον καὶ θεοῦ δωρήματα, 34-35). At the

---

1. The fragments are found in Eusebius, *Praep. Ev.* 28 and 29 and have been edited with a fine commentary by H. Jacobson, *The EXAGOGE of Ezekiel* (Cambridge: Cambridge University Press, 1983); Jacobson has a full discussion of date and provenance, pp. 5-17.

2. For arguments that it was intended to be staged see H. Jacobson, 'Two Studies on Ezekiel the Tragedian', *GRBS* 22 (1981), pp. 147-78. For extensive parallels with Aeschylus's *Persae*, the Danaid trilogy and Euripidean style, see Jacobson's commentary.

palace he was given 'a royal education' (τροφαῖσι βασιλικαῖσι καὶ παιδεύμασιν, 37), which, at the time Ezekiel was writing, would clearly be understood as Greek education (the Ptolemaic dynasty was, of course, Greek, not native Egyptian). Thus Moses is an educated and religious Jew as well as being fully conversant with the fruits of Greek civilization—precisely the 'ideal' which Ezekiel himself embodied with his intense loyalty to the Jewish people intricately combined with his Hellenistic training.[1]

The account of the slaying of the Egyptian, given in full biblical detail, is at first sight surprising. Moses simply recounts finding a Hebrew and an Egyptian fighting, without explicitly recording who was the aggressor or persecutor (contrast LXX ὁρᾷ ἄνθρωπον Αἰγύπτιον τύπτοντά τινα Εβραῖον and other accounts to be discussed below). Although the apportionment of blame may be partly implied by the context, there is remarkably little effort here to whitewash Moses' action.[2] The most plausible reason, suggested by H. Jacobson, is that Ezekiel saw here a parallel to some of the great heroes of Greek tragedy whose passions led them to commit murder and forced them into exile (Oedipus is the most obvious case).[3] In this way, murderer though he may be, Moses can still elicit the sympathy and attract the interest of the audience; in fact, his crime adds spice to a drama which would otherwise bore its spectators with faultless characters!

Finally, we may note a subtle change in the account of Moses' inter-

---

1.   It is striking how often Ezekiel refers to the Jewish nation as a race (γένος / γέννα lines 7, 12, 35, 43, 135 in Jacobson's edition) and identifies Moses as a national hero. Yet his literary and linguistic learning, and the social status required to produce and stage such dramas, indicate training in the gymnasium. It is interesting that the only education mentioned in the more parochial and Palestinian text, *Jubilees* (47.9), is the teaching of writing by Moses' father, Amram.

2.   In the context lines 40-41 refer to the king's ἔργα and τέχνασμα, echoing the oppression mentioned in lines 4-10; but Jacobson, *ad loc.*, is right to highlight the apparent oddity here.

3.   In the prologue to *Oedipus Coloneus*, the hero arrives on stage as a fugitive murderer; further parallels are noted in Jacobson, 'Two Studies'. Aristotle (*Ars Poetica* 13.5) discusses the need for a tragic hero to suffer misfortune by some great ἁμαρτία; perhaps Ezekiel would not wish to describe Moses' action in terms as explicit as that, although some rabbinic sources do refer to Moses' sin in this affair (see M.M. Kasher, *Encyclopedia of Biblical Interpretation*, VIII [New York: American Biblical Encyclopedia Society, 1967], pp. 52-53).

vention in the fight on the following day. According to the biblical
text he tries to make peace between two Hebrew combatants, who
reject his authority. Ezekiel simply says that the two men were of the
same race (συγγενεῖς, 49); those familiar with the biblical story might
understand this as two Hebrews, but others in the audience could well
imagine Moses is intervening here in a fight between two Egyptians![1]
The effect of this ambiguity is to remove possible sources of embarrassment to Jews: the story no longer portrays Jews fighting among
themselves, rudely rejecting Moses' leadership or giving information
against him to Pharaoh.[2] There is nothing here to cause difficulty for
Alexandrian Jews and plenty to make them proud of their Jewish heritage and confident in their Hellenistic environment.

4. *Philo*

Philo gives a very full account of the episodes which concern us in the
course of his *De Vita Mosis*, drawing his information, he says, both
from the 'sacred books' and from 'the elders of the nation' (i.e.
legends). In fact, the picture of Moses is decisively moulded by Philo's
own philosophical perspective: he modernizes Moses as flagrantly as
Christian scholars have usually modernized Jesus! The accent
throughout is on Moses' exceptional qualities; he was simply the
greatest and most perfect man (1.1), remarkable in his physical development (1.18-19) and with a mind so uniquely gifted that everyone
wondered whether it was human or divine or a mixture of both
(1.27).[3]

According to Philo, Moses was transferred to the Egyptian palace as

---

1. I owe this observation to Jacobson, *EXAGOGE*, pp. 79-81. As he points
out, the ambiguous identity of the combatants is maintained by having the insolent
questioner refer to Moses' previous killing of 'the man' rather than 'the Egyptian'
(which would suggest a Hebrew perspective).

2. In the biblical account it is not recorded who informed against Moses, but if
there was no one else present (Exod. 2.12) it must have been the Hebrew he saved!
In line 55 of Ezekiel's play (if the text is secure) it is the insolent (Egyptian?) combat-
ant who is explicitly said to report matters to the king.

3. The most accessible edition is in the Loeb Classical Library (*Philo*, VI) with a
translation by F.H. Colson, utilized at some points below. Philo is keen on the LXX
description of Moses as ἀστεῖος (1.9, 15, 48 [his λογισμὸς ἀστεῖος]); his 'divine'
qualities are further suggested by the reference to him as θεὸς καὶ βασιλεύς
(1.158, drawing on Exod. 7.1).

soon as he was weaned (unusually early, 1.18), and the princess, who had previously enlarged her womb with divine help, was able to pass him off as her own son; and since she was an only child, that made Moses the heir to the Egyptian throne (1.13-19). This exalted status, with its prospects of extraordinary wealth and power, heightens the force of Philo's insistence that Moses did not renounce his family or ancestral customs (1.30-33); with his eye on fellow Jews whose wealth and social status had led them into apostasy, Philo is keen to present Moses as the model of loyalty to Judaism in the midst of social success.[1]

The royal education which Moses received in the palace was provided by teachers from Egypt and surrounding nations, as well as tutors specially summoned from Greece (1.21-24). The curriculum covered the whole gamut of Egyptian lore, including the philosophy conveyed in symbols through Egyptian inscriptions and animal-cults; Philo is careful to distance Moses from the divine honours *they* pay to such beasts, while suggesting some, unspecified, philosophical symbolism behind it all (1.23). It also included, from the Greek tutors, the rest of the ἐγκύκλιος παιδεία (1.23) and it is not fanciful to find echoes here both of Philo's own education in Alexandria and of the ideal curriculum for philosopher-kings as described by Plato.[2] True to his general tendency, Philo describes Moses' educational development as exceptional: he soon outstrips his teachers, devising problems they could not solve, penetrating beyond contradictory doctrines to the ultimate truth and appearing, says Philo, to exhibit ἀνάμνησις rather than μάθησις (1.21-24).[3] What is, perhaps, even more striking is the way Moses is portrayed throughout in ascetic terms: even as a child he

---

1. *Vit. Mos.* 1.30-31 shows that Philo is thinking of known cases of Jewish apostasy; his own nephew, Tiberius Alexander (Josephus, *Ant.* 20.100-101), was an obvious but by no means isolated example. It is important that Philo insists that Moses could have stayed in the palace (and even inherited the throne?) but for the new 'impiety' against the Jews (1.33): in other words, there is no *necessary* contradiction between loyalty to Judaism and high social status in Egypt (as enjoyed by Philo himself).

2. For Philo's understanding of the value of education see, e.g., *Congr.* 11.79-80, 140-150. Holladay (*THEIOS ANER*, pp. 109-12) finds many parallels with the Platonic ideal for philosopher-kings (*Republic* 7.522-31), in which category Moses is expressly included, *Vit. Mos.* 2.1-2.

3. This is the closest Philo comes to the famous Platonic theory, but he is careful to qualify it with δοκεῖν (1.21)!

eschewed laughter and sport (1.20), he showed exemplary control of the passions, especially those of the stomach and 'below' (αἱ ὑπογάστριοι ἡδοναί, 1.28), and in his disciplined preference for the soul over the body was a model of moral and spiritual excellence.[1] In Philo's hands, Moses is the ultimate philosopher in the Cynic–Stoic tradition.

Philo's treatment of the death of the Egyptian is replete with apologetic motifs. He rearranges the Exodus account of the oppression of the Hebrews, making their harsh enslavement a new development after the completion of Moses' education: Moses could not be accused of years of comfortable complicity while his people were oppressed! Philo also builds up a highly rhetorical picture of the cruelty of the Egyptian overseers as ferocious task masters 'in savageness differing nothing from venomous and carnivorous animals' (1.43). At the climax of this rhetoric Philo describes 'the cruellest of them all', a man who refused to listen to the pleas of Moses, persecuting and torturing the Hebrews to death (1.44). This was the man whom Moses killed, considering his action holy (δικαιώσας εὐαγὲς εἶναι τὸ ἔργον, 1.44). Philo is quick to register his assent: it was right to destroy someone who lived only to destroy others. He accordingly omits all mention of Moses' attempt to hide the body in the sand; that would smack too much of guilty secrecy.[2]

Finally, after treating so many other details in imaginative fullness, Philo passes over the incident of the two Hebrew disputants, and their rejection of Moses' leadership, in complete silence.[3] The king was dismayed to hear of Moses' slaughter of the Egyptian, not because it was unjust but because it showed disloyalty, and when the mood at court turned against him, Moses decided to 'retire' (ὑπανεχώρησεν,

---

1. Note especially 1.25-26, 28-29 (ψυχῇ γὰρ ἐπόθει μόνῃ ζῆν, οὐ σώματι), and the list of his virtues in 154; in 158 he is explicitly called a παράδειγμα.

2. Of course Philo knew very well that the text included this detail, and elsewhere can make allegorical use of it, *Leg. All.* 3.37-39; *Fug.* 147-48. But in *De Vita Mosis*, where he cannot 'explain' such matters allegorically, they are best left out. Among the rabbinic attempts to justify Moses' action here are the suggestion that the Egyptian slain had just raped a Hebrew woman and the notion that Moses, inquiring into the future, realized that no proselyte or righteous person would ever spring from that man's progeny so no harm would be done by his death (*Exod. R.* 1.28-29; *Lev. R.* 32.4; Palestinian Targum, *ad loc.*)!

3. Again there is an allegorical use of the incident elsewhere, *Fug.* 147-48.

1.47)!¹ He thus renounced Egypt for its moral turpitude and threw in his lot with the Hebrew nation, not out of any narrow nationalism but because 'it was destined to be consecrated above all others to offer prayer for ever on behalf of the human race that it may be delivered from evil and participate in what is good' (1.49). Put in these broad terms Moses is thus a symbol of Philo's universalist understanding of the divine favour to Israel.

Interpretations in the New Testament

1. *Acts*

Stephen's speech in Acts 7 surveys a panorama of biblical stories, but there is an interesting concentration on the Mosaic incidents we have been studying, which are here put to novel and highly polemical use. Although he may be employing an earlier source for some of the material in this speech, Luke clearly retains editorial control and, in this case particularly, has moulded the speech very precisely according to his design.²

After a somewhat breathless survey of the story of Abraham and Joseph, the narration suddenly slows down at the birth of Moses (described as ἀστεῖος τῷ θεῷ, v. 20). All the main features of Exod. 2.10-15 are then described—Moses' upbringing in the palace, the death of the Egyptian and Moses' unsuccessful attempt to mediate between two Israelites (Acts 7.22-29). The significance of these incidents for Luke is signalled by their detailed treatment, the inclusion of an explanatory commentary (v. 25), and, especially, by the renewed reference to the Israelites' rejection of Moses' leadership at the start of a rhetorical application of the lessons of history (v. 35). This application also makes clear the overall purpose for this focus on Moses.

---

1. In *Leg. All.* 3.12-14, Philo makes much of the distinction between withdrawal (to fight another day) and flight: the latter would be ignominious.
2. M. Dibelius (*Studies in the Acts of the Apostles* [London: SCM Press, 1956], pp. 167-70) suggested that Luke used here an older non-polemical survey of Jewish history but reworked it to sharpen its impact; his thesis is followed by most scholars, with varying analyses of Luke's additions and alterations. For the contrary opinion, that the whole speech is original to Luke, see J. Bihler, *Die Stephanusgeschichte im Zusammenhang der Apostelgeschichte* (Munich: Hueber, 1963).

BARCLAY Manipulating Moses: Exodus 2.10-15   41

By quoting Moses' promise that God would raise up a prophet like him (Deut. 18.15, cited in Acts 7.37), Luke carefully reminds the reader of his prophet-Christology (e.g. Lk. 7.16; 13.33-34; 24.19) and signals his intention to draw a close comparison between Moses and Jesus (cf. also Acts 3.19-24). It is this parallel with Jesus which decisively shapes the narration of the Moses story in this speech, and nowhere more so than in the details of the incidents which are our particular concern.

After describing the discovery and adoption of the baby Moses, the speech refers to Moses' education 'in all the wisdom of the Egyptians' and concludes that he was δυνατὸς ἐν λόγοις καὶ ἔργοις αὐτοῦ (v. 22). It may be too fanciful to find any special 'Tendenz' in the reference to Egyptian wisdom: perhaps it is no more than an echo of the proverbial pre-eminence of the Egyptian cultural heritage, without any attempt to emphasize (or to limit) the effect of the Egyptian environment on Moses' development. If any parallel with Jesus is implicit, it may be with his early growth in wisdom (Lk. 2.40, 47, 52, without the need for education?); and it could be significant that Jesus claimed greater wisdom than Solomon, who was himself admired by the 'queen of the south' (Lk. 11.31). In any case, the Jesus parallel is crystal clear in the exact verbal link between this verse and Lk. 24.19. Moses, like Jesus, was powerful in speech and action (despite Exod. 4.10!); both were naturally fitted to be leaders of Israel.

Far from attempting to cover up Moses' killing of the Egyptian, the speech highlights this action; however, it is presented not as a secretive event but as a symbolic overture to the salvation which Moses meant to bring for his people. Moses decides to visit his brethren (ἐπισκέψασθαι τοὺς ἀδελφοὺς αὐτοῦ, v. 23, with echoes of the salvific visitation of God to his people through Jesus, Lk. 1.68, 78; 7.16). Seeing one being oppressed, he defends and vindicates him (ἠμύνατο καὶ ἐποίησεν ἐκδίκησιν, v. 24, echoing the ἐκδίκησις of God's salvation, Lk. 18.7-8; 21.22). He strikes the Egyptian, but does not (except in text D) hide the body. In fact the context requires that he intended his action to become known since 'he thought his brethren would understand that God was giving them salvation (σωτηρία) by his hand' (v. 25). Here God's authority is understood to lie behind Moses' action and Moses is presented as a would-be saviour (cf. v. 35 and the repeated references in Luke–Acts to the σωτηρία wrought by

Jesus).[1] Moses' sense of mission, which in the biblical text arises only after the encounter at the burning bush, is here shifted to an earlier point;[2] thus Luke makes Moses as much a forerunner of Jesus as possible.

But for Luke the central point in the whole story is that, while trying to bring salvation to Israel, Moses is misunderstood and rejected by his people. The editorial comment at the end of v. 25 is crucial (οἱ δὲ οὐ συνῆκαν) and sets up resonances with the key text from Isaiah 6 used by Luke to describe Israel's failure to understand the preaching of Jesus and Paul (Lk. 8.10; Acts 28.26-27; cf. Lk. 2.50; 18.34). It is this failure which Luke sees illustrated in the Exodus story of the hostile reaction by the Israelite to Moses' friendly attempt to break up a fight.[3] Although the biblical text (cited verbatim in vv. 27-28) records hostile questions from only one of the combatants, Luke takes this as symptomatic of rejection by the whole of Israel ('this Moses whom *they* denied, saying. . . ', v. 35).[4] And where the biblical text records that Moses fled out of fear of Pharaoh, Luke omits all mention of the Egyptian threat so that his flight (ἔφυγεν, v. 29) is purely motivated by Israel's rejection. Israel denied her leader and saviour (ἄρχοντα καὶ λυτρωτήν, v. 35) and forced him to flee: and this, in Acts 7 and in Lukan theology, is an outstanding example of her rejection of all the prophets, a tendency which has now reached its tragic climax in her betrayal and murder of Jesus.[5]

1. σωτηρία: Lk. 1.69, 71, 77; 19.19; Acts 4.12, etc. Jesus as σωτήρ: Lk. 2.11; Acts 5.31. While Acts 7.27 and 35a cite the LXX exactly with the question whether Moses is ἄρχοντα καὶ δικαστήν, it is significant that in v. 35b the emphasis is shifted to a salvific role in ἄρχοντα καὶ λυτρωτήν. Thus, while Jesus can decline to be a Mosaic figure in the sense of κριτὴς καὶ μεριστής in Lk. 12.14 (where there are clear echoes of Exod. 2), he is clearly a deliverer in the broader sense (cf. λύτρωσις in Lk. 1.68; 2.38; cf. 24.21).

2. Well observed by J.J. Kilgallen, *The Stephen Speech: A Literary and Redactional Study of Acts 7* (Rome: Biblical Institute Press, 1976), p. 69.

3. What might appear a meddlesome intervention in Exod. 2.13 is toned down here by talk of Moses trying to reconcile the opponents and by the addition of ἄνδρες, ἀδελφοί ἐστε, which immediately gives the reason for Moses' objection (Kilgallen, *Stephen Speech*, p. 70).

4. E. Haenchen, *The Acts of the Apostles* (Philadelphia: Westminster Press, 1971), pp. 281-82. Note the parallel to Jewish denial of Jesus in Acts 3.13-14.

5. Note the climax of Stephen's speech, 7.51-53 and the repeated accusations against the Jews in Acts 2.23; 3.13-15; 4.10-11; 5.30; 13.26-29; etc. For a recent

Acts 7, then, provides an interpretation of the Moses stories different in key respects from all the examples we have seen in Egyptian Judaism. The figure of Moses is important not for his own sake, or as an ideal figure of cultural or philosophical significance, but because his story foreshadows that of the final Mosaic prophet, Christ. Moreover, far from omitting (Artapanus, Philo) or neutralizing (Ezekiel) the story of the Israelites fighting and the rejection of Moses' leadership, Luke makes these the pivotal events; for his ultimate purpose is not to advance a positive portrait of Judaism but to explain and expound what he understood, from the perspective of late first-century Christianity, to be the disastrous failure of most Jews to respond to God's salvation.[1] He can thus exploit the inherent Jewish self-criticism in the biblical text to advance the cause of a new movement rapidly separating from its Jewish matrix.

2. *Hebrews*

An interpretation of Exodus 2 is included in Hebrews 11 as one in a chain of examples of faith. The πίστις which is rhetorically emphasized at the start of each section is rarely a constituent part of the original biblical story. Both in the case of Moses' parents (who hid the baby Moses when they saw he was ἀστεῖος, v. 23), and in the case of Moses himself (who renounced his royal status to identify with the suffering people of God, vv. 24-26) the motif of faith is imposed upon the story and has an important influence on its retelling. It is no accident, for instance, that no mention is made here of the killing of the Egyptian or the subsequent Israelite hostility to Moses: it would be hard to see how those details could be made examples of faith![2] Rather, the story is told in very general terms with the accent on the theme of renunciation. In order to understand this emphasis, and the tenor of much of the vocabulary used in this account, it is necessary to survey briefly the purpose of the letter.

---

treatment of this theme see J.T. Sanders, *The Jews in Luke–Acts* (London: SCM Press, 1987) (together with the judicious review by C.K. Barrett in *JTS* 39 [1988]).

1.   See the discussion of Stephen's speech by J.C. O'Neill, *The Theology of Acts in its Historical Setting* (London: SPCK, 2nd edn, 1970), pp. 71-93.

2.   A few MSS, in fact, include a reference to the killing of the Egyptian, but, as H.W. Attridge notes, this story is 'hardly a good example of the faithful endurance that the pericope as a whole inculcates' (*The Epistle to the Hebrews* [Philadelphia: Fortress Press, 1989], p. 338).

One of the passages which reveals much about the historical and social context of the letter is 10.26-39. The author here issues a terrifying warning against lapsing into sin and reminds the readers of their initial Christian commitment, when they had willingly supported those who suffered and had themselves been exposed to hardship in the form of abuse (ὀνειδισμοί, v. 33) and loss of property (v. 34). They had endured all this for the sake of a better and abiding possession (v. 34) and need now to be reminded in earnest tones to continue to endure in the struggle (v. 36; cf. 12.1, 3, 7). They must combat the allures of sin (12.1, 4), identify with those who are still imprisoned (13.3) and look to the great reward (10.35). It is clear that their Christian faith could involve a considerable loss of social status; they need to be told that this is both inevitable and, in an eternal perspective, infinitely rewarding.[1]

In this context, the emphasis of Hebrews 11 makes excellent sense, with its definition of faith in terms of transcendent realities (11.1) and its long catalogue of those who suffered alienation and insecurity because of their loyalty to God. The story of Moses, in the portion we are specially concerned with, is particularly apposite. By a careful choice of vocabulary, and a subtle handling of the story-line, Moses is made here the model of suffering faith. He renounced the wealth of Egypt and his high status as son of Pharaoh's daughter; rather than enjoy these 'fleeting pleasures of sin' he was willing to share in the suffering of the people of God (vv. 24-26).[2] All this was possible because he looked to the reward (v. 26) and endured as one who saw the unseen (v. 27). The parallels with what the author hopes for from the readers are obvious and are made fully explicit in the startling reference to Moses' willing embrace of 'the abuse of Christ' (τὸν ὀνειδισμὸν τοῦ Χριστοῦ, v. 26). This sudden reference to Christ, whose name is mentioned nowhere else in this whole chapter, demonstrates how fully Christianized the figure of Moses has become.[3] He

---

1.   This general description of the situation of the addressees is about as much as can be gathered from the document; further details (date, ethnic identity, location, etc.) remain unclear and therefore still controversial.

2.   It was apparently necessary to remove any more specific reference to 'the sons of Israel' in order to make the parallel with the church as the people of God (cf. 4.9; 8.10; 10.30; 13.12).

3.   Although the phrase has echoes of LXX Pss. 68 and 88.51-52, attempts to read into this verse some theology of Moses as precursor of Christ or representative

has been turned into a model of the discipleship required of Christian believers.

It is worth noting the subtle alterations of the story required to make Moses this model of Christian faith. In the first place, his 'suffering' with the people of God has to be expressed in these very general terms: in the biblical story he leaves Egypt, but the rest are left behind making bricks! Further, one advantage of omitting the story of the killing of the Egyptian is that the motif of secrecy can also be left out; it is difficult to see how a Moses who hides the body of his victim and is shocked at the public knowledge of his action could be seen as a figure who consciously and deliberately renounced his public prestige. Finally, the most flagrant adaptation of the story comes in v. 27 where the author insists that Moses left Egypt 'not fearing the wrath of the king'; this is despite the fact that the biblical story explicitly mentions Moses' fear (Exod. 2.14)! The reason for this contradiction is not hard to find: the author wishes to project an image of fearless faith (cf. 10.36; 11.23) and a Moses who flees Egypt in fear for his life will hardly fit the bill.[1]

The author of Hebrews thus sees an entirely different lesson in these stories of Moses from that detected by the author of Acts, who has christological patterns to weave. As in the texts we have studied from Egyptian Judaism, Moses is a model in behaviour and character. But the type of example Moses becomes in Hebrews is sociologically a very different entity from that projected by the Egyptian Jews. For all their diversity, Artapanus, Ezekiel and Philo all depict Moses from the perspective of cultural security, whether that be within the traditions of Egyptian culture, the refined tastes of Alexandrian theatre-goers or the common presuppositions of philosophy. Even though Philo also has Moses practising renunciation, it is clear that he understands this in terms of moral discipline rather than social ostracism.[2]

---

of the 'anointed' people are unconvincing. The author is using language loosely in adumbrating the Christian duty to bear the reproach of Christ (13.13); cf. Attridge, *Hebrews*, pp. 341-42.

1.   Some commentators attempt to deny a contradiction here by taking this verse as a reference to the later flight from Egypt at the exodus. Most, however, recognize that to be an unconvincing harmonization, e.g., F.F. Bruce, *The Epistle to the Hebrews* (Grand Rapids: Eerdmans, 1964), pp. 321-22.

2.   See the full discussion comparing the accounts of Hebrews and Philo in M.R. D'Angelo, *Moses in the Letter to the Hebrews* (Missoula, MT: Scholars Press, 1979), pp. 59-64. He also compares the theme of endurance (11.27) with Josephus,

But for the author of Hebrews and the community he exhorts life is far less comfortable: they need Moses not to celebrate his cultural prowess or his intellectual abilities but to show them that abuse, poverty and hardship are the necessary prelude to the ultimate reward. Moses is a model of the outcast from society who endures suffering with the assurance of faith and hope.

We are fortunate in having these two detailed, but very diverse, New Testament interpretations of the same cluster of Moses stories. We can only speculate what Paul would have made of the biblical source at that point: on the occasions he uses Moses material, it can serve typological (1 Cor. 10), polemical (2 Cor. 3) and even allegorical purposes (1 Cor. 9.8-10). The stark differences between Acts and Hebrews certainly illustrate once again that there was never any univocal Christian interpretation of the Bible: Christian exegesis was as diverse as the Jewish tradition from which it sprang.[1]

These five/six interpretations of Exodus 2 (five of the LXX, itself an interpretation of the Hebrew) demonstrate how extraordinarily different meanings can be found in the one text. This is especially so when, as in each example we have studied, the base story is manipulated by additions, expansions, paraphrases and convenient omissions. In each case the interpretation is particularly revealing of the historical, social and theological perspective of the interpreter; each one recreates Moses in his own image. Without such treatment Moses would have been no more than a figure of past history and legend. Perhaps it was only by manipulating Moses that he could be made a living and relevant part of Jewish and Christian religion.

Ant. 2.256-57 (pp. 27-33). As R. Williamson has argued, it is unlikely that Hebrews is dependent on Philo in this context (*Philo and the Epistle to the Hebrews* [Leiden: Brill, 1970], pp. 469-80).

1.   As it continues to be: I was interested to find in a Children's Bible from a conservative stable (by M. Batchelor [Oxford: Lion Publishing, 1985]) a paraphrase of these stories insisting that Moses 'never forgot that he was an Israelite. He remembered and loved the God of his own people, not the many strange gods and goddesses of Egypt.' He struck out at the Egyptian 'bully' only because he 'beat an Israelite slave to death'. I doubt whether the author was aware how close she was in some respects to Ezekiel and Philo!

EPHESIANS 2.11-22: A CHRISTIAN VIEW OF JUDAISM

Ernest Best

There have been many Christian views of Judaism down the centuries, some of them framed in very unfriendly terms. That of Eph. 2.11-22 comes from almost the beginning but is not expressed in a hostile manner, although the author (I take him not to have been Paul, although whether he was Paul or not has no bearing on the nature of the view expressed here) clearly believes that his Christian faith is superior to Judaism. Before we examine his view it is appropriate first to enquire if it was one that would have been readily recognizable in the ancient world. The readers of the Ephesian Epistle came largely from a Gentile background (cf. 2.11; 3.1), probably in Asia Minor; to what image of Judaism had they been accustomed in their pre-Christian days?

This question can only be answered in very general terms for all of us are affected both by the general beliefs of society about any group of people and by the actual contacts we have with individual members of it in forming our opinion of the group. Gentiles of the time who had been helped in some way by Jews would have thought very differently from those who believed they had been cheated in business by them. There are, however, some general points that we can make, for many Greek and Roman authors have commented on the Jewish people, and Jewish writers such as Josephus and Philo, by the rebuttals they make of what they take to be slanders on their people, indicate views held by others.[1] We need, however, to remember that the views

---

1. On views held about the Jews in the ancient world see, e.g., M. Whittaker, *Jews and Christians: Greco-Roman Views* (Cambridge: Cambridge University Press, 1984), pp. 14-130; M. Stern, 'The Jews in Greek and Latin Literature', in *The Jewish People in the First Century*, II (ed. S. Safrai and M. Stern; Amsterdam: Van Gorcum, 1976), pp. 1101-59; *idem, Greek and Latin Authors on Jews and*

pagan authors express, often in passing, are those of educated people, and the less well-educated may have judged differently. Those, moreover, who had never encountered Jews would depend very much for their opinions on rumour, and rumour rarely preserves good views. Allowing for all this, we can say that it was widely known that Jews were circumcised.[1] Even if a few were not circumcised (a few proselytes were excused circumcision for one reason or another[2]) the great majority were, and were probably despised because of their circumcision. It was also generally accepted that they kept one holy day in the week and did not eat pork. Authors either deduced from these beliefs, or learnt from deliberate enquiry, that the Jews were controlled by an unusual system of law or custom.[3] Apparent also, and partly arising from these practices, was a view that the Jews kept to themselves and did not mingle in society as others did; they formed an exclusive community within the general populace, a community which was centred on their place of worship. It would also have been widely recognized that they did not take part in the normal religious rites and ceremonies (i.e. what went on in every city and village) but worshipped only one God of whom they made no images; indeed there were those who called them atheists because they did not worship the generally recognized gods or the gods specific to their area.[4] Their exclusiveness, combined with their rejection of the worship of their pagan neighbours, could also lead to such wild rumours as that they secretly worshipped pigs (so Petronius, *Satyricon*, frag. 37) or asses (as reported by Josephus, *Apion* 2.114; 2.80).

If it is difficult to determine the opinion of non-Jews on Jews and

---

Judaism (3 vols.; Jerusalem: The Israel Academy of Sciences and Humanities, 1974–1984); V. Tcherikover, *Hellenistic Civilisation and the Jews* (New York: Atheneum, 1979), pp. 344-77.

1.   It is true that other peoples practised circumcision; Paul may have known this since he had lived in Arabia (see L. Gaston, 'Israel's Enemies in Pauline Theology', *NTS* 28 [1982], pp. 400-23) but in the ancient world circumcision was regularly connected only with Jews.

2.   Cf. N.J. McEleney, 'Conversion, Circumcision and the Law', *NTS* 20 (1973–74), pp. 319-41.

3.   Diodorus Siculus, *World History*, 34/35.1.3; 1.94.1-2; 40.3.3; Josephus, *Ant.* 16.162-65.

4.   Cf. H. Conzelmann, *Heiden–Juden–Christen* (Tübingen: Mohr, 1981), pp. 43-46, 130-31, 231-32.

their beliefs, it is equally difficult to determine the way in which first-century Jews would have described themselves and their faith in distinguishing themselves from others. There were then a number of groups within Judaism, each of which might have characterized Judaism in different ways and might not have been prepared to acknowledge the Jewishness of all the other groups; but in practice, most of the groups seem to have been prepared to accept most of the other groups.[1] The leaders of the Qumran community were probably hesitant to acknowledge as true Jews those who controlled the temple, and the Jewishness of the Samaritans may not have been widely recognized. While it may be true that the later rabbis disenfranchised other groups, that would take us beyond our period. It is, however, clear that the exclusion of some who did not come up to recognized standards began to appear within the first century, as the existence of the *birkat ha-minim* testifies, and this holds true whether the relevant prayer is regarded as directed against Christians or sectarian Jews.[2] The Qumran community practised both partial (1QS 6.25-27; 7.15-16) and total (6.27–7.2; 7.17, 22-25) exclusion from its membership, but whether in the latter case the Jewishness of the excluded member was denied is not certain. The exclusion of some from Judaism did take place, or was at least advocated in one earlier period. Ezra compelled Jews who had married non-Jews to put away their wives; presumably if they had not done so he would no longer have acknowledged them as Jews (Ezra 9; 10; cf. Tob. 4.12; 6.15). The basis for his judgment seems to have been behaviour rather than belief. This raises one of the basic issues in relation to the definition of Judaism: is it more a way of life than a way of thought, or to put it differently, is Judaism to be conceived as an orthopraxy or an orthodoxy? But even to put the alternatives in this way is not sufficient. Being a Jew is not

---

1. On the whole area see *Jewish and Christian Self-Definition. II. Aspects of Judaism in the Graeco-Roman Period* (ed. E.P. Sanders with A.I. Baumgarten and A. Mendelson; London: SCM Press, 1981), and a series of papers by N.J. McEleney, 'Orthodoxy in Judaism of the First Christian Century', *JSJ* 4 (1973), pp. 19ff.; D.E. Aune, 'Orthodoxy in First Century Judaism', *JSJ* 7 (1976), pp. 1-10; L.L. Grabbe, 'Orthodoxy in First Century Judaism?', *JSJ* 7 (1976), pp. 149-53; N.J. McEleney, 'Orthodoxy in Judaism of the First Christian Century: Replies to David E. Aune and Lester L. Grabbe', *JSJ* 9 (1978), pp. 83-88.
2. See the articles by R. Kimelman and E.E. Urbach in Sanders *et al.* (eds), *Jewish and Christian Self-Definition*, II, pp. 226-44, 268-98.

just a question of believing a certain number of doctrines (e.g. that there is only one God) and/or practising a certain number of rules (e.g. not eating pork) but of belonging to the Jewish group either through birth, or exceptionally, through conversion, in which case the children of the converts are Jewish. Thus one of the Maccabaean martyrs speaks of dying for his *patris* as well as for the law (2 Macc. 8.21).

One of the more important factors which made it difficult for one group of Jews to deny the Jewishness of another group was birth; so long as its members had been born within the nation, their Jewishness could hardly be denied. Christian churches have regularly made decisions defining their membership through a legal process of some type, but there was no body in the Judaism of the first century which was able to determine in particular cases whether a person was or was not a Jew. Yet for practical purposes, for example marriage, Jews needed to know who were Jews and who were not. In the Mishnah, we find clear instructions about the differing attitudes that should be adopted to Jews and non-Jews. A benediction is not to be said over the lamp or spices of Gentiles (*Ber.* 8.6). A Jewish woman may not assist in the birth of a child of a Gentile woman, although a Gentile woman may assist in that of a Jewess (*'Abod. Zar.* 2.1). The same practical concern is found in one of the Qumran writings (CD 12.6-11), probably because this writing was designed for members living outside the actual community who would be in contact with both other Jews and Gentiles. The need to identify who was a Jew and who was not would also arise in the case of the conversion of someone who had been previously held to be non-Jewish. The ritual connected with conversion may or may not at this period have included immersion, but if it did there was no way afterwards of determining whether a person had been immersed or not except through the testimony of eyewitnesses. The same difficulty would apply in relation to the offering of sacrifice at the temple (or after 70 AD of the readiness to sacrifice). But someone who had been circumcised could always be thereafter identified. Also required of converts was acceptance of Torah; this would not mean that every prescription of the law was observed but only the more important,[1] for example charity, and the avoidance of pork and idolatry. The avoidance of pork and idolatry were two easily observ-

---

1. Cf. L. Schiffmann in Sanders *et al.* (eds.), *Jewish and Christian Self-Definition*, II, p. 124.

able indicators and were regarded as important as can be seen from
the stories of the martyrs or possible martyrs (Dan. 3.1-18; 6.1-15;
2 Macc. 6.18-31; 7.1-42). Another obvious sign of the Jew was his
joining with other Jews in worship, although this in itself would not
serve to determine whether a person was a Jew or not since there
were others than Jews who attended synagogue. Also, although it is
not often expressed, probably because it was so obvious, all Jews
would have been believers in the God of the Old Testament.

I now turn to Eph. 2.11-22. It is, in fact, a discussion of the disadvantages under which Gentiles suffered as seen from the position of a
Jewish Christian, assuming that Ephesians was written by such a
person. The Jewishness of the author is not certain, yet even if Paul is
not the author, it is still very probable; but granted this Jewishness we
do not know whether he (or she) was a first-generation Christian, that
is, converted directly from Judaism, or a second-generation Christian,
one whose Jewish parent(s) had been converted and who, while aware
of their Jewish inheritance, had never in fact personally lived as a
Jew. As a discussion of the disadvantages under which Gentiles suffered it may be read in mirror fashion to disclose the advantages of
Jews. It is also not a sociological presentation; for example, it does not
deal with the moral failures of the Gentile world, an approach which
is made at two other points in the letter (4.17-24; 5.13-14). It is rather
a theological characterization of the Gentile world and so, in mirror-
image, it provides a theological characterization of Judaism.

It begins not unnaturally with circumcision and we have seen how
largely this featured in Gentile views of Judaism and in Jewish views
of itself. In 2.1-10 both Jewish and Gentile Christians have been
depicted as once dead in trespasses and sins; Gentile Christians
however lacked the physical sign by which, despite this, Jews knew
they belonged to God's people, and the author of Ephesians is writing
to Gentile Christians for he explicitly identifies his readers as Gentile
by birth, τὰ ἔθνη ἐν σαρκί. Left to themselves, Gentiles would not
have distinguished themselves in any essential way from Jews; Jews
were just another race or nation among the many on earth; educated
Gentiles would have been more concerned to distinguish themselves
from barbarians than from Jews. Only the presence of Jews among
them would have made them aware of Jewish feelings on Gentile
identity as being on a different plane from Jewish identity and in some
way inferior to it. Why the author of Ephesians should have thought it

necessary to remind Gentile Christians of the distinction Jews drew between themselves and others is not clear; perhaps as one from Jewish stock he felt Gentile Christians too easily forgot their origins, although he can hardly be said to feel his own Judaism with the same emotional involvement as does Paul in Rom. 3.1-2 and 9.1-5. From Marcion onwards, Christians have regularly ignored their Jewish origin, or forgotten it, or taken it for granted without understanding its implications.

So far as circumcision goes, the author does not wish to emphasize it as an important part of the distinction between Jews and Gentiles; it is only a physical (ἐν σαρκί) thing, made by human hands, χειρο-ποιήτου. In the LXX this word is used of idols (Lev. 26.1, 30; Isa. 2.18; Dan. 5.4, 23; cf. Acts 17.24) and in the New Testament of the Jewish people (Mk 14.58; Acts 7.48; 17.24; Heb. 9.11, 27), and always with the intention of stressing the inadequacy of that to which it refers. Paul himself had already said that neither circumcision nor uncircumcision was of any value (Gal. 5.6; 6.15) and one of his school who particularly influenced the writer of Ephesians had spoken of a circumcision 'not made with hands' (Col. 2.11). But the writer of Ephesians does not go as far as Paul in making a positive attack on the practice (Phil. 3.2) or spiritualizing it (Rom. 2.29), nor does he suggest baptism as a substitute for it as many have done. It is the physical rite separating Jews and Gentiles. Since, for our author, this distinction no longer exists within the Christian community, he does not have to find a place for it and can simply give up speaking about it.

There is a sense in which 2.11 is really parenthetical. Its author had begun by calling on his Gentile readers to 'remember'; it is not, how-ever, circumcision that he wishes them to remember but certain other factors to which he moves in v. 12. In recalling their past their non-circumcision had been relatively unimportant; what had been impor-tant was their separation from the messiah, their alienation from the commonwealth of Israel, their non-participation in the covenants of promise, and the fact that they had been without hope and without God in the world. Their pre-Christian condition is thus not described in sociological or moral terms but in theological. That the writer had a dim view of their earlier moral behaviour is seen in 4.17-24; 5.3, 14. They had come from a sinful past described in the way many a Jewish moralist would have viewed Gentile life. But this aspect of their past existence is not the author's concern at this point. We now need to look item by item at the description he gives of their previous condition.

Of the five items, the second and third are coupled by 'and', as are the fourth and fifth. There is no reason to take this 'and' as indicating that the third and fifth items explain the second and fourth or are their consequences.[1] Nor should the first be understood as qualifying what follows, 'you (in the time when you were) without Christ were alienated. . . ',[2] but taken predicatively, that is, as a distinct item in the chain. It is not surprising that the reference to the messiah should be set first, for throughout the letter it is the relation of the readers to Christ which is positively stressed. They have been redeemed by him, they are 'in him', they are members of his body, they have been made alive with him, raised with him and sit with him in the heavenlies. We may note here the difference from the list of Jewish advantages which Paul gives in Rom. 9.4-5 where the reference to Christ is the climax. In Ephesians all begins from Christ.

I commence with the first phrase: what does it mean to be 'without Christ'? Christ can be conceived as being present with Israel in his pre-incarnate state (cf. 1 Cor. 10.4; 1 Pet. 1.11; Jn 12.14[3]) or as the Jesus who lived and died as a historical person in Israel[4] or as the messiah for whom Israel hoped.[5] As for the first possibility, there are no indications elsewhere that the author of Ephesians believed in a pre-incarnate presence of the messiah with Israel. To limit the reference to the historical Jesus makes only a trivial point and one which

1. So H. Merklein, *Christus und die Kirch: Die theologische Grundstruktur des Epheserbriefes nach Eph 2,11-18* (SBS, 66; Stuttgart, 1973), pp. 17-18.
2. So J.A. Robinson, *St Paul's Epistle to the Ephesians* (London: Macmillan, 1909); C. Masson, *L'épitre de saint Paul aux Ephésiens* (Commentaire du Nouveau Testament; Paris: Delachaux & Niestlé, 1953).
3. So H. von Soden, *Die Briefe an die Kolosser, Epheser, Philemon* (Hand-Commentar zum Neuen Testament; Leipzig: Mohr, 1893); M. Barth, *Ephesians 1–3* (AB; New York: Doubleday, 1974); for the idea see A.T. Hanson, *Jesus Christ in the Old Testament* (London: SPCK, 1965).
4. So E. Haupt, *Die Gefangenschaftsbriefe* (KEK; Göttingen: Vandenhoeck & Ruprecht, 1902); H. Rendtorff, *Der Brief an die Epheser* (NTD; Göttingen: Vandenhoeck & Ruprecht, 1955); Merklein, *Christus*, p. 18.
5. So H. Schlier, *Der Brief an die Epheser* (Düsseldorf: Patmos-Verlag, 1971); J. Gnilka, *Der Epheserbrief* (Freiburg: Herder, 1971); F. Mussner, *Christus, das All und die Kirche* (Trier: Paulinus-Verlag, 1955), p. 77.

would have been true for only a limited period. Thus the third view is
to be preferred. There is, however, a sense in which it cannot be separated from the second; for Gentiles there had never been a time when
they had hoped for a messiah; when they first came to hear of a
messiah he was already identified as Jesus. Although our author begins
his list with a reference to a messiah it is important to note that in the
brief summaries I gave of Gentile and Jewish views of Judaism there
was no reference to such. It would be natural that Gentiles would
know little about Jewish expectations of a messiah (before their
conversion Gentiles would probably never even have heard the word
'Christ' and if they had they would have thought it referred to someone anointed with oil after a hot bath!) What emerges here then is
how much more important to Christian views of Judaism than to
Jewish views was the messianic expectation.

It is more difficult to give an exact significance to the second item in
the list, 'outside the πολιτεία of Israel'. 'Outside' is the translation of
the perfect participle from ἀπαλλοτρίοω (the use of the word here
probably derives from Col. 1.21) more usually rendered by something like 'alienated' or 'excluded'; such translations would wrongly
suggest a definite action in which Gentiles had been excluded or that
there had once been an original harmony from which they had alienated themselves. They have always been outside. But of what are they
outside? πολιτεία has a wide range of meanings.[1] Since it does not
appear in the LXX as the translation of any Hebrew word but only in
the Jewish texts for which we have no underlying Hebrew it probably
entered Judaism in the Hellenistic period when Jews had to explain
their life and nation to others. It can signify 'constitution' (Josephus,
Ant. 4.45; 13.245) or 'way of life' (2 Macc. 8.17; *4 Macc.* 8.7). The
former is too legalistic for the present context; in any case at this time
the Jews did not have a constitution. The latter by itself hardly goes
with the idea of being outside, excluded or alienated. A meaning
therefore which suggests membership of a community with the rights,

1.   Cf. LSJ; W. Bauer, *Wörterbuch zu den Schriften des Neuen Testaments*
(Berlin: Töpelman, 1952); C. Spicq, *Notes de lexicographie néo-testamentaire*
(Friburg, Switzerland: Editions Universitaires, 1978–82), II, p. 710; Strathmann,
TWNT, VI, pp. 516-55; R. Schnackenburg, 'Die Politeia Israels in Eph 2,12', in
*De la Torah au messie: Etudes d'exégèse et d'herméneutique bibliques offertes à
Henri Cazelles pour ses 25 annés d'enseignement à l'Institut Catholique de Paris*
(Paris: Desclée, 1981), pp. 467-74.

privileges and way of life associated with that membership seems most suitable, and in 2 Macc. 13.14 Jews are bidden to struggle for their laws, temple, city, country and πολιτεία; cf. *4 Macc.* 17.9. This understanding would make it accord with the 'fellow-citizens' of v. 19 if the 'saints' mentioned there are the Jews, though such an identification of the 'saints' in v. 19 is doubtful; there is in fact no need for it to accord; words coming from the same root but formed differently can vary in meaning within a paragraph provided always that both are customary meanings. Our term is not, however, the equivalent of 'nation'. In modern parlance it has both a political and a religious (including moral) aspect. In our context it means that Gentiles were once outside the community of Israel. Israel is not of course here a substitute for the church.[1] Whenever it denotes anything other than the Jewish people, or a part of that people, this is made clear (for example, Gal. 6.16; even here it is not clear if the church is intended).[2] The phrase used in Eph. 2.12 is not out of keeping with the indefinite way in which, as we have seen, Jews tended to describe themselves, and for the writer as for the Jews it is clearly a description intended to give honour.

The third phrase in the series 'strangers to the covenants of promise' is again unusual, perhaps because it is intended to carry a lot of meaning. Like the preceding phrase, it expresses the condition of the Gentiles in Jewish terms (for Gentiles as strangers or foreigners see Jer. 5.19; Mt. 27.7). The plural διαθῆκαι with the meaning 'covenants' is unusual; in the New Testament it is found only at Gal. 4.24, where only one of the two covenants which are mentioned refers to Israel, and Rom. 9.4.[3] Generally speaking the view of the Old Testament is that God had one covenantal relationship with Israel which he renewed on a number of occasions and the plural is not used to describe this.[4] Often the plural means 'promises' but this is impossible here, as it is also at Rom. 9.5, where we have covenants and promises as separate items in the list. Probably, then, we have to

1. S. Hanson, *The Unity of the Church in the New Testament, Colossians and Ephesians* (Uppsala: Almqvist & Wiksell, 1946), p. 142.
2. Evidence for the description of the church as Israel is scarce; cf. P. Richardson, *Israel in the Apostolic Church* (SNTSMS, 10; Cambridge: Cambridge University Press, 1969), pp. 70ff.
3. The singular is an alternative reading here but should be rejected.
4. Cf. C. Roetzel, 'Diathekai in Romans 9,4', *Bib* 51 (1970), pp. 377-90.

recognize an unusual use of the plural. This may be occasioned because Christians thought of two covenants, the old first one made with Abraham and a new second covenant made with Christ (Jer. 31.31-34; cf. 32.40; Isa. 55.3; Ezek. 37.26) of which they were reminded every time they celebrated the Eucharist. It is possible, although highly unlikely, that the covenant made with Noah has occasioned the plural. More probable, but still unlikely, would be the idea that the author of Ephesians looked on the covenant, originally made with Abraham, when renewed with Isaac and Jacob as being a new covenant. Wherever the covenantal idea appears in the Old Testament, a promise, or promises, is associated with it, although the term 'promise' is not an Old Testament term, appearing only in later Jewish writing (2 Macc. 2.17-18; *3 Macc.* 3.15; *Ps. Sol.* 13.8; Josephus, *Ant.* 2.219; 3.77; etc.). But what within our context is the content of the promise? Although Christians may associate the covenant with the Eucharist, and see in Christ the fulfilment of the promise of the new covenant, this can hardly be the idea here, for Christ has already featured in the list as its first item. The word recurs at 3.6 and is again undefined and may refer either to the total promise of the Old Testament with its many aspects as promise of salvation, or the particular promise made to Abraham on which the position of the Jews as the people of God depended and which Paul argues can be understood as including Gentile Christians (Gal. 3.29). The style of the author of Ephesians suggests that he may be expressing in fresh words what he had already said in the previous phrase ('strangers' to some extent parallels 'outside') but pushing it in a new direction. From the Christian point of view there is something inherently forward-looking in the community of Israel; not only is there the expectation of a messiah but also that of the creation of a new community, the community of the new covenant (2 Cor. 3.6; Heb. 8.6; 12.24), and indeed a great part of Ephesians is taken up with describing the nature of this new community; the passage with whose beginning we are dealing ends with such a description (2.19-22).

The final two phrases 'having no hope and without God in the world' do not appear to be directly related to Israel[1] and therefore

---

1.   Cf. Schnackenburg, 'Zur Exegese von Eph 2,11-22 im Hinblick auf das Verhältnis von Kirche und Israel', in *The New Testament Age. Festschrift B. Reicke* (ed. D. Brownell and W.C. Weinrich; Macon, GA: Mercer University Press, 1984), pp. 467-91.

sound more like value judgments than theological descriptions. However, to Jews looking out on the Gentile world, they would appear as indicating its non-spiritual condition and their judgment would not change in this respect if they became Christians.[1] Most Gentiles, while they would not have worried very much about their failings in respect of the first three phrases, would, however, have rejected the final two charges as untrue. The reference to hope follows naturally after that to promise, for promises give hope. Hope should not be limited to the hope of an afterlife but taken in the broadest way possible in line with the promise. If, as is possible, 'in the world' also qualifies it, then every material thing is rejected as the object of hope. If hope follows on promise it is also linked to belief in God. Atheism,[2] without God, could be an accusation that Gentiles were godless or impious, but this would be a value judgment (see 4.17-24 for Gentiles as impious), and therefore more probably means they did not worship the true God, the Jewish God, or had been abandoned by him. The description of Gentiles as without hope and God would be one that the readers of Ephesians would themselves have made about those around them who were neither Jews nor Christians. I am not concerned to evaluate its truth as a judgment on Gentiles; most of them would have denied that they were without God; genuine atheism was on the whole rare at that time. Hope was also not something confined to believers in Yahweh.

Thus we see that all five phrases, when taken as they stand, give a description of the Gentile world, yet their mirror-images are a description of Judaism as at least one Christian saw Judaism. It looks forward to the messiah, it is the community of God's people with whom God has entered into covenants with their promise, it believes in the true God and has hope. Before we begin to compare this with pagan and Jewish views of Judaism we need to turn to the one other

1. It is interesting to note that when the early fathers refer to our verse it is largely the second and third phrases which they quote as a brief glance at *Biblia Patristica*, I–III will show. Moderns would probably choose the fourth and fifth as descriptive of the world outside the church.

2. On atheism in the ancient world see J. Thrower, *A Short History of Western Atheism* (London: Pemberton Books, 1971), pp. 37-48; Conzelmann, *Heiden*, pp. 43-46, 130-31, 231-32.

place in the New Testament where we have a description of Judaism. In Rom. 9.4-5, the privileges or advantages of Judaism are set out directly and there is no need for mirror reading. On this occasion they are detailed also by someone, Paul, whose relationship to Judaism is known and of whose firsthand experience of it in its rabbinic and Hellenistic forms we can be certain. This list runs

> They are Israelites, and to them belong the sonship, the glory, the covenants, the giving of the law, the worship, and the promises; to them belong the patriarchs, and of their race, according to the flesh, is the Christ. God who is over all be blessed for ever.

The list appears to be carefully constructed[1] yet is probably not pre-Pauline but his own creation since it contains so many of his favourite concepts; he may, of course, have formulated it prior to the writing of Romans. There are elements here which correspond to the list of Eph. 2.11-12: the reference to Israel, the covenants, the promises, Christ (he is now the climax of the list), God, if we include the final clause of v. 5 and do not regard it as a statement of Christ's divinity, or if we regard the 'glory' as that of the Shekinah indicating his presence, or if we regard him as the object of the worship. Unique to Romans then are the giving of the law,[2] sonship, worship, and the fathers, though our understanding of πολιτεία would probably suggest that both the worship and the fathers would fall under that heading. Unique to Ephesians is the reference to hope.

The two lists of Ephesians and Romans serve different purposes.[3] In the latter, they form part of an argument that God has not forsaken Israel and that it continues to have a place in his purpose. The words are set with a verb in the present tense and so are to be regarded as still being true after Christ. In Ephesians, the list is set in a once/now

1. Cf. M. Rese, 'Die Vorzüge Israels in Röm. 19,4f. und Eph. 2,12: Exegetische Anmerkungen zum Thema Kirche und Israel', *TZ* 31 (1975), pp. 211-22; F. Dreyfus, 'Le passé et le présent d'Israël (Rom. 9,1-5; 11,1-24)', in *Die Israelfrage nach Röm 9–11* (ed. L. de Lorenzi; Rome: Abtei von St Paul, 1977), pp. 131-51; J. Piper, *The Justification of God* (Grand Rapids, 1983), pp. 6-7.

2. E.J. Epp ('Jewish–Gentile Continuity in Paul: Torah and/or Faith? [Romans 9:1-5]', in *Christians among Jews and Gentiles: Festschrift K. Stendahl* [ed. G.W.E. Nickelsburg with G.S. MacRae; Philadelphia: Fortress Press, 1986], pp. 80-90) argues that Paul has deliberately used a word which refers to the giving of the law so as to avoid a direct reference to the law.

3. Cf. Rese, 'Vorzüge Israels'.

contrast; Christian Gentiles once were without Christ, etc., but now they have him. No conclusion is drawn as to the Jews, although certainly Christ, etc., was once theirs. It is not at this point said that Jews no longer enjoy the listed privileges; all that can be said is that Gentile Christians now enjoy the privileges that once belonged to Israel. In Romans, of course, nothing is said at that point to suggest that Gentile Christians participate in what are the privileges of Israel. Finally, we should note that there are no extant equivalent lists of Jewish privileges compiled by Jews. The nearest approaches are found in 2 Macc. 2.17-18; *4 Ezra* 3.13-24; *2 Bar.* 57.1-3. In them, however, the activity of God is stressed rather than actual privileges.[1]

The picture of Judaism which Eph. 2.11-22 presents is very different from that which Gentiles held, and it is also, though not to such a great extent, different from that of Judaism itself. The only factor common to all three is circumcision. The differences between Judaism's own picture or pictures and that of Ephesians must lie in the reason why the latter's author wishes to give a picture at all. Before looking at that, we note that the factors he has picked out are those of which he can make positive use as a Christian. The church believes in a messiah, sees itself as in some way related to Israel, as enjoying the promises, understood in a Christian way, made to Israel, as related to God in a new covenant, as believing in the same God as Israel believed in and not some other, and as having a hope of salvation just as Israel had. Since the letter is a round letter written to a number of Christian communities, none of which can be identified, we know little about its recipients. The stress, however, on continuity with Judaism (for this in fact is what the list indicates) suggests that there were those in these communities who were forgetful of the rock from which they were hewn. It would go too far to say that they were renouncing their Jewish heritage as Marcion did, but the probable absence of many Jews among them had left them in a position similar to that of many Christians today who seem unaware of their Jewish inheritance. Our author might have chosen to remind them of this by copious quotation from the Old Testament in the manner of the author of Hebrews but instead has chosen another and more subtle approach. It is interesting that when we first find the early fathers quoting this section of

---

1.　For references to possible lists see L. Cerfaux, *Recueil Lucien Cerfaux*, II (BETL, 7; Gembloux: Duculot, 1954), pp. 339-64 (p. 340 n. 1).

Ephesians they sometimes use it to refute Marcion and various Gnostics and to demonstrate the link between Christianity and Judaism.[1]

I have suggested that our author selected those concepts from Judaism which suited him as a Christian, those, moreover, which he could take up and use in expressing his Christianity; it is therefore interesting to note what he has left out that a Jew might have inserted. Surprising is the omission of any reference to the law and in this our list contrasts with that of Rom. 9.4-5. There is in fact very little about the law in Ephesians; it is mentioned only in 2.15 where it is said to be abrogated. Commentators differ here as to whether 'the law of commandments in ordinances' means the many commandments of the ceremonial law or is intended to refer to the whole law. The matter was apparently not important enough for the author to spell out. This absence of reference to the law is in striking contrast to what we find in Paul. Indeed there is an almost total absence of hostility towards Judaism. The author is not concerned with the continuing existence of Judaism and the fate of unbelieving Jews as was Paul in Romans 9–11. There is nothing to suggest that Jews are rejected as God's people, but nothing either to suggest that they remain his people.

Yet the author should not be taken to be indifferent to Judaism. He goes on directly after this list to deal with the relation of Gentile and Jewish Christians. The Gentiles who were once far off (2.13, 17) are now near; but this nearness is not a nearness to the Jews but of both Jewish and Gentile Christians to God. Gentiles on becoming Christians have not thus become Jews. With Jewish believers they have been formed into a new group, the community of believers (2.15, 16).[2]

---

1.   Cf. W. Rader, *The Church and Racial Hostility* (Tübingen: Mohr [Paul Siebeck], 1978), pp. 12-16; Irenaeus, *Adv. Haer.* 5.14.3; Tertullian, *Adv. Marc.* 5.11.13.

2.   The position which M. Barth has argued for in a number of writings as well as in his commentary on Ephesians (e.g. *Israel und die Kirche im Brief des Paulus an die Epheser* [Munich: Kaiser Verlag, 1959]; 'Conversion and Conversation: Israel and the Church in Paul's Epistle to the Ephesians', *Int* 17 [1963], pp. 3-24; *The People of God* [JSNTSup, 5; Sheffield: JSOT Press, 1983]) that Gentile Christians have entered Israel, the Israel of v. 12, is thus to be rejected. For criticism see Schnackenburg, 'Exegese'; A.T. Lincoln, 'The Church and Israel in Ephesians 2', *CBQ* 49 (1987), pp. 605-24. See also E. Grässer, *Der alte Bund im Neuen Testament* (WUNT, 35; Tübingen: Mohr, 1985), pp. 25-34.

THE DISCOMBOBULATIONS OF TIME AND THE DIVERSITIES OF TEXT: NOTES ON THE *REZEPTIONSGESCHICHTE* OF THE BIBLE

Robert P. Carroll

> Hegel remarks somewhere that all great, world-historical facts and personages occur, as it were, twice. He has forgotten to add: the first time as tragedy, the second as farce.
>
> Karl Marx[1]

> The history of ideas is not without its ironies.
>
> Isaiah Berlin[2]

> Tell all the Truth but tell it slant—
> Success in Circuit lies. . .
>
> Emily Dickinson[3]

The teaching of Bible and Theology in the Faculties of Arts and of Divinity in the ancient Scottish Universities involves an enormous amount of lectures, seminars, tutorials and general teaching duties. Robert Davidson's great strength in the Faculty of Divinity at Glasgow has been his contribution to the teaching of Hebrew, Greek and English Bible. Apart from his teaching of texts, especially Hebrew texts, his particular contribution to courses popular with students were his Old Testament theology course and his history of the interpretation of the Bible (Old Testament) course. Elsewhere in this collection

1.   'The Eighteenth Brumaire of Louis Bonaparte', in *The Marx–Engels Reader* (ed. R.C. Tucker; New York: Norton, 1972), p. 436.

2.   'Hume and the Source of German Anti-Rationalism', in *Against the Current: Essays in the History of Ideas* (ed. H. Hardy; Oxford: Oxford University Press, 1989), p. 162.

3.   Poem No. 1129 in *The Complete Poems of Emily Dickinson* (ed. T.H. Johnson; London: Faber & Faber, 1975), p. 506.

Graeme Auld has addressed the subject of Old Testament theology,[1] so I want to focus on Robert's other great strength and offer a few observations on a very complex subject.

The history of the interpretation of the Bible or, as I would prefer to call it, the history of the reception of the Bible (*Rezeptions-geschichte*) is by its nature too complex and too comprehensive to be analysed intelligently in a short article, so these notes are intended to acknowledge Robert's interest in the subject by way of sketching a few features of the terrain. If I confine my remarks to a few general observations followed by a very limited number of examples drawn from biblical books on which Robert has written commentaries, I shall have matched my intention with my performance to my own satisfaction. Readers can make good my defects from their own superior knowledge.

I

Writing an adequate *Rezeptionsgeschichte* of the Bible is an impossible task. The Bible—whether in Hebrew, Greek, Latin, English or any other language—has been in existence for far too long for any single author or even collectivity of writers to be able to encompass the range and content of its interpretation through time. As a library of books in itself it exceeds the normal range of literature constituted by ordinary books and as a book recognized by many different religious traditions as their 'holy book' its influence and significance also outstrip those of other books. Among classicists, Homer and Virgil might be said to occupy a similar position to that of the Bible, but throughout history there have been far fewer classicists than religious and theological groups relating to the Bible. The different languages represented in the Bible (Hebrew, Aramaic, Greek) and by translations of the Bible constitute other factors bearing on the history of its interpretation. So a proper *Rezeptionsgeschichte* would have to be a multilingual enterprise which took into account all the many uses made of the Bible in all the various languages of societies, communities and groups for whom the Bible had had any significance. Such an enterprise would inevitably escape the competence of any but the

---

1. See 'Can a Biblical Theology also be Academic or Ecumenical', above pp. 13-27.

largest group conceivable of scholars, historians, hermeneutists and
other interested parties.

If the production of a comprehensive *Rezeptionsgeschichte* of the
Bible is a task beyond realization, then it must also be admitted that
various attempts to produce single to multi-volumes of works dealing
with the subject generally have been miserable failures. Works such as
the Cambridge History of the Bible or the *Bible de tous les temps*
project or Ludwig Diestel's great work—to mention but three notable
enterprises—must be regarded as having but scratched the surface of
the subject.[1] Lesser works—which must remain unnamed in order to
protect the innocent—do not even make that much of an impression
on the topic. Volume after volume in series after series make a
contribution to the working materials of an adequate *Rezeptionsgeschichte*, but the subject itself eludes the combined attentions of the
encyclopaedists and historians because it is too varied and large to be
encompassed in a practical manner. Contrary to what sometimes
passes for the belief and practice of scholars, the *Rezeptionsgeschichte*
of the Bible is a topic much larger than many scholarly works imagine. It is larger because it includes a vast amount of reading of the
Bible done outside the confines of the academies and the religious
institutions revering the Bible as sacred.

As a literary work or, perhaps better, as a collection of literary
works the Bible belongs fundamentally to literature and therefore is
part of literary history and criticism. As such its *Rezeptionsgeschichte*
belongs as much to the history of the study of literature as it does to
religious and theological categories. The category of the sacred may
be a special subset of literature in general, but the literary dimension
of the Bible cannot be gainsaid. Hence the literatures of the world
must be combed for their contributions to the *Rezeptionsgeschichte* of

1. *The Cambridge History of the Bible* (3 vols.; Cambridge: Cambridge
University Press, 1963–70); *Bible de tous les temps* (8 vols.; ed. C. Kannengiesser;
Paris, 1984–89); L. Diestel, *Geschichte des Alten Testamentes in der christlichen
Kirche* (Jena, 1869). Mention perhaps should be made of H.G. Reventlow's *The
Authority of the Bible and the Rise of the Modern World* (London: SCM Press,
1984) and of K. Scholder's *The Birth of Modern Critical Theology: Origins and
Problems of Biblical Criticism in the Seventeenth Century* (London: SCM Press,
1990) as examples of specialized studies of certain aspects of the enterprise. For
glimmerings of the subject see *A Dictionary of Biblical Interpretation* (ed. R.J.
Coggins and J.L. Houlden; London: SCM Press, 1990).

the Bible. Now that is a task which will outstrip the competence of any biblical scholar and which makes the enterprise of producing a comprehensive *Rezeptionsgeschichte* necessarily a collective endeavour and a multi-disciplinary one at that. So a suitable modesty will cloak the observations which are made in this brief set of notes.

The Bible as literature and its many contributions to literature are topics which will keep the mills of scholarship grinding for millennia. And as no text can be read without taking into account the many levels of interpretation which it has generated through time, the *Rezeptionsgeschichte* of the Bible is virtually a limitless subject. Thus a reading of the book of Jonah will inevitably entail reading Herman Melville's novel, *Moby Dick*, which embraces the Jonah legend of the great fish as well as making use of the story of Jonah in Father Mapple's sermon. The *Rezeptionsgeschichte* of Jonah encompasses a colossal amount of work in Jewish and Christian interpretations of the book, not to mention the wide range of books and paintings which make use of the story of Jonah. From the New Testament to Simon Louvish's novel, *The Last Trump of Avram Blok*,[1] that story has gripped the imagination and called forth an endless stream of influence and resignification. A similar individual *Rezeptionsgeschichte* of the story of Joseph in Genesis could be developed around a study of Thomas Mann's tetralogy, *Joseph and his Brothers*.

The examples of Mann and Melville are too well known to warrant further attention. What is less known because less obvious are the multitudinous *influences* of the Bible on literature which the modern reader absorbs without really noticing. A simple if banal example is that of the revelation of the divine name in the story of the burning bush and among the many things said to Moses is the very famous utterance 'I AM WHO I AM' (English versions of this saying tend to favour an upper case I AM, though there are no warrants in the Hebrew text for this treatment of the word 'I am'). Such a phrase as 'I am' is too common and too ordinary to be of any significance and yet it echoes throughout English literature as a distant but distinct allusion to the burning bush affirmation. Its use in the Fourth Gospel in the dialogical encounters between Jesus and the Jews, or Jesus and his

---

1.   Louvish's novel (London: Collins, 1990, pp. 343-45) contains an episode based on the Jonah legend in the Bible but updated to fit into the flow of the novel's plot.

followers is too well known to invite further comment. Henry Vaughan catches it nicely in the lines:

Each Bush
And Oak doth know I AM;[1]

It trips off the pen of the great *Sprachschöpfer*[2] himself, William Shakespeare, on a number of occasions of which perhaps Iago and Viola provide the best examples. Iago's 'I am not what I am' (*Othello* Act I, Scene 1, line 65) negates Exod. 3.14 and so constitutes the outer limit of the history of the assertion 'I am what I am'. Viola and Olivia offer a subtler set of variations on the seminal phrase:

Viola: Then think you right: I am not what I am.
Olivia: I would you were as I would have you be!
Viola: Would it be better, madam, than I am? I wish it might, for now I
    am your fool.[3]

The divine tautology of Exodus 3 combines the utterly banal with the elusively profound, offering a commonplace which every person throughout history employs without thinking and yet which also recapitulates echoes of the divine being.[4]

The intertextuality of the divine self-assertion raises the spectre of the Sisyphean nature of the quest for an adequate *Rezeptionsgeschichte* of the Bible. Who could produce even the equivalent of a *catalogue raisonné* of the history of the reception of phrases, idioms and metaphors from the Bible in the literatures of the world? If in this article I offer a few examples of such intertextuality it is not in the hope that a task already started elsewhere can be brought to a successful conclusion but in order to underline the nature of the enterprise and to iterate my conviction that such a project will defeat even the most industrious team of historical and literary researchers. While such a *catalogue raisonné* of biblical intertextuality (within the Bible itself and between Bible and literature) may be a desideratum of

1. 'Rules and Lessons', stanza 3 in *Silex Scintillans 1650* (Menston, Yorkshire: The Scolar Press, 1968), p. 54.
2. The term ('creator of language') is Ludwig Wittgenstein's; see his *Culture and Value* (ed. G.H. von Wright; Oxford: Basil Blackwell, 1980), §§ 84, 84e.
3. *Twelfth Night*, Act III, Scene 2, lines 138-40.
4. An interesting discussion of these aspects of the phrase appears in O. Barfield, *Saving the Appearances: A Study in Idolatry* (New York: Harcourt, Brace & World, 1965).

current biblical scholarship and its cognate studies in literature, it is so unlikely to be produced that an adequate *Rezeptionsgeschichte* of the Bible must remain more a dream than a realizable goal.

The matter is, of course, much more complex and complicated than these remarks may lead the reader to believe. A proper and comprehensive treatment of the history of the reception of the Bible would have to include accounts of all the pictorial and iconic representations of biblical material. From mosaics and murals to movies and magazines, the visual representation of the Bible constitutes a series of different histories of its reception. The intertextual nature of so much of this representation adds a further dimension to the study of the subject. For example, a familiarity with Rembrandt's depiction of Belshazzar's Feast needs to be supplemented with a knowledge of representations of that *topos* which preceded Rembrandt's activity and then with an awareness of all subsequent reproductions of that famous scene—especially of paintings influenced by Rembrandt's actual painting such as Frank Auerbach's recent painting. All such visual representations of a biblical scene, story or moment are themselves highly interpretative acts which reflect a *reading* of the text and are therefore a natural part of the history of the interpretation of the Bible.[1] Yet much of mainstream biblical scholarship is blind to such visual representations and their contributions to the *Rezeptionsgeschichte* of the Bible. To be an expert in Aramaic and Hebrew or Greek and Latin may be a *sine qua non* of being a competent interpreter of the Bible, but to be a truly adequate reader of the Bible requires also a competence in reading visual representations of the book and a much wider range of knowledge of its less mainstream interpreters.

The academic slant on the Bible is only one part of the world of *Rezeptionsgeschichte* and, perhaps, one of the least important because least popular. There are many worlds of biblical interpretation and reception outside the academy, though the academy may be the only one competent enough to produce an adequately comprehensive account of all the different interpretative histories of the Bible. From

---

1.   I have not yet seen Mieke Bal's book *Reading Rembrandt* (Cambridge: Cambridge University Press, 1991), but knowing her work elsewhere on pictorial representations of the Bible, I am sure this book will have much to instruct us on the matter.

the popular perceptions of the Bible embedded in such notions as 'the Bible and Shakespeare' (the radio programme 'Desert Island Discs' embodies a universe of assumptions in that combination of two collections of English literature produced in the late sixteenth and early seventeenth centuries) and the many, many fundamentalistic sects all over the Western world, to the uses of the Bible inherent in the English language (e.g. a *jeroboam* of champagne or *Balaam*[1] as printers' jargon for the nonsensical matter kept in type to fill up odd spaces), there are worlds to be explored, charted and written up as necessary contributions to a comprehensive *Rezeptionsgeschichte* of the Bible. The world of music also has much to contribute to such a history. Not simply the setting of biblical texts to music where the music has only a contiguous connection with the text—see Iain Matheson's contribution to this volume where such matters are more competently discussed (below, pp. 200-214)—but also beyond the world of hymns and liturgies the exploration of the Bible by composers seeking a direct musical expression of different worlds of discourse. In all these worlds of sound and sight the question must strike the intelligent reader 'Where would one start?'[2] Other questions follow quickly on that one and relate to structures, categories, limitations and coherence. In what follows here I will limit my remarks to just a few observations which may indicate to the reader something of the complicatedness of the project.

II

According to Qoheleth 'time and chance happen to them all' (9.11), and he might have added, in the light of the observations in 12.12, that time and chance happen also to books. The Bible is very much the product of time and, to a great extent, a production of chance. Time also happens to things and alters them (radically or otherwise). This is perhaps what is behind Karl Marx's observation on Hegel's notion of

---

1. The biblical character Balaam would require a separate book for an adequate treatment of the *topos*. Nick Cave's novel *And the Ass Saw the Angel* (London: Black Spring, 1989) touches on it, as does J. Magonet's chapter 'How a Donkey Reads the Bible—On Interpretation', in *A Rabbi's Bible* (London: SCM Press, 1991), pp. 60-72.
2. For a start one might try teasing out all the biblical allusions in the lyrics of Bob Dylan's song cycles (e.g. those in 'John Wesley Hardin' or 'Saved').

the recurrence of significant persons and things. Somewhere else Hegel remarks 'Christ died for our sins so long ago it can hardly be true any more' (see his Jena diary). Both remarks of Hegel, including Marx's important glossing of one of them, underline the contribution time makes to anything and a proper *Rezeptionsgeschichte* of the Bible would be an effective study of its continual change through time, including the discombobulations brought about by time.

Time which permits reflection, development, transformation, resignification and all the negative aspects of such changes also provides a running commentary on the Bible (in all its many versions). If I focus here on the discombobulations brought about in the reading of the Bible by time it is only in order to emphasize an aspect of biblical interpretation which is often ignored by more mainstream sources. A simple reversal of a biblical statement or observation will serve as an example. In one of his poems Edmund Blunden writes:

> I have been young, and now am not too old;
> And I have seen the righteous forsaken,
> His health, his honour and his quality taken.
> This is not what we were formerly told.[1]

This of course depends almost entirely for its words and sense on a well-known verse from one of the Psalms:

> I have been young, and now am old;
> yet have I not seen the righteous forsaken
> or his children begging bread (37.25).

Any treatment of Psalm 37 which aspired to be comprehensive or to include an element of its history of interpretation would have to taken Blunden's observation into account. The two belong together, because the statement in the Psalm gave direct rise to the poet's observation. The truth or falsity of the psalmist's somewhat optimistic account of life may be determined by observation and experience—various lament psalms or the books of Job and Qoheleth would challenge such sanguine piety and the rabbinic controversy aroused by Elisha ben Abuya has as its focus this very question of the relationship between virtue and reward. Time has shown the psalmist's optimism to be false: too many Jewish children begged in the streets and ghettoes of

---

1. 'Report on Experience', in *The Poems of Edmund Blunden* (London: Cobden-Sanderson, 1930), p. 284 (originally published in his *Near and Far*, 1929).

the Third Reich (not to mention throughout the long history of Christian Europe) for the modern reader of Psalm 37 to be impressed by its writer's faith. Perhaps in the writer's experience it was as stated, in which case we may note the psalmist's narrow outlook and move on to more realistic accounts of the matter. Time has not so much discombobulated the text as allowed for the emergence of comments on it which have effectively undermined it. We cannot *now* read the text without reflecting on how false it sounds in the light of the passage of time and all the other writings in the Bible.

All the many uses to which the Bible has been put by ecclesiastical institutions through time include many instantiations of what I have chosen to call 'the discombobulations of time'. A really good, comprehensive *Rezeptionsgeschichte* of the Bible would take full account of what the poet Robert Lowell meant by the lines 'O Bible chopped and crucified/in hymns we hear but do not read. . . '.[1] But a history of the reception of the Bible via hymns, prayers and liturgies would furnish a section of a library and its production must be regarded as further evidence of the Sisyphean nature of the task of producing such a project. Most of the great liturgies of the Christian churches consist of amalgams of biblical texts weaved into narratives which constitute rather different stories from those told in the Bible. The beginnings of this kind of imaginative intertextual construction are to be found in the Passion narratives in the Gospels where the different writers have told the story of the sufferings of Jesus by means of textual fragments drawn from the LXX (in particular from the book of Psalms). Whether these stories reflect in any historical sense what happened to Jesus or are themselves purely readings of ancient texts shaped by belief in the 'facts' of Christian tradition (that 'Christ died for our sins *according* to the Scriptures, that he was buried, that he was raised on the third day *according* to the Scriptures', 1 Cor. 15.3-4) is a matter for debate beyond the competence of this article. In the mediaeval period, the Old Testament continued to be read in such a way that it

1. 'Waking Early Sunday Morning', stanza 7, lines 1-2 in *Near the Ocean* (London: Faber & Faber, 1967), pp. 13-16 (p. 14). As Lowell's poem was a response to Wallace Stevens's 'Sunday Morning' poem (*Collected Poems* [London: Faber & Faber], pp. 66-70), there is a nice intertextual issue going on here which must complicate matters further. Lowell's substantive point is worth offering to hymnologists for reflection on as well as making a point for those interested in the history of the Bible's reception.

afforded substantive elements in the depiction of the Passion of Jesus in narrative and liturgy, as well as in iconographical representations.[1] Rhetorical flourishes and tropes in the biblical text were transformed into historical elements in the story of the murder of Christ by the Jews. Such transformations of metaphors and figures of speech into descriptive narrative necessarily discombobulates the text and makes for endless mischief. Thus the christological interpretation of the Old Testament text became a mechanism whereby Jews in mediaeval times suffered terribly on account of a literalistic twist given to figurative language.[2] While we may regard such readings of the text as essentially *mis*readings, they belong fully to any competent *Rezeptionsgeschichte* of the Bible and demonstrate the sense in which time may be said to a discombobulating factor in the interpretation of the Bible.

Time may also be kind to texts and bring them back into fashion. Social mores may change or reading sensibilities may develop which allow ancient texts to be read in a new light. A very good example of this kind of change is the *topos* in the New Testament 'the illegitimacy of Jesus'. This is not a subject which receives much attention from commentators.[3] They prefer to discuss 'virgin births' and other theological conundra rather than focus on the illegitimacy (or bastardy) of Jesus, even though the dogma of the Virgin Birth has as its necessary corollary that illegitimacy. Dogma and doctrine overwhelm the concerns of exegetes and the text is read in accordance with the demands of ideological correctness. However, in the late twentieth century, radical changes in social mores have removed the scandal from illegitimacy and the figure of the 'single parent' is too common to excite obloquy. So it is now possible to focus on the illegitimacy of Jesus and

---

1.   See J.H. Marrow, *Passion Iconography in Northern European Art of the Late Middle Ages and Early Renaissance: A Study of the Transformation of Sacred Metaphor into Descriptive Narrative* (Brussels: Van Ghemmert, 1979).

2.   Cf. Marrow, *Passion Iconography*, pp. 146-49 for the transformation of stone-throwing/mocking incidents in the Old Testament to features of the sufferings of the Christ in his Passion. Jewish children will suffer greatly at the hands of Christian masses in European history because of that transformation. Cf. R.P. Carroll, *Wolf in the Sheepfold: The Bible as a Problem for Christianity* (London: SPCK, 1991), pp. 89-116.

3.   It is most illuminatingly discussed in J. Schaberg's *The Illegitimacy of Jesus: A Feminist Theological Interpretation of the Infancy Narratives* (San Francisco: Harper & Row, 1987).

in theological terms to allow for a solidarity between all bastards and Jesus. Mary then becomes a figure of all women betrayed by a man somewhere in their background. The text remains unchanged but the circumstances in which it is read have changed fundamentally and therefore the readings must inevitably change.

The story of Jesus which will bear many, many different tellings—tellings governed by other texts and the passage of time—is given a particularly twentieth-century telling in Mikhail Bulgakov's masterpiece *The Master and Margarita*.[1] I mention this novel in particular in order to avoid having to list the many novels and treatments of the Gospel story while drawing the readers' attention to a very important aspect of the *Rezeptionsgeschichte* of the Bible. A narratological collection of so many narratives such as the Bible contains grafts the Bible into the tree of narrative which flourishes in human history. Each telling of a biblical story becomes part of the history of the reception of the Bible. Each use of an element of a biblical story contributes to that history. And it must be admitted that cataloguing all the elements in that history is a task beyond the scope of this article and the wit of most scholars. For example, Housman's well-known poem 'Easter Hymn' is a brilliant expression of an agnostic's view of the death and 'resurrection' of Jesus. Its famous line 'The hate you died to quench and could but fan' tells the story of the death of Jesus from the viewpoint of the time which has passed since then.[2] It recognizes the fact that Christian history has been marked by hatred and killing and so can build that aspect of things into his portrayal in a way that the New Testament could not because it was produced in the period before Christians really committed themselves to killing each other in the name of Christ.

Housman's sentiment reminds me of the fact that in 1697 the Church of Scotland had the Edinburgh student Thomas Aikenhead *executed* for, among other things, his views on the authorship of the Pentateuch. Aikenhead's opinion that Ezra had written the Pentateuch

---

1. The Russian version was completed in 1938 and an English version was published in 1967. Among other things it tells the story of the last days of Jesus from the perspective of Pontius Pilate. Paperback editions of the novel are plentiful (e.g. Collins Harvill, 1988).

2. A.E. Housman, 'Easter Hymn', in *Collected Poems and Selected Prose* (ed. C. Ricks; London: Penguin Books, 1989), p. 147.

rather than Moses is not one which would even raise eyebrows today, although in his time Presbyterianism in Scotland was struggling to hold on to power, so that opinions such as his were regarded as scurrilous and even 'atheistical'. Any *Rezeptionsgeschichte* of the Bible which lacked a mention of Thomas Aikenhead would be a very inadequate one, although space is seldom available for an adequate discussion of the history of biblical interpretation in relation to state and ecclesiastical power structures.[1] I mention Thomas Aikenhead because I want these notes to include some acknowledgment of Robert Davidson's prominent position in the Church of Scotland—he was Moderator of the General Assembly of the Church of Scotland in 1990–91—and am of the opinion that the execution of Aikenhead is perhaps an outer boundary of the Presbyterian discombobulations of Scripture brought about by the passage of time.

No account of the Church of Scotland and the Bible could ignore the fact that the Kirk has as its symbol a picture of the burning bush.[2] So any history of the reception of the story in Exodus 3 would of necessity have to have a chapter on the Church of Scotland. Whatever the image of the bush which burned without being consumed may have stood for in the Bible—it is not a topos of any significance outside of Exodus 3 in the Bible—it is used in Presbyterian circles in a very different way. More akin to rabbinic interpretation of the symbol, the Kirk's appropriation of the image reflects its consciousness of itself as being rooted in Scripture. What is said in Scripture is said to and of the Kirk: thus Jesus may have committed the keys of the kingdom of heaven to Peter (according to Matthew's account of the matter in Mt. 16.19), but *The Westminster Confession of Faith* is clearly of the opinion that the keys were committed to the officers of the church.[3] While no critical or modern reading of Matthew 16

---

1. On this criterion the *Cambridge History of the Bible* passes muster quite well (cf. *CHB*, III, pp. 241-42).

2. See G.D. Henderson, *The Burning Bush* (Edinburgh: The Saint Andrew Press, 1957), pp. 1-22.

3. Cf. Chapter XXX which states

> The Lord Jesus, as king and head of his church, hath therein appointed a government in the hand of church officers, distinct from the civil magistrate.
> II. To these officers the keys of the kingdom of heaven are committed, by virtue whereof they have power respectively to retain and remit sins, to shut that kingdom against the impenitent, both by the word and censures; and to open it unto penitent

would understand the text in that way, an adequate *Rezeptions-geschichte* of the Bible would have to take due cognizance of Roman Catholic and Reformed readings of the text.

As important as the passage of time for the interpretation of the Bible is the fact that the Bible consists of a wide diversity of texts. This diversity includes contradictions, contraries, errors and cruces of interpretation as well as the surplus of meaning which accrues to a highly figurative text so dependent on metaphor and metonym. Now such a collection of material which by its very nature includes the contradictory—for those who still insist on the dogma of the non-contradictory nature of Scripture please read 1 Samuel 15 in the light of v. 29 or answer the question 'who killed Goliath?'—inevitably must give rise to a highly hermeneutical form of exegesis over the centuries. Harmonies of the Gospels will proliferate among the early churches and the post-Reformation emergence of the critical method will come to power on the strength of biblical contradictions. Contradictions and discrepancies generate different interpretations as hermeneutists opt for distinctive possibilities or develop what Morton Smith has called 'a system of harmonistic exegesis'.[1] Such a diversity of texts as is constituted by the Bible will guarantee over time a very rich and complex tapestry of interpretation. If a multiplicity of inter-pretative communities use the Bible, then there will emerge many different families of tapestries. Cataloguing all these discrete and

        sinners, by the ministry of the gospel, and by absolution from censures, as occasion shall require.

The *mélange* of proof-texts cobbled together to underwrite this reading of a biblical text affords an interesting insight into the kind of narrativity used by certain Reformed churches' reception of the Bible (*The Confession of Faith* [Edinburgh, 1928], p. 45).

    1.   See M. Smith, 'Pseudepigraphy in the Israelite Literary Tradition', in *Pseudepigrapha. I. Pseudopythagorica—Lettres de Platon. Littérature pseudépigraphique juive* (Entretiens sur l'antiquité classique, 18; ed. K. von Fritz; Geneva: Vandoeuvres-Genève, 1971), pp. 191-215, with 'Discussion' on pp. 216-27; see pp. 225, 227 for the cited phrase. The death of Morton Smith on 11 July 1991 removes from the world of biblical scholarship one of its finest practitioners and one of its most colourful characters. The silencing of his rational voice is a great loss to us all and one mourns his passing, while recognizing the significance of his scholarly contribution to our profession.

distinctive creations will make the *Rezeptionsgeschichte* of the Bible virtually a never-ending task.

III

Robert Davidson's main contributions to the commentary form—and the commentary genre is of the essence of any *Rezeptionsgeschichte* of the Bible—are his commentaries on Genesis and Jeremiah. So in this section I will offer a few notes on the books of Genesis and Jeremiah.

Genesis[1]
Science and modern critical thought have tended to relegate Genesis 1–11 to the realm of poetry and religious myth, so I shall offer no comments on that section of the book of Genesis. In fact, to keep these notes as brief as possible, I shall simply focus my attention on the famous story of Abraham's attempted murder of his son Isaac in Genesis 22.[2] In our contemporary age of child abuse, with all its horror stories and concomitant political interests striving to gain power from the real or imagined suffering of children, this narrative of Abraham's abuse of Isaac comes to us out of the distant past as if it were a tale in the morning newspapers of our own time. Like the illegitimacy of Jesus *topos*, the story of Isaac's near-slaughter is repristinated by the times in which we read it. As part of the ongoing story of divine violence against human beings (cf. Gen. 6.5-7; 19.1-29) the story is well contexted in the book of Genesis. As Robert Lowell observes, in a line the meaning of which has often baffled me, 'the Lord survives the rainbow of his will'.[3] That divine will to kill (cf. Hannah's confession in 1 Sam. 2.6) seems to find its echo in Abraham's uneasy relationships with his sons: the banishment of

---

1.   R. Davidson, *Genesis 1–11* (Cambridge Bible Commentary; Cambridge: Cambridge University Press, 1973); *Genesis 12–50* (Cambridge Bible Commentary; Cambridge: Cambridge University Press, 1979).

2.   Cf. Davidson, *Genesis 12–50*, pp. 91-98. Here I must acknowledge the work of my Indonesian research student, Robert Setio, who is writing a thesis on the Aqedah. Supervising him has allowed me to focus on the text in regular discussions with him and has helped me to learn again how to read texts.

3.   The line concludes Lowell's poem 'Our Lady of Walsingham' and nicely indicates YHWH's awful tendency to forget his will to peace (Gen. 8.20–9.17) in his will to destruction.

Hagar, Ishmael's mother, had threatened the life of both mother and
foetus (Gen. 16; cf. 21.8-21) and the attempt to sacrifice Isaac threatened the life of Sarah's son. The fact that the text reports the death of
Sarah almost immediately after the story of Isaac's near murder
(23.1-2) may be regarded as a statement about the connection between
the two events (the rabbinic interpretation of the juxtaposition of the
stories).

The absence of Sarah is pregnant with meaning in the story of what
may be regarded either as 'the testing of Abraham' (22.1) or as 'the
binding of Isaac' (22.9—hence the tendency to call the story the
Aqedah or 'Binding' of Isaac). Very much present in the expulsion of
the pregnant Hagar, Sarah is entirely absent in the story of how
Abraham almost killed *her only son* (shades of Clytemnestra and
Iphigenia). The disappearing of Ishmael in the text of 22.2—'take
your son, your only son Isaac, whom you love. . . '—is curious in the
context of the stories of Abraham in Genesis and seems to steal a line
more appropriate to Sarah than to Abraham. Perhaps the lapidary
nature of the narrative encourages the skipping over of all subtleties
and sophisticated subtextual matters, or perhaps the seams of the story
as now stitched into the larger Genesis canvas are showing here.
There is another more subtle possibility: Genesis 21 tells how Sarah
had had Hagar and Ishmael cast out for fear of rivalry with *her son*
Isaac (the women of Genesis and their sons!); now Genesis 22 will tell
how YHWH cast Isaac out of the family home and away from Sarah
forever. Vengeance belongs to YHWH yet. A silent (uninformed?)
witness to the absence of Isaac from the home, yet aware that he was
in the company of a man much given to looking after his own safety
above that of all others when away from home on journeys, Sarah
stands in Genesis for all those women throughout history who know
the wretchedness of motherhood in a world where men run things *in
public*.

If I focus on Sarah even though she does not appear *at all* in Genesis
22, it is because contemporary close readings of biblical texts have
taught us to gap-fill the silences of texts.[1] What is not said in a text is
as important as what is said in it (shades of Heidegger here control the

---

1. On the notion of gaps and gap-filling in literature see M. Sternberg, *The
Poetics of Biblical Narrative: Ideological Literature and the Drama of Reading*
(Bloomington: Indiana University Press, 1987), pp. 186-229.

hermeneutic turn). Today any reading of Genesis 22 is going to notice Sarah's absence because the reader is going to ask after a perusal of the text—'where was Sarah when all this was going on?' or 'what did Sarah have to say about Abraham's sinister activities?'. Sarah's highly active involvement in the affairs of Hagar and Ishmael (chs. 16 and 21) and her joy (laughter) in the birthing of Isaac (21.1-7) hardly presage a silent role for her in the story of the Aqedah. Hence her absence is remarkable. Equally remarkable is the absence of Isaac on the road home from the near tragedy on the mountain (in 22.19 Abraham returns to his servitors and together they return to Beersheba; Isaac disappears after v. 13). Sticking strictly to what the text says (without any attempt to fill the gaps) Isaac will now live apart from his father—who would not after the murderous encounter in the mountains!—until that day when he and his half-brother Ishmael will bury the old man in the cave of Machpelah, in Ephron's field (25.7-11). Small wonder that the text notes 'after the death of Abraham God *blessed* Isaac his son' (25.11). I should think the death of Abraham *was* Isaac's blessing.

These few observations on the story of the binding of Isaac are clearly influenced by a modern awareness of the problems of child abuse in society. My reading focuses on elements in the Genesis stories of Abraham which represent a consistent portrayal of Abraham as a (moral) monster in his dealings with other people. That may not be the approach of the biblical narrators—or there again it may well be their deconstructive approach to the presentation of Abraham—but the history of the reception of the Bible is determined by the reader's situational hermeneutics and not by the text's narratological values. On the other hand, a shelf-full of books could be produced on the *Rezeptionsgeschichte* of Genesis 22.[1] My notes here are only intended to comment on one aspect of the story and hence focus on the absences within the text rather than on its presences. Sarah's absence or her silence—'I shall be silent, Abraham./The years have accustomed me to silence'[2]—is one approach to a contemporary reading of the story.

---

1. See esp. S. Spiegel, *The Last Trial: On the Legends and Lore of the Command to Abraham to Offer Isaac as a Sacrifice: The Akedah* (Philadelphia, 1967).

2. Lines from Andrew Harvey's poem 'Abraham and Sarah', in *A Full Circle* (London: André Deutsch, 1981), pp. 32-36 (p. 34).

The history of its reception knows many other approaches. Whether it be the paintings of Rembrandt or Michael Ayrton or the writings of Kierkegaard, the Aqedah has attracted much attention over the centuries. I suppose one of the better-known treatments of the tale of the old man's near murder of his son is Wilfred Owen's poem 'The Parable of the Old Man and the Young' which updates the retelling of the story to the period of the First World War.[1] The awful slaughter of the young in the trenches of that war is justly incorporated into Owen's version of Genesis 22:

> Behold,
> A ram, caught in a thicket by its horns;
> Offer the Ram of Pride instead of him.
> But the old man would not so, but slew his son,
> And half the seed of Europe, one by one.[2]

This is not so much the discombobulation of the text by time as the enhancement of the text by time. So a climate of child abuse may assist us to read Genesis 22 with greater scrutiny and more awareness.

Jeremiah[3]

Robert Davidson and I both share a certain interest in the book of Jeremiah. Our approaches to the text are, however, very different and I do not intend to explore those differences here. A proper *Rezeptionsgeschichte* of Jeremiah would be a lengthy, complex enterprise. It would have to include recent uses of Jeremiah 50–51 with reference to Saddam Hussein and the Gulf War: YHWH's war against Babylon—YHWH is laying Babylon waste (51.54)—in the ancient oracles incorporated into the book of Jeremiah has been providing copy for journalists (especially Israeli journalists) and letter-writers to the newspapers. Some of this resurrection of ancient texts has been justified by Saddam Hussein's own propagandistic linking of himself with the famous emperor of ancient Babylon, Nebuchadnezzar. In Jeremiah's poems against Babylon, Nebuchadnezzar is likened to the

---

1. *The Collected Poems of Wilfred Owen* (ed. C. Day Lewis; London: Chatto & Windus, 1963), p. 42.
2. Some versions of the poem lack this last line.
3. R. Davidson, *Jeremiah*, I (Daily Study Bible; Edinburgh: The Saint Andrew Press, 1983); *Jeremiah*, II with *Lamentations* (Daily Study Bible; Edinburgh: The Saint Andrew Press, 1985).

dragon (51.34), that monstrous symbol of chaos (some would even say, symbol of evil itself), hence the modern journalistic attempts to demonize Saddam Hussein have very ancient roots in political propaganda against the territory now known as Iraq (ancient Babylon). Biblical texts can still fund abuse of opponents and serve the purposes of political copy-writers. The Iraqi attacks on the modern state of Israel during the Gulf War certainly provided warrants for repristinating the rhetoric of Jeremiah against an ancient enemy and employing it in new circumstances.

To keep these notes to a modest length I shall just focus on one brief set of tropes in the book of Jeremiah. In 8.22 a series of rhetorical questions states the community's plight as thus:

> Is there no balm in Gilead?
>   Is there no physician there?
> Why then has the health of my daughter people not been restored?

The commentaries invariably comment on the use of balm in ancient times as a medicinal substance, its trade route through the territory of Gilead, and often identify the storax tree as the source of the balm.[1] My own commentary on Jeremiah devoted remarkably little space to treating the verse and one of my most indefatigable critics has regularly commented on my failure to produce the trade figures for the importation of balm in the period.[2] While acknowledging my exegetical inadequacies, here I wish only to pick up that very well-known phrase 'balm in Gilead' and to note how it has entered the English language as an idiom. It is also the title of a reasonably well-known hymn.[3] Perhaps of more significance for the history of interpretation approach to the Bible is the fact that Edgar Allen Poe uses it in one of

---

1. Cf. Davidson, *Jeremiah*, I, p. 85. Illustration and comments in W. Paterson, *A Fountain of Gardens: Plants and Herbs of the Bible* (Edinburgh: Mainstream, 1990), pp. 24-25.

2. R.P. Carroll, *Jeremiah: A Commentary* (OTL; London: SCM Press, 1986), p. 237. Reasons of space dictated the paucity of my remarks there and to the justified criticism I can only respond by leaving my chief critic nameless here.

3. The hymn 'Balm in Gilead', which Christianizes Jeremiah's phrase, used to be associated with the singer George Beverly Shea. I mention this connection because in the summer of 1991, the Billy Graham crusade circus visited Scotland in order to bolster up the falling rolls of the Church of Scotland and as a follow-up to its 1955 visit to Scotland.

his most famous poems. In the fifteenth stanza of his poem 'The
Raven' are to be found the following lines:

> 'Prophet!' said I, 'thing of evil!—
> Prophet still, if bird or devil!—
>
> Tell me truly, I implore—
> Is there—*is* there balm in Gilead?—
> Tell me—tell me, I implore.'
> Quoth the Raven, 'Nevermore'.[1]

Poe's treatment of the half-line from Jeremiah takes the biblical poet's
rhetorical question further in the direction of the depressing possibility that there *is* no balm in Gilead. Whereas for Jeremiah, the point
seems to be that, in spite of there being balm in Gilead, Jerusalem is
not healed, for Poe a more fundamental question needs to be asked. Is
there balm in Gilead? The discourse of Poe's poem suggests that the
answer to that question is 'No'. All is therefore lost. Poe has taken
Jeremiah further along the road to despair without violating the words
of Jeremiah.

From the point of view of writing a *Rezeptionsgeschichte* of the
Bible, the Poe stanza is an important use and development of a half-
line derived directly from the biblical text. The poem is therefore part
of the history of the text's interpretation. It may be a very simple
example of the type of contribution literature makes to that history,
but it is one that could be multiplied a millionfold in the history of
literature. The text of Jeremiah provides ample resources for the
literature of depression and the laments in the book of Jeremiah
afford many opportunities for depressed poets to develop the
discourse of despair. Gerard Manley Hopkins's famous repristination
of Jer. 12.1ff. in one of his terrible sonnets is too well known (and too
complex) for me to have chosen it as a brilliant example of the reception of the text in literature,[2] so I have opted for the simpler Poe

---

1. *Poems* (London, 1875), p. 111. There are various typographical
arrangements of Poe's poems; cf. *The Collected Works of Edgar Allan Poe*. I.
Poems (ed. T.D. Mabbott; Harvard: The Belknap Press of Harvard University Press,
1969), p. 368.

2. Cf. Carroll, *Jeremiah*, p. 284. Davidson touches on it in his *The Courage to
Doubt: Exploring an Old Testament Theme* (London: SCM Press, 1983), p. 136
rather than in his Jeremiah commentary.

example. Any commentator on the book of Jeremiah will know the enormous difficulties of producing an adequate account of the *Rezeptionsgeschichte* of Jeremiah just because it is both complex and huge (the double tradition of Hebrew and Greek versions of the book guarantee those factors). A modern poet such as Allen Ginsberg acknowledges the profound influence of Jeremiah on his formation as a poet and thereby grafts himself on to any adequate account of the history of the interpretation of the book of Jeremiah.[1] But Ginsberg is only one such example. Add him to Poe and Hopkins just for a start and then think of the New Testament uses of Jeremiah and the importance of Jeremiah for Christian mystics and the homily writers of the early churches and a *Rezeptionsgeschichte* of Jeremiah begins to look like a task beyond the wit of the commentator.

IV

To complete this brief look at Robert Davidson's contribution to the commentary genre—no doubt a minor contribution because the five volumes of commentary are all in very minor series of commentaries—I shall offer a few remarks on the books of Lamentations, Qoheleth, and Song of Solomon.

Lamentations[2]
As a genre the lament is quite dominant in the book of Psalms and also in Jeremiah, Job and Isaiah 40–66. The human situation being what it is, human communities will always be bemoaning the cruelty of their situation and responding to catastrophes with poems and songs of unmitigated suffering. Little needs to be done by way of adaptation to the book of Lamentations to make it fit into the twentieth century. Throughout time composers have set its plaintive songs to music. The Christian churches adapted the substance of its laments to refer to Jesus and the sufferings of his Passion. For Jews throughout Christian

1. On Ginsberg and Jeremiah see P. Portugés, 'Allen Ginsberg's Visions and the Growth of his Poetics of Prophecy', in *Poetic Prophecy in Western Literature* (ed. J. Wojcik and R.-J. Frontain; London/Toronto: Associated University Presses, 1984), pp. 157-73, 216-17.
2. The traditional attribution of Lamentations to the prophet Jeremiah often survives in modern commentaries which append Lamentations to their treatment of Jeremiah.

history, its threnodies have been an expression of their continual suffering at the hands of cruel rivals. On the other hand, its focus on *deserved* suffering makes Lamentations less appropriate for much of the suffering which goes on in the world. The laments of an Akhmatova or a Mandelstam or a Celan may have some links with Lamentations, but the great crimes of the twentieth century have caused sufferings which elude the theological rectitude of Lamentations. In religious communities, guilt-ridden laments have an important place, but the common human experiences of undeserved suffering moves the focus from the book of Lamentations to the book of Job or to Qoheleth.

Qoheleth[1]

Modern readings of the Bible tend to find Job and Qoheleth (along with all those well-known stories and narratives of the Bible) the least irrelevant elements in the Bible. Qoheleth's famous dicta, for example, 'vanity of vanities', 'nothing new under the sun', 'for everything there is a season', etc., have contributed powerfully to the making of the English language and the philosophical discourse of commonsense observations. A *Rezeptionsgeschichte* of Qoheleth would make for another shelf of books—adding further spice to Qoheleth's observation, 'of making books there is no end, and much study is a weariness of the flesh' (12.12); an observation which has been much quoted and often adapted by other writers only all too well aware of the depressing truth of Qoheleth's dictum. The phrase popularized in the 1960s 'what's new pussycat?' was a distant relation of Qoheleth's 'there is nothing new under the sun'. Whenever we encounter something novel and it turns out to be just one more example of something old, Qoheleth's point is made yet again. On the other hand, something genuinely new would serve to rebut Qoheleth's contention and so would bring to mind Qoheleth's words. A good example of this point is the following observation by the scientist George Klein:

> 'There is nothing new under the sun' ('*Ein kol hadash tahat hashemesh*'),
> said Qoheleth, the son of King David, known as the Preacher. Or is there?
> Yes, there is. Its name is DNA.[2]

1. R. Davidson, *Ecclesiastes and Song of Solomon* (Daily Study Bible; Edinburgh: The Saint Andrew Press, 1986), pp. 3-92.
2. G. Klein, *The Atheist and the Holy City: Encounters and Reflections* (Cambridge, MA: MIT Press, 1990), p. 158.

Add that exchange to the *Rezeptionsgeschichte* of Qoheleth and of the Bible and ponder the complexities of writing an adequate history of the use and interpretation of the Bible.

Song of Solomon[1]

Few books of the Bible have been as at home in the twentieth century as the Song of Songs. The one volume of erotica in the Bible has had to wait a long time for Western society to catch up with it. Allegorization and typological exegesis have tended to defuse the raw sexuality of the book in the history of its interpretation and harnessed its tropes to the service of synagogue and church. That is perhaps understandable as religious communities have generally (in the West) preferred to transform sexual situations into discourse about sex as metaphor of something else. Since the so-called sexual revolution of the twentieth century, it has become easier to read the Song of Songs as a series of lyrical poems expressing the delight in each other felt by men and women in sexual relationships. As such a proper *Rezeptionsgeschichte* of the book would have to take into account other literary erotica and develop the discourse of sexuality in human communities (recent academic commentaries have begun to do this very competently and provide a fine contrast between contemporary readings of the text and the history of its interpretation). At a more general level, the Song provides all the problems touched on in this article of creating an adequate *Rezeptionsgeschichte*. The Victorian penchant for using the Song's phrase 'until the day breaks and the shadows flee away' (2.17) on tombstones is a nice example of trans-ferred meaning from sex until morning to death and its afterlife. A further example of literary allusion which belongs to the history of the text's reception is a line from a Samuel Beckett play. In *Krapp's Last Tape* this fascinating line is heard on the tape:

> At that time I think I was still living on and off with Bianca in Kedar Street.[2]

---

1.   Davidson, *Ecclesiastes*, pp. 93-160.

2.   S. Beckett, *Krapp's Last Tape and Embers* (London: Faber & Faber, 1965), p. 12. Beckett's most famous play *Waiting for Godot* furnishes a trope for all those failed prophetic, messianic and 'the return of Jesus' expectations in the Bible. Like Godot, none of these hopes ever arrived. Paul Celan's poem 'Shulamith' links the

Now that is a very clever part-inversion of a famous verse in the Song—Beckett is a master of the use of biblical allusion and his *oeuvre* constitutes an important chapter in any twentieth-century account of the reception of the Bible—alluding as it does to 1.5. The woman speaks 'I am black but comely. . . like the tents of Kedar'— the Dark Lady of the Song—and Beckett incorporates those two points in Krapp's reminiscences by inverting the black to white ('Bianca') and locating the shared domicile of Krapp and Bianca in Kedar Street. Such cleverness in a writer for whom the Bible is part of his language reservoirs should warn the historian of the interpretation of the Bible of the complexities of constructing an adequate *Rezeptionsgeschichte*.

V

It is time to draw this simplistic exploration of the history of the reception of the Bible to a conclusion. I have chosen a number of examples of how the Bible has been used in literature in order to underline the difficulty of the task of producing a good and compre- hensive *Rezeptionsgeschichte* of a collection of books which has had a profoundly creative effect on many writers over many centuries. If many of my examples have been very simple, or even trivial, that has been done on purpose. Too often scholarship, theological or academic, has ignored the ordinary and the popular and has only counted the orthodox or the institutionally defined important writers on the Bible. That is a slant, to use Emily Dickinson's word, which has its legiti- mate part to play in constructing a history of the interpretation of the Bible, but it is only one slant among many slants. I have focused on a literary-social usage of the Bible in order to remind readers that there are more things on earth than are often dreamt of by scholars and theologians. If the history of the interpretation of the Bible—how that lengthy half-sentence justifies the use of a German compound *Rezeptionsgeschichte*!—is the category of investigation then I must confess that much of what has passed for it in the past is a woefully inadequate representation of the subject.

Time and theory happen to everything, including texts. But just as time happens to the Bible and tends to discombobulate it, so time also

Song to the death camps of the Third Reich, but is too poignant for me to handle here.

happens to theories of reading and interpretation. So any good *Rezeptionsgeschichte* of the Bible will have to take into account the way theories of reading the Bible—be they academic (e.g. Marxist or post-modernist) or religious (e.g. fundamentalist or mystical)—are forced to change and give way to other theories of reading. The ethics of reading is always changing. I cannot help feeling that approaches to reading the Bible such as are entailed in political readings (e.g. liberation theology) dependent on Marxist values are very vulnerable to recent demolitions of Marxist theory. Nice theory, shame about the praxis. A proper *Ideologiekritik* of texts must also involve a thoroughgoing scrutiny of the ideological holdings of the theoreticians doing the readings. Different theoretical perspectives inevitably produce very different readings of texts, and texts as traditional and as ideological as the Bible are always vulnerable to changing paradigms of interpretation. Thus much modernist and post-modernist reading of the Bible reads against the grain of the text, while feminist readings of the Bible read against the groin of the text. So changing theories of reading will have to be part of the enterprise and will contribute greatly to the production of a more adequate *Rezeptionsgeschichte* of the Bible.

I have not attempted to illustrate the force of Karl Marx's remark about the farcical nature of repetition of significant events and persons. Most readers of the Bible will have had sufficient experience of bad preaching from the Bible in their youth to know *exactly* what Marx was on about. Homiletics, whether good or bad, is an important part of the story of the reception of the Bible and the use of homilies relating to the Bible throughout the history of the Christian churches has its own contribution to make to that story. Often the way the Bible is used by a preacher or a writer will tell us more about speaker and author than it will about the Bible. William Blake on Isaiah is a case in point. As has been said of Blake 'The Hebrew Bible is cancelled, not fulfilled, in the Christian mythology of Blake...'[1] But then I think it

---

1.   H. Bloom, *Ruin the Sacred Truths: Poetry and Belief from the Bible to the Present* (Cambridge, MA: Harvard University Press, 1989), p. 123. An analysis of William Blake's reception of Scripture would make a very good paradigm case of the many aspects of interpretation, resignification and usage of the Bible involved in a competent production of the *Rezeptionsgeschichte* of the Bible. Similar analyses of the use of the Bible in the work of Bertolt Brecht and Samuel Beckett would take the

would be true also to say that the New Testament started that particular rot by cancelling—colonizing or transforming may be words preferred by others—the Hebrew Bible (well, Greek Bible) originally. That factor must make any *Rezeptionsgeschichte* of the Bible a very complex matter because it has to work with Jewish *and* Christian canons of Scripture and canons involve very complicated hermeneutics which segregate communities rather than bringing them together. Any *Rezeptionsgeschichte* is therefore going to be *per definitionem* a political enterprise with concealed agendas and muted ideologies lurking behind the arras. At which point it might be wise to remember that this article is only offered as 'notes on the *Rezeptionsgeschichte* of the Bible' and not as *das Ding an sich*. That is, not so much scratches on the surface of the subject as a feeble attempt to polish up the surface so that others may make scratches on it.

subject out of the hegemonic control of theological and ecclesiastical systems of reference.

MARK 1.1: *ARCHĒ*, 'SCRIPTURAL LEMMA'

Robert B. Coote

archē in Mk 1.1 is usually taken to mean 'beginning' and to refer to the beginning of Mark, or to Mark as a beginning of something else. A few translators have taken it to mean 'principle', usually in reference to the whole of Mark as the principle of something else. I would argue that while such meanings are defensible, especially since there are a number of passages in early Christian literature where *archē* seems to refer in some way to a Gospel or to Christian learning, it makes more sense to understand *archē* in Mk 1.1 as 'beginning' or 'principle', referring to the Scripture cited in Mk 1.2-3. This Scripture then functions as a sort of scriptural foundation or principle, or in other words 'scriptural lemma', for the whole of Mark.

archē could mean 'beginning': 'The beginning of the report[1] concerning Jesus Anointed is as/as is written in the prophet Isaiah...' The prophecy from Isaiah (and Exodus and Malachi) might fairly be taken to foretell what Mark explains about John's and Jesus' baptism:

---

1. *euaggelion* and related terms represent forms of the root *bśr* in Hebrew or Aramaic. *bśr* does not mean 'announce good news', but 'deliver a war report', as can be seen by examining all its occurrences in the Hebrew Scriptures; cognates in Syriac, Arabic and Ge'ez have been influenced by Christian usage. The sole apparent exception in Hebrew, the man announcing Jeremiah's birth in Jer. 20.15, is followed immediately by a reference to war ('let that man be like the cities which Yahweh overthrew with no pity', 20.16) and alludes to Jeremiah's pre-birth appointment ('I have appointed you over warring classes, to tear up and break down, destroy and overthrow', 1.10); see R.P. Carroll, *Jeremiah: A Commentary* (Philadelphia: Westminster Press, 1986), pp. 402-403. Most if not all uses of *euaggelizein* and related terms in the New Testament follow this scriptural meaning. Note, however, that this point is not intended to address the question of the genre of Mark or the Gospels. Koester understands the term in Greek to mean 'news, message'; H. Koester, *Ancient Christian Gospels: Their History and Development* (Philadelphia: Trinity Press International; London: SCM Press, 1990), pp. 1-48.

'The beginning of the report. . . is as written in Isaiah. . . : John appeared. . . ' In this sense 'beginning' would refer to some portion of the beginning of Mark. Guelich lays out the options as to what portion and decides in favour of Mk 1.4-15, including Jesus' 'gospel' in 1.15, which he takes as the referent of *euaggelion* in 1.1.[1] This reading finds support in the three other occurrences of *archē* in Mark, all clearly meaning 'beginning',[2] and in the parallel texts in both Matthew and Luke, which I think were probably, but especially in Matthew's case, readings of Mark. Matthew and Luke present the appearance of John (only a part of Mark's 'beginning' as defined by Guelich) as the fulfilment of the Isaiah passage cited.[3]

However, the difference between Mk 1.1-2 and its Synoptic parallels again throws the spotlight on *archē*. In Matthew and Luke, the narrative precedes the citation which is fulfilled by it, while in Mark the supposed narrative fulfilment follows the citation. As noted, it is quite unlikely that 'as is written' (Mk 1.2) by itself refers to what follows the scriptural citation rather than to what precedes it, leaving 1.1 as a title. In any case, the normal pattern shows the referent preceding the formula 'as is written' with the citation over 20 times in the New Testament, including in Mk 9.13 and 14.21; only 1 Cor. 2.9-10 goes against the rule (compare Dan. 9.13).[4] The formula and citation in Mk 1.1-2 therefore probably refer in the first instance back to *archē*, not forward to the following narrative. Here is reason for hesitation.

Also, the lack of the definite article with *archē* poses a difficulty,

<hr/>

1. R.A. Guelich, ' "The Beginning of the Gospel": Mark 1.1-15', *Papers of the Chicago Society of Biblical Research* 27 (1982), pp. 5-15. For earlier versions of this interpretation, see A. Wikgren, '*Archē tou euaggeliou*', *JBL* 61 (1942), p. 12 n. 2. Alternatively, *euaggelion* could refer to the whole of Mark, as many have thought. Guelich shows that 1.1 by itself cannot be a self-contained heading for the whole of Mark, contrary to the usual interpretation. I do not find the interesting and useful attempt by Gerhard Arnold to find parallels to such a heading in Greek and Latin literature convincing: 'Mk 1.1 und Eröffnungswendungen in griechischen und lateinischen Schriften', *ZNW* 68 (1977), pp. 123-27.

2. Mk 10.6; 13.8, 9.

3. In each of the three Gospels of course in a significantly different form; Mt. 3.2-3; Lk. 3.2-6.

4. See also H.G.M. Williamson, 'History', in D.A. Carson and H.G.M. Williamson (eds.), *It Is Written: Scripture Citing Scripture. Essays in Honour of Barnabas Lindars, SSF* (Cambridge: Cambridge University Press, 1988), p. 28.

given that 1.1 is probably not a title:[1] in what sense could Mk 1.4-15 be *a* beginning? Moreover, the 'beginning' of Mark, Mk 1.4-15 or some portion thereof, is too limited an antecedent for such a scriptural citation: the Scripture cited substantiates the whole of Mark, not just the beginning of Mark.

The latter point should not be passed over lightly. It is now commonly recognized that Mark's beginning itself forms the basis for, or substantiates in principle, the whole of Mark. The motif of 'baptism' for Jesus' royal (re)birth, death, and return is basic to Mark, as are many *pervasive* ancillary motifs derived from parallels between Jesus and Moses, Joshua, Elijah, Elisha, and the 'servant of Yahweh', and their 'way' suggested by the citation from Exod. 23.20, Mal. 3.1 and Isa. 40.3.[2] Since this is so, however, the meaning of *archē* must be, in relation to the whole of Mark, not simply 'beginning', but 'root, basis, principle' as well, and, as it refers in the first instance to the Scripture cited, 'scriptural basis', or 'scriptural lemma'. The Scripture cited is the beginning point, principle and lemma for the war report represented by the whole of Mark—the text to be exegeted, the text that makes the entire exposition true. 'The principle, or scriptural basis, of the [following] report. . . is written in Isaiah.'[3]

---

1.   In Hellenistic titles the first term often lacks the article, as in Mt. 1.1, Rev. 1.1 and many LXX and Apocryphal titles.

2.   For a recent concise exposition of many of these motifs, see H.C. Waetjen, *A Reordering of Power: A Socio-Political Reading of Mark's Gospel* (Minneapolis, MN: Fortress Press, 1989). Waetjen shares the view, which I find compelling, that the whole of Mark can be regarded as the 'beginning' of a recurrent Gospel narrative that cycles from the end of Mark to its beginning.

3.   Cf. Wikgren, '*Archē tou euaggeliou*', pp. 11-20; for earlier scholars who understand the syntax in this way, see p. 12 n. 3. For recent scholars who understand *archē* as 'principle', see Guelich, '"The Beginning of the Gospel"', p. 13 n. 6. Wikgren cites several early Christian parallels with this meaning of *archē* in reference to the 'gospel'. The most interesting of these is perhaps a third- or fourth-century letter referring to a 'catechumen in the principle of the gospel', *kathēkoumenon en archē tou euaggeliou*. However Wikgren takes *archē* in Mk 1.1 to refer to the whole of Mark and *euaggelion* to some general 'gospel' beyond Mark: 'The principle [Mark] of the gospel [*viz.* in general] (is) *as* written in Isaiah. . . '; similarly R. Pesch, *Das Markusevangelium*, I (Freiburg: Herder, 1976), pp. 75-76, and H. Weder, '"Evangelium Jesu Christi" (Mk 1,1) und "Evangelium Gottes" (Mk 1,14)', in U. Luz and H. Weder (eds.), *Die Mitte des Neuen Testaments: Einheit und Vielfalt neutestamentlicher Theologie. Festschrift für Eduard Schweizer* (Göttingen:

The 'basic' nature of the scriptural citation is confirmed by its position at the very inception of Mark, before anything has happened of which it might be a fulfilment (in contrast to Matthew and Luke). We must imagine the urgent question foremost in readers' minds to which Mark's opening is the swift answer, imparted before a single other subject is broached. It is likely that Mark represents a significant shift in understanding Jesus Anointed, particularly in relation to the First Judaean War and the fall of the Temple, however the specifics of such a shift are to be understood. Of course it is always to be recalled that there was no single, uniform 'Gospel' spanning the first century, or even the pre-War years, of which Mark is coincidentally one more variant, or from which every shift would be equally significant. The key question confronting the writer of Mark, as one of the first Christian writers to attempt to make sense of the meaning of the Judaean War and the destruction of the Temple, is whether his 'Gospel', involving *such* a shift, conforms, like any competing understanding of Jesus Anointed which claims validity, to Scripture. This is a fundamental issue throughout early Christian writings: is the Gospel scriptural?[1]

Furthermore, readers would want to know more than whether just the 'beginning' of Mark's version of the war report regarding Jesus was in line with Scripture. They would want to know whether the *whole report* was in line with Scripture. And they would want to know *what* Scripture. Mark wastes no time answering their questions: 'Rest assured', we might paraphrase, 'the basis for *this* version of the war report regarding Jesus Anointed *is according to* the following *scripture* from Isaiah [and Exodus and Malachi]. . . '[2] This report,

---

Vandenhoeck & Ruprecht, 1983), pp. 400-402. This seems to make too much of Mk 1.1-3 as a title and to understate the representation of the 'principle' in the scriptural citation. The lack of article can be better accommodated with the meaning 'principle': 'A principle scriptural basis. . . is as written in Isaiah. . . '

1. Compare the following comments of Ignatius: 'I heard some people saying, "If I don't find it in the charter documents [*en tois archeiois*], I don't believe it in the Gospel", and when I said to them, "It *is* written [in the Scriptures]", they answered me, "That's just the question!"' (*Phil.* 8.2); '. . . whom neither the Prophets nor the Law of Moses have persuaded. . . ' (*Smyrn.* 5.1).

2. Although none of these texts individually or together are cited in Christian texts before Mark (i.e. in Paul), I am not necessarily arguing that Mark was the first

Mark affirms, different though it may be from what you may previously have heard, is according to Scripture and has scriptural authority. Accordingly, Mark's entire report is authoritative midrash on its opening scriptural lemma. Mark's unfolding narrative then proves this claim in practically innumerable ways from beginning to end.

The importance of this point, it seems to me, is considerable, given that it concerns the beginning and basis of the earliest of the canonical Gospels, from which, it could be maintained, the entire New Testament *as a collection* stemmed.[1] In this sense, *archē* may be regarded as nothing less than the first word of the New Testament.

Does *archē* in Mk 1.1 mean 'scriptural basis, lemma' or 'beginning'? There is no need to choose one meaning to the exclusion of the other. The one Greek word may simultaneously entail both English meanings,[2] in that the 'principle' of Mark's 'war report' is represented equally well by the *Scripture* that substantiates both the beginning and the whole of the report,[3] and by the *beginning* of the report in its own right. In either case, the *euaggelion* of Mk 1.1 is not some generalized Gospel, but Mark's report, based on scriptural principle, regarding the war all along expected to usher in Jesus' rule, in light of and in terms of the outcome and meaning of the most important event in Palestine for many generations, the Judaean War.[4]

to use them as Christian proof-texts. It is not the texts themselves, but what is made of them, that is significant.

1. See R.B. Coote and M.P. Coote, *Power, Politics, and the Making of the Bible* (Minneapolis, MN: Fortress Press, 1990), pp. 110-23.

2. For a concise statement, see Pesch, *Markusevangelium*, I, p. 76; Weder, ' "Evangelium Jesu Christi" ', p. 401. As noted by them and others, the Hebrew term *rē'shit* behind many instances of *archē* in translation provides a further foundation for this dual meaning. In at least one rabbinic text, *rē'shit* refers to the whole of Torah as a substantiating text; see H.G. Perelmuter, *Siblings: Rabbinic Judaism and Early Christianity at their Beginnings* (New York: Paulist Press, 1989), pp. 11-12, on *Gen. R.* 1.1.

3. Including as a beginning: see p. 87 n. 4, above.

4. I wish to express my appreciation to Chandler Stokes, Newhall Fellow in Classics, Judaic Studies, and History at the Graduate Theological Union in Berkeley, for his assistance in the preparation of this article.

THE MIDST OF THE YEARS

Paul E. Copeland

> O LORD, I have heard the report of thee,
>   and thy work, O LORD, do I fear.
> In the midst of the years renew it;
>   in the midst of the years make it known;
>   in wrath remember mercy (Hab. 3.2 [RSV]).

The opening lines of the 'Prayer of Habakkuk' have generated an ingenious array of interpretations and reconstructions, ranging from the exegetical traditions of the ancient Greek translations and Aramaic Targums to modern efforts to restore the text through the application of principles of prosodic composition. In this essay I propose to draw attention to various attempts since the Reformation to give the sense of the enigmatic 'in the midst of the years' (בקרב שנים), and, against that background, to examine the earlier efforts reflected in the ancient Greek and Aramaic versions. Such an examination will suggest, on the one hand, that the Old Greek, which offers two different vocalizations of our phrase, attempted to resolve the ambiguities of the consonantal text within an exegetical framework dominated by liturgical associations with Pentecost. The Targum, on the other hand, also offers two interpretations of בקרב שנים, but from the perspective of theodicy, and in reliance upon a Masoretic-type textual tradition.

1. *Exegesis of the Masoretic Tradition since the Reformation*

Since the time of the Reformation, expositors who have adopted the Masoretic form of Hab. 3.2 have explained בקרב שנים along one of two general lines. A significant minority relate the phrase to the general sweep of salvation history, while others understand it in a contemporizing manner of the years of trouble that overtake God's people from time to time. There are, of course, numerous variations on these

themes. A few examples must suffice to illustrate the development of
these two approaches.

Calvin, for example, suggested that Habakkuk saw his own generation standing in a sort of 'mid-life' crisis in the history of Israel.

> By the *middle of the years*, he means the middle course. . . of the
> people's life. For from the time when God chose the race of Abraham to
> the coming of Christ, was the whole course, as it were, of their life, when
> we compare the people to a man; for the fulness of their age was at the
> coming of Christ. . . Hence the Prophet prays God not to take away the
> life of his people in the middle of their course; for Christ having not come,
> the people had not attained maturity, nor arrived at manhood.[1]

J.A. Bengel offered a different approach within the history of salvation framework, identifying 'the midst of the years' as the point of
transition between the Old and New Testament eras. In his *Ordo
Temporum*, Bengel utilized Hab. 3.2 in an elaborate attempt to calculate the time between creation and the advent of Christ, and between
Christ's advent and the end of the world.[2]

It may be said for Calvin that he at least relates the phrase to the
situation of the nation in the days of the prophet. However, both
Calvin and Bengel refer 'in the midst of the years' to a historical
'midpoint' which they have perceived in hindsight. As Delitzsch
pointed out, it is doubtful that the prophet foresaw the course of salvation history in a manner that would permit him to calculate the
'midpoint' with such precision.[3]

Luther, on the other hand, explained בקרב שנים as a general statement about the timely character of God's help. Beginning with the
persuasion that 'to impart life to the work means nothing but to help
in time of need',[4] he explained 'in the midst of the years' as an indication that the Lord adheres to a 'golden mean' when aiding his people,
as befits the nurturing of faith.

---

1. J. Calvin, *Commentaries on the Twelve Minor Prophets*, IV (trans. Rev. John
Owen; Edinburgh: Calvin Translation Society, 1848), p. 137.
2. See the editor's introduction to J.A. Bengel, *Gnomon of the New Testament*, V
(ed. A. Fausset; Edinburgh: T. & T. Clark, 1868), pp. xix-xxi. Cf. also
F. Delitzsch, *Der Prophet Habakuk* (Leipzig: Karl Tauchnitz, 1843), p. 131.
3. Delitzsch, *Habakuk*.
4. M. Luther, *Works*. XIX. *Lectures on the Minor Prophets II Jonah-Habakkuk*
(ed. H.C. Oswald; St Louis: Concordia Publishing House, 1974), p. 228.

'In the midst of the years' expresses as much as 'at the right time'. It signifies that God does not appear as soon as the need begins, as though any time were the right time. Nor does help remain away forever, as though every time for helping had passed. But he comes in the midst of time, that is, he knows how to follow a middle course, so that he does not help too soon and also not too late. For if he would help too soon, we would not learn to despair of ourselves but would remain arrogant. If he would be too tardy with his help we would not learn to believe but would despair of him. But now that he adopts a middle course, he also holds us in the middle.[1]

Luther has not been widely followed in seeing Hab. 3.2b as a statement of faith concerning the inscrutable wisdom of the divine timing. Likewise, other attempts to refer בקרב שנים to the critical midpoint or decisive turning point in a period of trouble have been rightly criticized on linguistic grounds.[2] However, there are not a few who have agreed with Luther's general premise by referring 'in the midst of the years', in some manner or other, to years of distress through which the nation was, or soon would be, passing.[3] Moreover, those who approach the text in this way often embrace its petition as a paradigm for prayer and faith in troubled times generally.

As one surveys the exegesis of MT Hab. 3.2 from the Reformation well into the twentieth century, one senses that the phrase 'in the midst of the years' has been explained more or less intuitively, by men who have been quick to adapt the text to the work of pastoral encouragement. That is not to say that they were unaware of the linguistic difficulties inherent in the phrase. Luther recognized a problem, but in his loyalty to MT located it in his imperfect knowledge of Hebrew, rather than in a fault in the text. 'The text is obscure here; that is to say, it is very Hebrew. Therefore many have tripped over it.'[4]

In more recent times, G.W. Wade and J.H. Eaton have also recognized the enigmatic character of the expression and then offered interpretations within the second general framework. Wade writes,

---

1. Luther, *Works*, XIX, pp. 228-29.

2. See Delitzsch, *Habakuk*, p. 131.

3. One of the most precise attempts to specify the referent of בקרב שנים was that of Franz Delitzsch, who related it to the interval between the time of Habakkuk's vision and the מועד of fulfilment mentioned in 2.3. See C.F. Keil, *The Twelve Minor Prophets*, II (trans. Rev. J. Martin; Edinburgh: T. & T. Clark, 1868), p. 95.

4. Luther, *Works*, XIX, p. 228.

'The expression is difficult to interpret, but possibly means "in the midst of a protracted period (of trouble)"'.[1] Eaton concedes that the phrase is 'difficult to penetrate', and then ventures, 'But whatever the precise sense, the phrase seems to amount to a request for help "here and now"'.[2]

John Mauchline offered an individual, rather than corporate, contextualization, suggesting that the phrase could refer to the loss of spiritual vitality in middle age.[3] However, the corporate application has been far more influential. The evocative power of this view is perhaps best illustrated in the work of George Adam Smith—a giant in Old Testament scholarship who certainly was not beyond criticizing MT, and who characteristically aimed at precision in stating the meaning of a text. However, Smith is content to leave the reference of בקרב שנים open.

> Israel cries from a state of life in which the years are huddled and full of turmoil. We need not wish to fix the date more precisely than the writer does, but may leave it with him *in the midst of the years.*[4]

It may be that discretion led Smith not to attempt to fix the date more precisely than the writer. However, his hesitance is certainly intelligible in the light of the practical exhortation which he draws from the text.

> For ourselves it is useful to fasten upon the poet's description of his position in the midst of the years, and like him to take heart, amid similar circumstances, from the story of God's ancient revelation, in the faith that He is still the same in might and in purpose of grace to His people. We, too, live among the nameless years. . .[5]

Thus Smith begins one of the most eloquent statements of an exegetical tradition concerning Hab. 3.2 which is at least as old as Luther in its general outline. It is a tradition which exercises a great deal of

1. G.G.V. Stonehouse and G.W. Wade, *Zephaniah, Nahum and Habakkuk* (London: Methuen, 1929), p. 196.

2. J.H. Eaton, *Obadiah, Nahum, Habakkuk and Zephaniah* (London: SCM Press, 1961), p. 110.

3. J. Mauchline, *Prophets of Israel. III. The Twelve* (London: Lutterworth Press, 1964), p. 65.

4. G.A. Smith, *The Book of the Twelve Prophets*, II (London: Hodder & Stoughton, 1928), p. 150.

5. Smith, *Prophets*, p. 158.

influence in the present, owing to its incorporation into such modern translations as the Good News Bible, the NIV, and the Jerusalem Bible. These versions freely translate בקרב שנים as 'in our day', or 'in our time', making the triumph of the contemporizing tradition quite explicit.

2. Critical Reconstructions of Hab. 3.2

Nevertheless, the textual foundation for this popular view of MT Hab. 3.2 has not gone unchallenged in the twentieth century. Critical scholarship has focused renewed attention on the linguistic obscurity of parts of the verse, and also re-examined its structure on both form-critical and prosodic grounds. The tricola structure of the verse, the hapax use of בקרב governing an object denoting time, the use of חיה with an inanimate object, and the unusual רחם תזכור have all aroused varying degrees of critical suspicion. The following examples illustrate the range of proposals for revision which have been offered, from rather wholesale emendation to the repointing of only a few words.

The fruit of criticism is seen, for example, in the New English Bible. The NEB excises בקרב שנים חייהו as an 'addition' and reads:

> O LORD, I have heard tell of thy deeds,
> I have seen, O LORD, thy work.
> In the midst of the years thou didst make thyself known
> And in thy wrath thou didst remember mercy.

NEB is unusual in that it seems to find no objection to the expression 'in the midst of the years', *per se*, but gives weight to other criteria which, unfortunately, are not identified. The following reconstructions, however, may reflect concerns shared by the editors of the NEB.

In 1942, William A. Irwin brought forward sweeping criticisms of the structure and syntax of MT Hab. 3.2.

> 2b is unquestionably disordered beyond all semblance of its original meaning. The first feature to rouse suspicion is that it is a tristich. . . and the occurrence of an isolated tristich in a series of distichs unless marking the conclusion of a strophe . . . is an almost infallible mark of corruption.[1]

---

1. W.A. Irwin, 'The Psalm of Habakkuk', *JNES* 1 (1942), p. 18.

Moreover his frustration with critical scholarship on syntactical points
bears indirect witness to the power of the popular exegetical tradition.

> All exegetes have felt the difficulty of 'the midst of the years', not to
> speak of the final stichos which is but undiluted nonsense. An astonishing
> aspect of critical scholarship is that a passage such as this has so long
> been accepted at face value, with expositors inventing every sort of
> ingenious explanation for words that are patently ludicrous.[1]

Taking a cue from the possibility that רחם (to have mercy) might be
a corruption of רהב (Rahab), Irwin reconstructed the text on the
assumption that it originally rehearsed Yahweh's victory over the
forces of chaos, using mythical imagery similar to that found throughout the rest of the psalm. Careful emendation along those general lines
led to the approximate reconstruction בקרב תנין תרע ברגז רהב
תדכה/חפר and the possible translation, 'In battle dost thou shatter the
dragon; in tumult (or by thy might) dost thou crush Rahab'.[2]

A less radical textual reconstruction of Hab. 3.2b was proposed by
Baruch Margulis in 1970. Like Irwin, Margulis dismissed בקרב שנים
הייהו בקרב שנים תודיע as 'virtually unintelligible' and ברגז רהם תזכור as
'impossible Hebrew'.[3] Drawing upon well-established principles of
Semitic prosody, Margulis offered a reconstruction which aimed at a
clearer *parallelismus membrorum* than that which appears in MT. Like
Irwin and the NEB editors, he concluded that one of the בקרב שנים
phrases is a spurious doublet, and excised it to bring the other into
parallel construction with the final hemistich. However, unlike the
NEB, he excised the second, and proposed בקרב שני-היים תודע ברגז
רחם תזכור, which he translated, 'When a twin-life looms you "appear";
when a womb throbs you "remember"'.[4]

Margulis displayed great skill and ingenuity in producing a text-
book perfect parallelism. In contrast to Irwin, one must particularly
admire the ease with which his reconstruction emerges from the
consonantal text passed on by the Masoretes. On the other hand,

---

1. Irwin, 'Habakkuk', p. 18.
2. Irwin, 'Habakkuk', pp. 18-19.
3. B. Margulis, 'The Psalm of Habakkuk: A Reconstruction and Interpretation',
ZAW 82 (1970), p. 412.
4. Margulis, 'Habakkuk', p. 413.

Irwin's reading seems to make a little more sense, drawing as it does upon standard ideas and expressions. Margulis related the proposed 'when a twin-life looms you "appear"' to the kind of oracular experience related of Rebekah in Gen. 25.22-24. However, he acknowledged that the idiom is otherwise unknown. It may be that he has simply substituted one obscure hapax for another!

A somewhat different, but equally creative, approach to the text was offered by W.F. Albright in 1950.[1] On the basis of form-critical analysis Albright identified four originally independent sections in Habakkuk 3, of which 3.2 constituted the first. Following the evidence of Ginsberg for the appearance of tricola between normal bicola,[2] Albright retained the tricola structure of MT Hab. 3.2b. He further proposed only one change in the text, the repointing of בְּקֶרֶב to בִּקְרֹב, citing structural parallels to the Song of Deborah (Judg. 5.2, 4), Ps. 27.2 and 114.1, and linguistic parallels to Gen. 27.41, Deut. 15.9, and Ezek. 12.23.[3]

However, despite the minimal change to the text, Albright's analysis of the original setting of 3.2 gives rise to a translation that breaks completely with the popular exegetical tradition. Suggesting that 3.2 originated as 'a very ancient prayer for the prolongation of (a king's) life, on the order of the hymn to Ishtar praying for the life of Amiditana',[4] he translated, 'As the years advance, "Give him life"—as the years advance—thou proclaimest'. Albright argued that the repetition of בקרב שנים was a 'stylistic device' which 'should not be allowed to interrupt the normal syntactic sequence of the bicolon'.[5]

The complexity of the textual problem emerges even from these few examples. The NEB, Irwin and Margulis agree (against Albright) that the tricola form of Hab. 3.2 preserved in MT is suspect. Further, Irwin, Margulis and Albright agree (against NEB) that the phrase 'in the midst of the years' is unacceptable. Irwin, Margulis and Albright agree that the repointing of בקרב is a necessary starting point in the

1. W.F. Albright, 'The Psalm of Habakkuk', in *Studies in Old Testament Prophecy* (ed. H.H. Rowley; Edinburgh: T. & T. Clark, 1950), pp. 1-18.
2. H.L. Ginsberg, 'The Rebellion and the Death of Baʿlu', *Orientalia* 5 (1936), p. 171.
3. Albright, 'Habakkuk', p. 13.
4. Albright, 'Habakkuk', p. 8.
5. Albright, 'Habakkuk', pp. 11, 13.

recovery of the proper sense of the phrase. Irwin repoints as בְּקְרָב ('in battle'), while the latter two opt for the infinitive construct—a choice at least as old as the Septuagint. However, Irwin, Margulis, Albright (and the LXX, as will be seen below) all part company when dealing with the elements reflected in both שׁנִים and הייהו. Moreover, they all send the revivalist looking elsewhere for a sermon text!

3. *The Exegetical Traditions of the Targum*

Before examining the Septuagint's exposition of Hab. 3.2, it is appropriate to note, in passing, the traditions reflected in the Targum. This translation, clearly based on a Masoretic-type text, offers two different interpretations of the phrase 'in the midst of the years'. The interpretation focuses on Yahweh's 'work', which the prophet fears. This work appears to be the judgment which he will bring upon the wicked, to whom he has granted an extension of time (ארכא) in which to turn to the Torah. The Targum then reads, 'But, if they do not turn, but provoke you to anger *in the midst of the years* in which you have given them life (= MT הייהו), thus it will finally happen, that you will make your power known to them *in the midst of the years*, of which you said that you would again renew the world (= M T הייהו) . . . '[1] The Targum goes on to make it clear that Yahweh's wrath will be visited on the godless, while he will remember the righteous with mercy.

Thus the Targum offers two possible ways of understanding 'in the midst of the years'. The second, which identifies the phrase with the years in which God will renew the world, has affinities with the historical approaches of Calvin and Bengel noted above. However, the first explains the phrase as the years in which Yahweh has given life, understood as an extension of time, to the wicked. Moreover, by understanding the wicked as the object of הייהו, the Targum succeeds (like Albright) in supplying a personal object for the verb. Construed as a perfect, rather than an imperative, any sort of petition for revival is also ruled out.

The Midrash Rabbah on the Song of Songs has an intriguing reference to Hab. 3.2 in its explanation of the word עלמות in Cant. 1.3:

---

1. See the text and translation in L. Reinke, *Der Prophet Habakuk* (Brixen: A. Weger's Buchandlung, 1870), pp. 46-47.

'Therefore maidens (עלמות) love thee'. Here it is suggested, by a process of reasoning impenetrable to this writer, that עלמות may be a reference to proselytes, and cites Hab. 3.2 in support of the interpretation.[1] Perhaps there is some remote connection between the Targum's extension of time granted to the wicked in Hab. 3.2, and Midrash Rabbah's suggestion that Hab. 3.2 has something to do with proselytes.

4. The Exegetical Traditions of the Greek Translations

The Greek exegetical traditions for Hab. 3.2 are of particular interest, owing to the fact that two distinct renderings of the Psalm of Habakkuk have come down to us in the ancient Greek translations. In addition to the Septuagint version, another 'anonymous' version is preserved in five manuscripts.[2] Best represented by 86, a ninth-century Italian manuscript from the Barberini collection in Rome,[3] it has become known as the Barberini version. The distinctive features of the Barberini text of Habakkuk 3 have been presented in a number of studies, but no consensus has emerged respecting its origin or relationship to LXX.[4] However, despite the extensive differences between the two texts, there is a striking agreement in the rendering of Hab. 3.2—an agreement that raises many questions about the origin and usage of this portion of the ancient translation.

LXX and Barberini present a text of Hab. 3.2 abounding with doublets and glosses. For ease of reference, the Göttingen text is presented here in sections, with numbered lines. Barberini variants are presented in brackets.

---

1. H. Freedman and M. Simon (eds.), *Midrash Rabbah*. IX. *Song of Songs* (trans. M. Simon; London: Soncino Press, 1939), p. 40.

2. J. Ziegler (ed.), *Septuaginta*. XIII. *Duodecim Prophetae* (Göttingen: Vandenhoeck & Ruprecht, 1984), p. 137.

3. H.StJ. Thackeray, 'Primitive Lectionary Notes in the Psalm of Habakkuk', *JTS* 12 (1911), p. 192.

4. Cf. M.L. Margolis, 'The Character of the Anonymous Greek Version of Habakkuk, Chapter 3', in *Old Testament and Semitic Studies*, I (ed. R.F. Harper, F. Brown and G.F. Moore; Chicago: University of Chicago Press, 1908), pp. 133-42; Thackeray, 'Habakkuk', pp. 191-213; H. Bevenot, 'Le Cantique d'Habacuc', *RB* 42 (1933), pp. 499-525; E.M. Good, 'The Barberini Greek Version of Hab. iii', *VT* 9 (1959), pp. 11-30; Ziegler, *Duodecim Prophetae*, p. 137.

(a) 1 Κύριε, εἰσακήκοα τὴν ἀκοήν σου καὶ ἐφοβήθην /
      <εὖ λαβήθην>
   2 <+κύριε> κατενόησα τὰ ἔργα σου καὶ ἐξέστην.

(b) 1 ἐν μέσῳ δύο ζῴων γνωσθήσῃ,
   2 ἐν τῷ ἐγγίζειν τὰ ἔτη ἐπιγνωσθήσῃ
   3 ἐν τῷ παρεῖναι τὸν καιρὸν ἀναδειχθήσῃ
   4 ἐν τῷ ταραχθῆναι τὴν ψυχήν μου ἐν ὀργῇ ἐλέους μνησθήσῃ

It is obvious from a comparison with MT that the doublets preserve diverse exegetical traditions. G's extremely diverse translational approaches to בקרב שנים may even suggest that one of the phrases in the *Vorlage* originated as a gloss or dittographic doublet.[1]

Significantly, the structure of the verse suggests that the doublets are not incorporated in a haphazard manner, but are carefully crafted into an expanded translation that aims at a symmetry and parallelism of its own. κατενόησα, for example, reflects the oft-repeated proposal that ראיתי is preferable to יראתי as a parallel to שמעתי.[2] ἐξέστην may serve to reinforce a preference for יראתי, but, in any case, it provides a structural parallel to ἐφοβήθην. The same is evident in 3.2b. Here, the addition of γνωσθήσῃ in line 1 and of an explanatory gloss in line 3 serves to create a climactic sequence of prepositional phrases beginning with ἐν and concluding with a future passive verb, second person singular. This carefully structured expansionism is consistent with the view that the translation was used for liturgical purposes, rather than as mere depository for variant readings.

Focusing specifically on the interpretation of בקרב שנים, two distinct efforts appear in (b) 1 and 2. The first vocalizes שנים as שְׁנַיִם, that is, 'two' (δύο), construing it adjectivally with the חיה element, which it takes as הַיּוֹת, that is, 'animals', or 'living creatures' (ζῴων). This results in the translation, 'between the two living beings'. The second attempt simply vocalizes בקרב as an infinitive construct governing שנים, resulting in 'as the years draw near', a proposal which has been encountered in the later work of Albright.

---

1. Cf. Margulis, 'Habakkuk', p. 412.

2. See, e.g., Margulis, 'Habakkuk', pp. 412-13; G. Fohrer, 'Das "Gebet des Propheten Habakuk" (Hab. 3,1-16)', in *Mélanges bibliques et orientaux en l'honneur de M. Mathias Delcor* (ed. A. Caquot, S. Légasse and M. Tardieu; Neukirchen–Vluyn: Neukirchener Verlag, 1985), p. 164; for a defense of MT cf. J.H. Eaton, 'The Origin and Meaning of Habakkuk 3', *ZAW* (1964), pp. 144-71.

With respect to the problematic בקרב שׁנים, it is worth noting that the Greek translation reproduces the MT vocalization for both elements, individually considered, but does not propose MT's combination of the two. Thus ἐν μέσῳ in (b) 1 stands for בְּקֶרֶב, while τά ἔτη in (b) 2 is straightforward for שָׁנִים. But if the concept 'in the midst of the years' was known or intelligible to the translator, it was not accepted. Such an interpretation certainly would not have harmonized well with the climactic view of time suggested by ἐν τῷ παρεῖναι τὸν καιρόν.

The radical differences between the Greek and Masoretic traditions respecting Hab. 3.2 point to diverse interpretive frameworks. On the one hand, it seems reasonable to assume that the tradents responsible for both MT and G understood Hab. 3.2, in some sense, of Yahweh's self-disclosure. This understanding is quite explicit in G with the sequence γνωσθήσῃ, ἐπιγνωσθήσῃ, ἀναδειχθήσῃ. It must have been present to some degree in the mind of the Masoretes as well, given the presence of the verb תודיע, and the theophany commencing in 3.3. On the other hand, G and MT conceive of this self-disclosure in distinctively different ways.

The crucial interpretive differences between the Greek and Masoretic traditions of Hab. 3.2 lie in the treatment of the היה element, and in the conception of time to be associated with בקרב. MT הייהו implies a renewal, apparently of Yahweh's work, in which he manifests himself in awe-inspiring power and majesty. Even the Targum, despite its twofold speculation on הייהו, interprets Yahweh's work from the framework of theodicy and emphasizes that Yahweh will *make his power known* to the wicked. MT places this renewal in the undefined 'midst of the years'. G, however, with its δύο ζῴων leaves the concept of renewal entirely out of consideration. Instead, G engages in a description of *where* the Lord's self-disclosure will take place, and offers a more suggestive description of the time. He will reveal himself between the two animals, or 'living beings', when the critical time (καιρός) arrives.

Very little attention has been given in modern times to the original intent of ἐν μέσῳ δύο ζῴων. Christian expositors who relied on G linked it with Isa. 1.3 as a prophecy that Jesus would be born in a stable between an ox and a donkey,[1] but this could hardly have been in the mind of the ancient tradents! Bevenot, however, appears to have

1. See Delitzsch, *Habakuk*, p. 132.

pointed the way with his suggestion that it may have been originally
understood of Yahweh's appearance between the cherubim in the Holy
of Holies, above the ark of the covenant.[1] Although Bevenot does not
elaborate upon this, several considerations give weight to the
suggestion.

The first is the fact that Hab. 2.20 closes with the declaration that
the 'Lord is in his holy temple'. Moreover, the call to 'keep silence'
(הַס) in 2.20 is rendered in G by the verb εὐλαβεῖσθαι, 'to show reverence', which is also chosen in Barb. Hab. 3.2 to render יראתי, suggesting that the translator linked the two passages in his mind. Thus,
in Barberini, the worshipper is called to show reverence in 2.20, and
in 3.2 the prophet responds that he has done so. Indeed, the divergent
interpretations of MT and G may owe much to the decision as to
whether the close of ch. 2, or the theophany at 3.3 offered the decisive
interpretive context.

Secondly, the choice of γνωσθήσῃ to fill out 3.2 (b), line 1, may
reflect more than just the arbitrary selection of a good parallel to
ἐπιγνωσθήσῃ.[2] Line (b) 1 is highly evocative of LXX Exod. 25.22
καὶ γνωσθήσομαί σοι ἐκεῖθεν καὶ λαλήσω σοι ἄνωθεν τοῦ
ἱλαστηρίου ἀνὰ μέσον τῶν δύο χερουβιμ. Significantly, in this
text, and in all but one of the texts where the verb יעד, niphal, is used
of Yahweh's meeting with Israel between the cherubim, the LXX
translates with the passive of γινώσκειν.[3] Thus, unless one assumes a
virtual wholesale confusion of the roots in the Pentateuch, it is likely
that γινώσκειν, passive, was used as a free translation to give the sense
of יעד, niphal, here,[4] and in other Pentateuch texts.[5] This raises the
interesting possibility that the *Vorlage* of G may even have contained
a doublet in line (b) 1 which proposed תועד as an alternative reading
to תודע.

The LXX translation of יעד in these Pentateuch settings could reflect

1. Bevenot, 'Habacuc', p. 505.
2. Cf. Margolis, 'Character', p. 135.
3. Cf. in MT and LXX the following: Exod. 25.22; 29.42, 43; 30.6, 36; Num.
17.19. In Exod. 29.43 LXX translates with τάξομαι, showing that יעד, niphal, was
known in another well-attested sense.
4. *Contra* J.I. Durham, *Exodus* (Waco, TX: Word Books, 1987), p. 357.
5. No less a Hebraist than William Holladay suggests that יעד, niphal, in Exod.
25.22 can mean 'let (oneself) appear, reveal oneself'. See *A Concise Hebrew and
Aramaic Lexicon of the Old Testament* (Leiden: Brill, 1971), pp. 137-38.

the view that the 'Tent of Meeting' (אהל מועד, Gr. τῆς σκηνῆς τοῦ μαρτυρίου) was a place where revelation took place and not merely a place to assemble.[1] When one keeps in mind the LXX use of γινώσκειν for יעד in the cherubim texts, and also notes that in Ezek. 10.15 the 'living creatures' (LXX τὰ ζῷα!) that uphold Yahweh's throne are specifically identified as the cherubim, an association of G Hab. 3.2 with divine self-disclosure between the cherubim in the Holy of Holies is not at all far-fetched.

The Greek tradition's predominating concern with the Lord's self-disclosure is also noteworthy in the light of Thackeray's theory that there are traces of liturgical notations for Pentecost in the two Greek textual traditions.[2] Thackeray pointed out that the use of Habakkuk 3 as a *haftarah* for Pentecost could have originated as early as the third century BCE, which would have roughly coincided with the beginning of the efforts to render portions of the Old Testament into Greek.[3] Thus, even though Thackeray's explanation of particular expressions as liturgical notations has not won complete acceptance, he certainly raised the level of scholarly awareness respecting the possibility of liturgical influence on the form of the Greek texts of Habakkuk 3.

It was noted above that G Hab. 3.2 carefully weaves doublets and glosses into a balanced composition consistent with liturgical usage. The close agreement of LXX and Barberini in Hab. 3.2 is also highly suggestive of liturgical influence, in view of their almost word by word divergence in the other major sections of the chapter. Indeed, it is hard to account for their agreement in 3.2 without recourse to the kind of strong traditional influence that is exercised by liturgy. Thackeray explains the agreement as a result of the inter-conflation of readings of LXX and Barberini. But he does envisage the conflation as the fruit of an effort to obtain a uniform text for lectionary purposes.[4]

It also seems possible that the Greek versions preserve an early translation portion that antedates either extant version of the Psalm. The exegetical traditions reflected in the two texts certainly could have

---

1. Cf. A. Dillman, *Exodus and Leviticus* (Leipzig: S. Hirzel, 1880), p. 282; B. Baentsch, *Exodus–Leviticus–Numeri* (Göttingen: Vandenhoeck & Ruprecht, 1903), p. 226.
2. Thackeray, 'Habakkuk', pp. 191-213.
3. Thackeray, 'Habakkuk', pp. 191-213.
4. Thackeray, 'Habakkuk', pp. 212-13.

existed prior to the time of these translations and could have been brought together for liturgical use by a means other than the inter-action of these two text types. It is clear that 3.2 is a text that revisors did not feel free to alter to any degree. Whether this was the result of an official textual standardization, or the result of a status achieved through usage in Greek synagogues prior to the appearance of full translations of the Book of the Twelve Prophets is perhaps a moot point.

The possibility that G Hab. 3.2 (probably with 3.3a) preserves an ancient *haftarah* for Pentecost raises the question of possible tradi-tional associations between 3.2 and Pentecost as a celebration of the giving of the law, indeed as a Festival of Revelation.[1] Now, the simi-larity between Hab. 3.3a and Deut. 31.2, which celebrates Yahweh's appearing at Sinai, was undoubtedly the decisive factor in the selection of Habakkuk 3 as a Pentecost *haftarah*. However, the likely reference in the Greek version to Yahweh's appearing between the cherubim, and the obvious focus there on divine self-disclosure, also suggest links with the theme of the giving of the law.

The connections between the law and the description of Yahweh's activity between the cherubim are well known. From texts like Exod. 25.22, a picture emerges of Yahweh manifesting himself to Moses between the cherubim, above the ark which contained the tables of the law, apparently to explain and augment the commandments of the law. Thus, it is not unlikely that the celebration of Pentecost as a Feast of Revelation may have reinforced, or even helped to produce, the exegetical tradition embodied in ἐν μέσῳ δύο ζῴων γνωσθήσῃ.

How a tradition of Yahweh's appearing between the cherubim at some critical time in the future would have been viewed by Jews cele-brating Pentecost can only be a subject of speculation. Perhaps Mal. 3.1, 'the LORD whom you seek will suddenly come to his temple', with 4.4, 'Remember the law of my servant Moses, the statutes and ordinances that I commanded him at Horeb for all Israel' (RSV), would lead one into interpretive paths similar to the ones that they have followed in this regard.

---

1. J. Hertz (ed.), *The Pentateuch and Haftorahs*. III. *Leviticus* (London: Oxford University Press, 1936), pp. 246-47. That the association of Pentecost with the theme of revelation is very old is evident in the Christian tradition that the Holy Spirit was poured out on the day of Pentecost.

Clearly, Hab. 3.2 has served as 'pretext' to widely divergent expositions, several of which have shaped the text form of ancient translations. In spite of their diversity, however, these expository traditions manage (for the most part) to converge in hopeful expectation of the divine self-disclosure. The text's potency as pretext originates in the uncertainty surrounding its original form, and in the obscurity of the predominant attempts to resolve that uncertainty—the phrase 'in the midst of the years'. That such an enigmatic expression should become part of the Judaeo-Christian idiom owes much to our tendency to think that what seems sufficiently clear to us must also appear so to others. Yet its power as pretext must ultimately lie in the hope of each generation that theirs may be one in which God will decisively act for the vindication of his cause in the world.

CRITICISM AND TRADITION*

Christopher F. Evans

The Alexander Robertson Lecture, which I have the honour of being invited to deliver this year, is specified as being 'for the defence of the Christian religion'. This could be said to have a late nineteenth- or early twentieth-century ring about it. It could also be said to have a Scottish flavour. That remark is meant as a compliment. It is made from south of the border, where not infrequently theologians have felt themselves compelled to admiration of notable foundations north of the border, such as this one and, for instance, the Gifford Lectures. For such foundations have been deliberately designed to secure that there shall be an open and continuing engagement of the Christian religion with philosophy, science, natural religion, ethics, and so on; and they have sometimes secured it in periods when the inclination of theologians elsewhere has been to run for cover.

It can hardly be denied, however, that in the course of the century such aims of apologetic—to give it its technical title—have become increasingly difficult to pursue. The time is long past when such an engagement was with a number of single identifiable attacks—concerned with creation perhaps, or with miracle—on a front which was otherwise comparatively solid and still holding. With the increasing fragmentation and departmentalization of Western thought itself the engagement has come to be on a larger and larger number of separate fronts, so that it has often been difficult to discern what is to be defended against which attack, and to distinguish between advance and retreat. And for some time in some quarters the situation could be said to have been, not so much that the Christian religion was under attack and was in need of defence, as that it has simply been

* The Alexander Robertson Lecture in the University of Glasgow given on 21 November 1985.

by-passed and ignored. In that death-dealing expression 'post-Christian', espoused even by some theologians, it had been relegated to a phenomenon of the past.

Moreover, there have been other discouragements to the enterprise coming not from outside but from inside. In the middle decades of the century there were not a few who regarded apologetics not as difficult or even impossible, but as 'grotesquely inappropriate', even profoundly unchristian. In an essay 'Has Apologetics a Future?', which was his contribution to the Festschrift for Davis McCaughey entitled *Imagination and the Future*, the philosopher of religion, Harry Wardlaw, wrote of that period as follows.

> The possibility of commending faith to its cultured despisers seemed like a dream which belonged to the old fashioned liberal tradition of the nineteenth century and could not longer be entertained by any Christian worthy of his calling. . . If apologetics is seen, as it often has been seen, as a matter of answering the unbeliever's questions, then this will seem to require accepting the question on its own terms, and this in turn may mean that the believer is asked to justify his belief in terms which are incommensurate with the belief itself. But to accept such a demand may surely lead to an abortive conversation which will certainly have no future.[1]

Still remembered with some glee in this respect is Karl Barth's *tour de force* in turning the Gifford Lectureship on its head by devoting it to an exposition of that revealed theology which natural theology—supposing *per impossibile* that such an entity could ever exist—would have to recognize as its opponent. In the sphere of biblical studies, this attitude to apologetic was particularly associated at that time with the movement of thought known as 'biblical theology'. This movement was confident in its ability to repristinate on critical grounds a unified Scripture as a self-contained whole, which could be made to yield a total and consistent viewpoint, which could then be the basis for a doctrinal and ethical system. This was to confront the world's thought and convert it, not to parley with it or enter into apologetic dialogue with it. But despite its considerable achievements, biblical theology undoubtedly overplayed its hand and claimed too much for itself. As a result it collapsed as a movement, leaving the situation once more

---

1. *Imagination and the Future: Essays on Christian Thought and Practice. Presented to J. Davis McCaughey* (ed. J. Henley; Melbourne: The Hawthorn Press, 1980), p. 204.

open and fragmented. Wardlaw himself goes on to devote the rest of his essay to an account of what is involved for Christian apologetic in three kinds of dialogue—namely that with empirical realists and their appeal to scientific objectivity, that with Marxists and their faith that politics can alone transform society, and that with liberal humanists and their attack on the intolerance and exclusive claims of Christianity. But he is not very sanguine about the enterprise beyond a conviction that dialogue must somehow go on 'so that we may be more open to each other in our authentic humanity perfected in Christ'.

In such circumstances what can a single individual expect to be able to say 'in defence of the Christian religion', even if he were giving a course of lectures and not a single lecture? I stress 'the single individual'. For it is not the case that the Christian apologist faces a fragmented world as himself the spokesman of something that is demonstrably a single architectonic whole. The Christian religion to be defended is itself fragmented, and in some respects rightly so. I am not here referring to the denominational divisions of Christendom, with their variant versions of what the Christian religion is, but to that separation of Christian thought into areas and departments, which has come about of necessity when it has submitted itself to—or rather has procured for itself—specifically modern forms of scrutiny and analysis. As a result biblical studies, itself capable of its own subdivisions, is separate from doctrinal studies, also capable of its own subdivisions, which is separate from ethics, and so on. These are no longer seen as evidently and naturally flowing in and out of one another. There can be hiatuses between them and within them. And since here, as elsewhere, the age of the polymath is past, the single individual, if he is to speak at more than a superficial level, cannot do so in all spheres at once, but only with effect in his own sphere. This may be illustrated by the person who would probably qualify as one of, if not the most effective apologist of our day, C.S. Lewis. He was forceful and convincing when bringing a rigorous philosophical mind combined with the sensitive imagination of a literary critic to the exposition of Christian doctrine in the face of secular thought; he was weak and unconvincing in his use of the Bible for the same purpose.

My own sphere, in so far as I can be said to have one, is that of New Testament studies. These, for obvious reasons, have often stood at the centre of the Christian enterprise, including apologetic, though there are signs that they no longer of necessity occupy that position. What then does the New Testament student have to say by way of defence of the Christian religion? That the answer to this question is not straightforward points to the difficulties. It depends on what kind of a New Testament student he or she is. For some—I trust I shall not give offence if I term them 'the biblicists'—the answer to the question remains, or has once more become, relatively immediate. To defend the Christian religion biblically is to reaffirm the Christian tradition by repeating in season and out of season, whether they will hear or whether they will forbear, the biblical text, and especially what are judged its primary proof-texts upon which the Christian doctrinal and ethical systems can be established; to do so either in the text's own language or in whatever modern language is deemed serviceable and faithful for the purpose; and in the process, if necessary, to rebut any attacks upon a four-square New Testament as to its correctness in respect of statement of fact or its coherence in respect of statement of religious truth, whether such attacks emanate from outside or inside the Christian community. For others, however, such a procedure is no longer possible. This is not only for the negative reason that the use of the New Testament as self-enclosed whole, with its parts potentially of equal value, both continues to appear dubious in theory, and also proves ineffective in practice for settling those doctrinal and ethical questions which are legitimately raised by believer and unbeliever alike. It is so also for the positive reason that something of profound and lasting importance is judged to have been taking place in critical study of the New Testament; something that, despite its many errors of method and judgment, is not temporary but permanent; not a disease caught from the outside world, a protracted bout of measles to be endured as a mysterious visitation from God like Job's boils, and from which the patient may be expected one day to recover; but a process that has profoundly altered the apperception of the New Testament text itself, and that, in consequence, calls for a method of handling the text corresponding to its character. The situation is, then, much more complex. For it is far less clear in advance what would constitute defence in the case of a text shown to be of this kind. It is less likely to consist in repetition and reaffirmation of the text as it stands than in a critical, and possibly highly controversial, dialogue with it, which may be engaged in, or overheard by, those who are concerned.

But let me attempt to be more specific. 'The radical and the liberals have no future, since they are simply parasites on the tradition.' This is a fairly recent statement by one who would, I think, accept that he was as a 'biblicist' voicing the 'biblicist' position. The statement has the advantage of being concise and forthright. It has the disadvantage that all the terms in it are ambiguous. This is so even of the emotive word 'parasite'. For it would not be entirely flippant to observe that in the order of God's creation it appears to be necessary for living things to have parasites to remain alive, which are replaced briefly by maggots when the living body has become a corpse, and to argue the conclusion 'no conservatives without radicals' as well as 'no radicals without conservatives'. I know of more than one theologian who would be happy with the word 'parasite' for what he thought he was trying to do for the health of theology.

But the same applies to the word 'radical', upon which there should surely be a moratorium in theological debate. For what is it supposed to mean? If by definition a radical is one who insists on going to the roots of a matter, then he is presumably doing what the fundamentalist thinks he is doing, and a radical is a kind of fundamentalist and a fundamentalist is a kind of radical, the dispute being over what the roots or fundamentals are, and over how you get at them. The word thus takes on the meaning you choose to give it. If it is a term of approval you use it of the Old Testament prophets, Jesus, Paul, or the theologians of your choice. If it is one of disapproval, doing service for the outmoded word 'heretical', you apply it accordingly. But is it of any use? And is it not the case that yesterday's so-called radicals prove to be tomorrow's conservatives, and that a person can be 'radical' in some things—liturgy or politics shall we say—and conservative in others—doctrine or philosophy, shall we say?

Similarly with the word 'liberal'. For what is this word, so charged with particular connotations in its history in this century, now supposed to convey? It was, after all, originally an adjective qualifying a noun. It denoted primarily a certain temper of mind and manner of approach to things rather than a fixed position or a set of beliefs. So John Morley wrote: 'Respect for the dignity and worth of the individual is its root. It stands for the pursuit of social and against class interest or dynastic interest. It stands for the subjection to human judgment of all claims to external authority, whether in an organized church, in more loosely gathered societies of believers, or in books held sacred.'[1] Already in such a description there is latent the possibility of conflict with religious tradition as such, which could lead to the very different definition of Newman that 'Liberalism in religion is the doctrine that there is no positive truth in religion, that one creed is as good as another. . . It teaches that all are to be tolerated, for all are matters of opinion'.[2] It is, however, somewhat fortuitous that this temper of mind came to be exercised at a time when progress had become a widespread dogma, and human self-sufficiency for the major purposes of life a deeply held presupposition. The two are not inseparable. In Dr Alec Vidler's description,

> A liberal man is free from narrow prejudice, generous in his judgement of others, open-minded especially to the reception of new ideas or proposals of reform. Liberal is the opposite not of conservative but of fanatical, bigoted or intransigent. . . It can be preserved even by those who once possessed it only by constant vigilance and exercise.[3]

But again does the word serve any useful purpose now?

Equally ambiguous in the statement I am considering is the word 'tradition', and here we come nearer to the heart of the matter. One might observe in passing that the presence of the word tradition in a 'biblicist' statement is somewhat surprising, since in the New Testament itself it is an ambivalent word, used both with approval and condemnation. In the history of doctrine, it has been for reformers an object of suspicion or violent attack. And no room is made for distinctions between Catholic, Orthodox, Reformed or other forms of tradition. But leaving these considerations aside, the main question at issue here is the relation between what comes to us as tradition and what is thought, spoken or written that is not already in the tradition. It has long seemed to me that a classic statement on this matter is that of T.S. Eliot in his essay, *Tradition and the Individual Talent.* There he wrote:

> Tradition is a matter of much wider significance (than simply that of taking possession of the past). It involves in the first place the historical

1. *Recollections* (1921 edn), I.19, quoted in A.R. Vidler, *Essays in Liberality* (London: SCM Press, 1957), p. 9.
2. In his address in response to the notification of his elevation to be a cardinal. See J. Lewis May, *Cardinal Newman* (London: Geoffrey Bles, 1929), pp. 214-15.
3. *Cardinal Newman*, pp. 21-22.

sense, which you may call nearly indispensable to anyone who would continue to be a poet beyond his twenty-fifth year; and the historical sense involves a perception, not only of the pastness of the past, but of its presence. . . This historical sense, which is a sense of the timeless as well as the temporal, and of the timeless and the temporal together, is what makes a writer traditional.[1]

Some years later Eliot returned to the subject in his Virgil Lecture, *What is a Classic?*, where he wrote as follows:

We may expect the language to approach maturity at the moment when it has a critical sense of the past, a confidence in the present and no conscious doubt of the future. In literature this means that the poet is aware of his predecessors, and that we are aware of the predecessors behind his work, as we may be aware of the ancestral traits of a person who is at the same time individual and unique. The predecessors should be themselves great and honoured, but their accomplishment should be such as to suggest still undeveloped resources in the language, and not such as to oppress the younger writers that everything that can be done has been done in their language. The poet, certainly in a mature age, may still obtain stimulus from the hope of doing something that his predecessors have not done; he may even be in revolt against them, as a promising adolescent may be in revolt against the beliefs, habits and manners of his parents; but in retrospect we can see that he is a continuer of their traditions, that he preserves essential characteristics, and that his difference of behaviour is a difference in the circumstances of another age. . . The persistence of literary creativeness in any people, accordingly, consists in the maintenance of an unconscious balance between tradition in the larger sense—the collective personality, so to speak, realized in the literature of the past—and the originality of the living generation.[2]

The force of these two quotations is that to remain in the tradition the artist has to do something fresh. He who imitates the past, and is content simply to reaffirm it by repeating it, does not remain in the tradition. According to this canon re-thinking could be, indeed would have to be asserted to be, a dogmatic necessity. While on the one hand there can be no reformation or innovation except in relation to an actual situation and on the background of a received tradition and belief, on the other hand re-thinking, if that is what is meant by radicalism, so far from being parasitic on the tradition and sucking its blood away, could be supplying life to it, could indeed be part of that

1.   T.S. Eliot, *Selected Prose* (Harmondsworth: Penguin Books, 1953), p. 23.
2.   *What is a Classic?* (London: Faber & Faber, 1945), pp. 14-15.

life. With a more specifically theological reference the French scholar George Tavard, in a study of the seventeenth-century debates on tradition in France and England, concludes with the judgment that what we have to do with here is a past that is moving and dynamic, the chief characteristic of which, when seen from the point of view of development, is no longer the preservation of tradition as a deposit, but its preparation of a future, and he pleads for the working out of a theology of tradition which shall be 'une théologie du devenir et d'avenir'.[1]

What is notable in these statements is the dynamic character given to tradition. This contrasts with what has generally been conveyed by the term in either its more general or its more specific sense, and in either Western or Eastern Christianity. There it has denoted what is fixed and static, a kind of package wrapped up at a certain point—the point at which this happened, and the way in which it happened, being matters of debate. And it is in a vocabulary determined for good and capable only of repetition. Hence apologetic has tended to demand that any alteration of tradition so conceived is to be met with blank rejection, as in Dean Burgon's reaction to the textual criticism of the Authorised Version, 'not a word, not a syllable, not a comma shall be changed'; or Liddon's conviction that once the Mosaic authorship of the Pentateuch is let go the whole of Christian belief collapses. Indeed, it has to be remembered that the word 'development' and the idea of it, upon which the statements I have quoted rest, was a comparative newcomer in Christian thinking. As Dr Owen Chadwick shows in his book *From Bossuet to Newman*, there was a real change of thought from the position of Bossuet—

> The Church's doctrine is always the same; The Gospel is never different from what it was before; there is no difficulty in recognising false doctrine; there can be no argument about it; it is recognised at once whenever it appears because it is new

—and the position of Newman that Christian doctrine may be compared to a broadening river which becomes fuller as it gets further away from its source.[2] The latter, about which the Roman Catholic

---

1. G. Tavard, *La tradition au XVIIe siècle en France et en Angleterre* (Paris: Cerf, 1969), p. 503.
2. O. Chadwick, *From Bossuet to Newman* (Cambridge: Cambridge University Press, 2nd edn, 1987), p. 17.

church is still undecided as to whether it is a welcome liberating force or a dose of deadly poison, presents a dynamic rather than a static concept of tradition. Far from being minimizing and reductionist, which has been the accusation often, and sometimes rightly, levelled against liberalism, it could be maximizing and additive. It allows it to be said that fresh things were done when Origen, with the help of Platonism and allegorizing, had been at work on the tradition as he had received it; or later when Augustine was at work with the help of Neoplatonism; or Aquinas with the aid of Aristotle; or Luther with justification by faith as arbitrator; or Calvin with election. It is, of course, necessary to maintain that in what happened to the tradition a theological continuity was to be observed. A living tradition is the product of a manner of receiving what is given such that a recognizable continuity and coherence emerge. But this raises the question of what is 'the given' that is to be received in this way. This question is raised acutely by the specifically modern method of critical analysis. Matters can then be more complex, and the shoe pinch hard.

In the first of my quotations from him, T.S. Eliot, in insisting that to be mature a poet must have a historical sense, defines that historical sense as a sense of the timeless as well as the temporal, and of the timeless and the temporal held together. He is speaking of literature, but what he says could go even more for theology, since it could be said to be pre-eminently the task of theology to have the timeless and the temporal together. However, in Eliot's statement there is more than a hint of Platonism. It is the Platonist approach that speaks of the timeless, and of the timeless and the temporal in juxtaposition; and for considerable periods of its life Christianity has gone hand in hand with Platonism. But what if, alongside a philosophical critique of Platonism, as well as of the Aristotelianism or other philosophies which displaced it, there develops an increasingly stringent and refined method of historical analysis in accordance with the oft-trumpeted claim that a distinctive feature of Christianity as a religion is its historical character. For this is a claim not to have the timeless alongside the temporal, but to a unique divine revelation in, with and under the historical. In Newman's time, historical analysis of the tradition had got little further than the removal of falsehoods in it—false decretals, bogus acts of councils, forgeries, which had previously propped it up, and whose removal purified it. What was to follow, stage by stage, was a penetration by which analysis into the core of the tradition itself, into the canon of Scripture, and into closer proximity to the historical events that formed its substance, with the discovery that the tradition at its core was of a significantly different kind than had been supposed.

I would wish to dwell on this a little, as it seems to be that the heart of the problem lies here in the use of the New Testament for apologetic, as for almost anything else. It is easy, and to some extent justifiable, to represent this approach and method—call it radical, liberal, critical, analytical, or what you will—as being inherently negative, destructive, and, in so far as their exponents remain Christians and value Christianity, reductionist. For this is how in their operation they have often represented themselves. Thus Adolf Harnack's *What is Christianity?* at the beginning of the century (when critical studies of the New Testament emerged from the first time from behind the closed doors of the divinity faculty) reduced, by a critical method, the core of the tradition to the proclamation by Jesus of the fatherhood of God and the brotherhood of man, and in his magisterial seven volumes on Christian dogma had presented it as the progressive Hellenization, and therefore degeneration, of an originally Hebraic message.[1] Rudolf Bultmann, in the middle of the century, crowned many years of technical New Testament work by a programme of demythologizing of the gospel, and especially the kerygma of the cross and resurrection, which located its force in the existential response of the believer. It may be noted in passing that both these reconstructions, which were also reductions, were made, not in a spirit of academic superiority and aloofness, but out of spiritual and apologetic passion. Harnack regarded his as a contribution to the solution of the grave problems of the Europe of his day. Bultmann's programme was his response to agonizing questions from pupils who had become army chaplains as to how the language of the New Testament could be made meaningful for the troops.

But to some extent this negative and reductionist quality has been fortuitous, and not of the essence of the critical enterprise. There is something involved here which goes much deeper, and which remains to be assimilated even when such reconstructions have been rightly repudiated and abandoned. This is the fact that historical analysis, in penetrating further into the core of the tradition, the Scriptures,

1. *History of Dogma* (London: Williams & Norgate, 1896–1905), *passim*.

shows them to have been themselves in movement—something like the interior of the once solid atom—and to be the kind of writings they are as the result of such movement. Thus, more important and far-reaching than any judgments on individual passages in the Old Testament—the creation story, the fall story, the exodus—was the demonstration that the Pentateuch was the end product of a process of movement and theological development over a considerable period, which still contained within itself as a finished whole abundant evidence of wide diversities and tensions. And, coming nearer to the core of the tradition for the Christian, more important and far-reaching than any particular judgment on individual passages or incidents in the Gospels is the fact that, under analysis, the Gospels are seen to have been, over a much shorter period and therefore in more concentrated fashion, in movement, and to be the end products of such movement.

It all began and begins with the Synoptic problem. The solution of this problem is, surprisingly for one of my generation, once more up for grabs, though I am not much impressed by the alternative solutions proposed to those on which I was reared. But whatever the solution, it will inevitably involve that some Gospels are what they are as the result of reaction to, criticism of, modification of, recreation of, even contradiction of, some previous arrangement of the tradition. The process continues with form criticism, with its attempt to discern from the shape of the tradition the forces that have been at work in shaping it so. And this is not something that is imposed on a recalcitrant tradition, but something actually demanded by it in its original form of separate and independent units, which had a previous history of use before being written down. And as the lecturer with his epidiascope twiddles the knob until the picture on the screen is in focus—in focus meaning that what is meant to stand out sharply in the foreground does so, and what is meant to be in the background is so—the form critic attempts to get his unit of tradition in focus; to detect, if he can, its *Sitz im Leben*, that is, where it is seen to be alive and doing its stuff. And in doing this he may well reach the conclusion that one constituent in the story, along with its previous form in the tradition, and what was in the mind of its teller, was the audience itself, whose needs and aspirations the story was framed to answer. And it was that that had made it fertile and not simply repetitive. The process continues in redaction criticism, which attempts to assess the actual situation, and the theological motivations belonging to it, which led each evangelist to do what he felt he had to do by way of re-ordering, reframing, restating and re-presenting such traditional material in the way he did. So it might be said that criticism, by a method which has at least some pretensions to be scientific, approximates to the verdict of Luther that the writing of the Gospels was a necessary evil, since neither the Lord nor his apostles wrote anything but only preached to particular audiences, and that the Gospels only function aright when turned back from the written to the spoken word.

And this is not confined to the Gospels. While it is still debated and debateable whether there is a development to be discerned in Paul's thinking, such as could have involved a jettisoning of parts of the previous tradition, as a physicist can jettison erroneous parts of his tradition, there would seem to be evidence of movement and development in the Pauline wing of Christianity. The Pauline corpus of letters (which as a collection of literature was to exercise such a powerful influence from within the larger collection of writings, the New Testament canon) appears on analysis, and especially if some Epistles are not by Paul himself but by disciples applying his thought to later situations, to be more a spectrum than a package. And the Epistles of John appear as belonging to a different kind of spectrum, or at the opposite end of the same spectrum; and when they are taken with the Gospel of John they raise in the acutest form the questions in what circumstances, and under what pressures and movement, the traditions about Jesus should have so altered both in form and content as to constitute almost a *metabasis eis allo genos*.

The upshot of all this in the present context is that it has radically altered the character of the given. For the given is now seen to have been itself in constant and exceedingly fertile movement from the start. The given consists not only in what is handed on or handed over (tradition as a passive noun), but includes the living situation in which this takes place (tradition as an active verbal noun). This is not only so now, but was the case then; and at no point do we reach a stage where what is before us is a fixed and solid core, from which all subsequent development can then be genetically traced. To judge from the character of the New Testament material under the hands of critical analysis, re-thinking was a process that was constantly taking place, and the necessity for it would seem to have been forced on the first Christian generations in the nature of the case. To understand the nature of the given differently is to understand the nature of the revelation differently, if we prefer to speak in terms of revelation rather than of tradition. The revelation has been of such a kind that movement and development were endemic to it from the first.

It is this which certain developments in the second and third centuries, however inevitable and justifiable they may have been at the time, have tended to conceal. With the creation of the New Testament canon, and some sort of apostolic succession of teaching in the face of heresy, the impression is given of a Christian golden age when everything went right, and anything apostles said was straight from the horse's mouth and true in all senses of the word, and that Christianity was now a fixed quantum of truth with firm and clear lines drawn round it. Any development of the tradition can come now only by way of exegesis of a canonical text, and its exegesis as a single and coherent whole. The Gospels are now received as part of a harmony, in which their individual characteristics, and hence the theological movement of thought which was responsible for those individualities, tend to be lost to view. And the non-Gospel material is received into a wider harmony with the Gospels, and both in harmony with the Old Testament. The effect of criticism has been to undo much of this, and to do so in the end with positive and not negative intent and results. If such a method of analysis is not a temporary disease caught from outside, but is something here to stay because it answers better to the character of the tradition, what are the implications for apologetic? What is received is to be received in accordance with the character of the given and with the way it is given. If radicalism means going to the roots, and the roots are shown to be of this kind, then, far from being parasitic, it may become profoundly illuminative. But what then will be its implication for apologetic? One implication would seem to be that a tradition which is shown to have this character cannot be defended simply by repetition and re-affirmation in its own terms, but only along with repeated attempts to retrace and appreciate its capacity for movement, and so to be on the track of its secret, namely that it proved so fertile and was able to capture one position of thought after another.

This undoubtedly makes the task more complex and difficult. In my own contribution to the Festschrift *Imagination and the Future*, to which I referred at the beginning, I animadverted briefly on one particular difficulty of a limited and technical kind, namely that the commentary form, which has been a principal mode of communicat-

EVANS *Criticism and Tradition*

ing exegesis of the biblical text at more than one level, is somewhat ill-fitted for the analysis of a tradition of this kind.[1] It can be very exact and informative on the text, but in being so can hardly escape first turning it into a corpse for dissection into separate sentences, phrases and words, while the fertile movement in and behind the text can seldom be evoked. I was also myself made aware of the difficulties on a wider front as a member of the last Doctrine Commission but two in the Church of England. Such Commissions are almost by definition apologetic in intent. Previous Commissions had been concerned to take individual items of Christian belief—the Virgin Birth, the Ascension, and so on—to discuss them individually, and to attempt to restate them in such a way that the shoe pinched less hard. And they undoubtedly did good work in this way, and enabled many to continue to be believers. This Commission, in face of the character of the tradition to which I have been referring, and also of contemporary pluralism in religious thought, deliberately eschewed this approach, and occupied itself with the question of what is now involved in the act of belief itself. Hence the title of its report was not Christian Belief, but Christian Believing.[2]

I would like now to try to be more specific still, and to relate these general observations to what might be regarded as a particular contemporary instance of apologetic in the form of a controversial dialogue among Christians about the tradition and its use, which has certainly been overheard by others to the extent that it has penetrated to the pages and correspondence columns of the press, and even to the House of Commons. I refer to the debate on resurrection initiated and maintained by my former pupil and colleague, David Jenkins, Bishop of Durham.

Now one thing may be said immediately on this from the standpoint of New Testament studies, which is that such a debate is entirely proper, and ought to be expected. For it is one of the conclusions of critical study that the resurrection of Christ, and what stems from it, are central and crucial to the New Testament as a whole and to many of its component parts. They are found to be so as early as we can trace back the Christian tradition, that is, to Paul's statements at the

---

1. 'How Shall They Hear?', in *Imagination and the Future*, pp. 231ff.

2. *Christian Believing: The Nature of the Christian Faith and its Expression in Holy Scripture and Creeds. A Report of the Doctrine Commission of the Church of England* (London: SPCK, 1976).

beginning of his exposition of resurrection in 1 Corinthians 15. And one of the curious features of Christian theology has been that after the second and beginning of the third century, when it was a storm centre of controversy, resurrection has lain comparatively unexamined and undebated, except as part of the subject of miracle in general; and that barely begins to do justice to it. To quote the author of the most recent extended study on the subject, Dr Pheme Perkins of Boston, 'Resurrection is not merely an assertion in the Creed, but pervades Christian speech in the New Testament. One might even go so far as to say that it is the condition for the emergence of Christian speech itself.'[1] But this very foundational character of resurrection speech has led to an awkward inability to explore the boundaries of resurrection as a category of Christian theology. To illustrate this the author quotes the judgment of a philosopher that 'the resurrection narratives are linguistically odd', but she proceeds that 'such judgements are not to be taken as signposts to tell non-believers and historical critics to keep out'.

> Rather, it would seem, that twentieth century Christians must explore the 'truth' of resurrection as the founding language of their tradition. Such explorations cannot stop with asserting that some symbols and concepts are 'untouchable'. It must ask instead what space such speech can occupy in the linguistic world of the twentieth century Christian. The question is not simply destructive meddling on the part of exegetes and theologians. . . One need not surround resurrection with 'do not touch' signs born of an apologetic instinct to bolster the foundations.[2]

She concludes from this that

> theological or reflective clarification seeks to explain in discursive terms what Christians mean by their use of resurrection language. Since resurrection emerges from the levels of symbol and story, even the first and second century authors found themselves called upon to explain what affirmations and consequences should or should not follow from belief in resurrection. That task is even more pressing for twentieth century Christians, who require such effective speech as a way back to the roots of their tradition.[3]

1.   P. Perkins, *Resurrection: New Testament Witness and Contemporary Reflection* (London: Geoffrey Chapman, 1984), p. 18.
2.   *Resurrection*, p. 18.
3.   *Resurrection*, p. 19.

How then is this task to be performed? And here a further point about the matter needs to be noted. Resurrection, as central and crucial in the New Testament, is not a private concern. Granted that the appearances of the risen Christ, upon which the resurrection faith came to depend, were made to insiders only—and that has often been for apologetic a point where the tradition has been most vulnerable to attack—the resurrection faith is in principle addressed to the world. Its intention is precisely to proclaim that Jesus of Nazareth is, as the risen Christ, the Lord of humanity and time. Indeed, strange as it may seem, one thing, and perhaps the only thing, which the otherwise varied accounts of these appearances have in common is that they are, each in its own fashion, vehicles for the command that the gospel is to break out of its Jewish boundaries and to go to mankind as a whole. This is so whether formulated in the message in Mark, 'He goes before you into Galilee'; or in Matthew 'Go into the whole world and make all nations my disciples'; or in Luke, 'You shall be my witnesses in Jerusalem, in all Judaea and Samaria and to the end of the earth'; or in John 'As my Father has sent me (i.e. into the world), even so I send you'. Thus resurrection is a public event, and is to be publicized. It is not the possession of a particular coterie for purely internal consumption. And its language therefore is not

> the private code of a group of initiates, who speak about things with no relation to the world, or to the lives of other human beings—or perhaps even their own lives apart from interactions with other members of the group.[1]

How, then, is the exploration of this crucial and public matter to be made? In the controversy I have referred to, along with the ups and downs, ins and outs, untidiness and clumsiness, exaggerations and over-simplifications that are almost inevitable in such a debate, two main positions would appear to have emerged. On the one hand the bishop has been from the first, and continues to be, primarily concerned with God, with the relation of God to the world and of the world to God, and with the language of resurrection as that which may enable and inform belief in God as we can now apprehend him in relation to the world as we now perceive it. On the other hand, some of his principal opponents appear to be primarily concerned with the

---

1. Perkins, *Resurrection*, p. 400.

tradition, with rebutting attacks on it and repairing breaches in it, so as to be able to reaffirm it as the truth in contradiction of what they take the bishop to be saying. Each of these two positions has its own difficulties, some of which are not unrelated to critical and historical analysis of the New Testament.

To take the second first, the reaffirmation of the tradition. Here indeed the position is startling. Despite the fact that resurrection occupies such a central position—or perhaps because of that very fact—the traditions about the resurrection exhibit almost a maximum of variation. This can be sketched here only very briefly. But analysis at one level has established that in Mark, previously established as the earliest of the Gospels, the last 11 verses are a later addition to the text, which originally ended with women fleeing from an empty tomb and not saying anything to anyone out of terror. And the majority opinion among scholars now is that this was not due to some subsequent accident to, or mutilation of, the text, but was deliberate. The author lays down his pen at this point as if to say 'the rest is silence', perhaps because resurrection is indescribable, and perhaps is so because it partakes of the character of the end of the world. Perhaps. We do not know. But at the heart of the tradition there is now a yawning gap, which is perhaps the gap of ineffable divine mystery. On one side of Mark stands Matthew. His contribution takes the form of a single sentence of four verses which says all that needs to be said; one of the most monumental sentences in the New Testament, compressed, formal, impersonal and hieratic, and bearing all the marks of Christian doctrine along one line of its development. In it the risen, or rather the already exalted Christ first states his divine omnipotence (all power has been given to me—i.e. by God—in heaven and earth), then commands a universal mission (go into the world and make all nations disciples) along with an initiatory sacrament couched in trinitarian terms (baptizing them in the name of the Father, the Son and the Holy Spirit), and a form of instruction of which Matthew's Gospel is particularly the repository (teaching them to observe all that I have commanded you), and concluding with a promise of his presence and assistance to the end of time (and behold I am with you until the consummation of the age).

On the other side of Mark stands Luke, whose contribution is also remarkable, but for the opposite reasons, which make it stand at the furthest pole from Matthew's. For here is an extended, direct, relaxed narrative of 23 verses, told in highly personal and circumstantial terms and with exquisite artistry, of the risen but not yet exalted Christ travelling incognito with two disciples on a seven-mile walk to an inn, and conducting on the way a Bible class to demonstrate that the whole of the Old Testament is to be understood as being about himself, and is recognized at the moment when he breaks bread and disappears. And this is followed by an appearance of a highly concrete kind, with the risen Lord eating fish, commissioning the apostles to a world-wide mission and repeating the Bible class; so that he becomes the originator of that interpretation of the Old Testament which was to dominate the development of Christian theology, and especially the theology of Luke–Acts. How different these two forms of the resurrection tradition are can be seen if they were made to change places. For them the Matthaean in Luke and the Lukan in Matthew would each stick out like a sore thumb. And this would be not only on account of the difference of style, but of content, as each would no longer be providing what it now provides, namely the climax and conclusion to that particular theological presentation of the Christ and his gospel in which it now stands. And similar observations could be made about the tradition in John, where the first appearance, that to Mary Magdalene, leans heavily on the specifically Johannine picture of the good shepherd who calls his sheep by name and they hear his voice; the second to the apostles is preceded by a breathing of the spirit on them as the second creation as God had breathed on the first; and the third, to Thomas, where the unique confession 'My Lord and my God' harks back to the developed theology of the Johannine prologue that the word was God.

This then is the character of the tradition here, and—if to save time I may be allowed to quote myself—

> it may be said to be strong. It is multiple and varied and has a wide spread. It is not single, uniform or stereotyped. But it should be noted where its strength lies. For there is a marked contrast between the centrality of the Easter faith in the New Testament and the almost fortuitous character of the traditions which now support it, and between the events on the one hand which remain so shadowy because the narratives are almost casual about the risen Lord's state and condition, and their interpretation on the other hand which is expressed so forcefully and

eloquently through the mouth of the risen Lord speaking in Matthaean,
Lukan and Johannine accents respectively.[1]

The religious mind is inevitably and very properly synthetic. There
is only one God, and one world known to us, and so there is one
Lord, one faith, one baptism, one God who is Father of all, as the
Epistle to the Ephesians puts it. The complex task now facing the
religious mind is that of achieving a synthesis by way of, and not
despite, analysis. For this purpose some have tended here to continue,
or revert to, the technique of harmonization. The first theological
book I ever read—I was a schoolboy at the time—was precisely a
book of apologetic on this subject—F.F. Morison's *Who Moved the
Stone?*[2] This was ably done, lively and, in its day, influential. Its
method was, by a series of imaginative hypotheses somewhat in the
manner of a whodunnit, to iron out the differences in the tradition and
to fill the gaps in it, so that it could be made to stand as a synthetic
whole speaking with a single voice. It is now evident that such a
method is doomed from the start, since it treats the material as that
which it is not. For analysis indicates strongly that what we are dealing with here is not scattered but potentially interlocking portions
from an originally single matrix. Rather are they separate expressions
of resurrection faith. Each is a complete whole in itself. Each has
developed along its own line so as to serve in the end as the proper
conclusion for each evangelist of his own presentation of the gospel.
And if there is a question of gaps, it is not of gaps within a whole,
which could perhaps be filled in by additional information, guesswork
or whatever. It is a question of gaps between wholes. A recent and
more powerful work of apologetic on the subject has been that of the
professor of law and lay theologian, Sir Norman Anderson, in his
book, *A Lawyer among the Theologians*.[3] But, despite its excellencies,
this also would appear to be misconceived. For it aims to arrive at its
results by seeing how the tradition stands up when put under examination in the witness box. But the material does not lend itself to this
method. It does not have the character of legal testimony. And while
'witness' is an important word in the New Testament, and especially in
connection with the resurrection, what is meant by it is not the eye-

1.   C.F. Evans, *Resurrection and the New Testament* (London: SCM Press,
1970), pp. 130ff.
2.   London: Faber & Faber, 1930.
3.   London: Hodder & Stoughton, 1973.

witness report it might be of a road accident, but testimony to the ultimate and theological significance of the resurrection. It is, therefore, couched largely in the symbolic language of faith, and varies in accordance with the varied theologies. Hence any reaffirmation of the resurrection tradition for apologetic or any other purpose is to be made with, and by way of, an adequate appreciation of its character of having been in movement from the start. And if it is to be defended from strength and not from weakness, full account must be taken of this dynamic and fertile quality, which enabled it from the first to move out and capture one stronghold after another: in Matthaean circles Jewish strongholds, in Lukan circles more Gentile strongholds, and in John and Paul even cosmological strongholds.

And now the bishop's position. The resurrection is about God or it is about nothing. Here he undoubtedly reproduces the emphasis of the New Testament—though it may be observed in passing that there are better and worse ways of doing this, and that references to 'a conjuring trick with bones' is one of the worst and will here cause the listening unbeliever as well as the believing participant to switch off. But, in the New Testament, resurrection is through and through theocentric, and is partly responsible for securing the theocentric character of the Christian gospel as a whole. Resurrection language is God language; it is not, except in a few aberrant passages, Christ language. The verb 'to raise' (i.e. from the dead) always has God as its subject, or it is used in the passive ('he was raised') which is only a reverential way of saying the same thing. Moreover it is language about God in his relation not primarily to individuals, nor even to the church, but to all things, and to individuals or the church in connection with his relation to all things, the universe; and, further, to the universe not as something static, but as heading somewhere. Thus resurrection, in securing the theocentric character of the Christian message, also secures its public, universal and cosmological dimensions.

But it is precisely here that the shoe now pinches most hard—as the bishop being sociologist as well as philosopher and theologian is in a position to know as well as anyone, and better than some. For it is the problem of God that has now moved into the centre of theological thinking. For some it fills the whole picture. For various reasons that it would take too long to attempt to trace even if one were capable of doing so, apologetic is not now primarily concerned with the church, its doctrines and sacraments, nor even with Christ, his incarnation and atonement, but with God and his relation to the world as his creation and as the object of his transformation. Whereas previously the word 'God' has tended to be 'the given', and could, as it were, be taken for granted and regarded as staying put, how to think the word 'God', how to use God language at all so that it conveys a sense of reality, and how to use it in a way that is meaningful in relation to the world as we know it, these are now the agonizing questions.

But secondly, there is a form of these questions that stems directly from critical study of the New Testament, and especially from the place of resurrection in it. In the earliest type of resurrection faith that we can trace, its force is derived from the eschatological symbolism in which it is couched. In Thessalonians, which is possibly the earliest document in the New Testament, Paul describes the experience of Christian conversion as 'You turned from idols to serve a living and true God, and to wait for his Son from heaven, whom he raised from the dead, Jesus, who delivers us from the wrath to come' (1 Thess. 1.9-10). Here the character of the resurrection lies in its being the beginning of the end of the world, and the operation in advance of God's ultimate relation to it of judging and saving it. Therefore part and parcel of such a faith, and not an optional extra, is the speedy return of Christ to those now embraced by it. For this character is only realizable by them when God through Christ consummates the process which he has already initiated through him. But this form of resurrection faith cannot be simply repeated or reaffirmed. For the return did not happen, and by definition there could never again be a situation in which matters were envisaged thus. It would seem here that the Christian religion was put into orbit from the launching pad of the Jewish religion on the back of a booster rocket, which, like all such, had to be jettisoned when it had done its work. And we can see this jettisoning already taking place during the creative period of the New Testament itself. Indeed some scholars would see it as one of the most formative factors in the development of early Christian thinking. For it was not just a jettisoning or abandonment of a concept that took place, but its restatement in fresh and equivalent forms corresponding to a changed perception of how things were and what was at issue. So, when in 2 Corinthians, Paul speaks of resurrection in language no longer of the end of the world but of new divine creation, or in Romans speaks of it as a present rising from the death of sin to a life of righteousness in anticipation of a consummated life called glory, or when 1 Peter speaks of it as divine rebirth to a life in principle heavenly, or John speaks of it as the means to a present existence that is in quality eternal, the dynamic can be seen at work in capturing the God position, and so in various ways establishing God to be God. In Eliot's terms the tradition maintains itself because something new is done with it and in it. And this could be the most significant thing about it, not only then but now.

For to quote Dr Perkins again, 'the modes in which contemporary theologians seek to recover the foundational character of resurrection symbolism are likely to be at least as diverse as the use made of that symbolism in the first century'.[1] And she cites as an example the work of Teilhard de Chardin in his attempt to marry the language and thought of theology and science. For he took the resurrection as the key indicator of the direction in which the world, understood now of necessity in evolutionary terms, was to be seen to be moving— moving, that is, not automatically but by divine influence towards a new hyper-personal stage of existence which he was prepared to call its Christification. And if his attempt has generally been pronounced a failure by theologians as too speculative and perhaps romantic, by scientists as deserting the language of science for that of vision, more important than the failure might be the conviction that the attempt has to be made, and that there are resources available for making it. The philosopher of science, Dr Stephen Toulmin, in himself judging it to be a failure, nevertheless sees it as possibly pointing to the shape of future reflection.[2] For Christian theology grew up in a world with quite different, static perceptions of cosmic history, with a much smaller scale of time and space; and the myths and images, including that of resurrection, were drawn against that scale. And whatever the weaknesses of this particular vision of Teilhard de Chardin, it indicates the necessity for Christian thought to establish its natural theology within a contemporary view of nature.

And I have paid some attention to this particular contemporary dispute over resurrection, not simply because it is contemporary, but because in some measure it affords a paradigm of what is likely to be

---

1. *Resurrection*, p. 413.
2. S. Toulmin, *The Return to Cosmology: Postmodern Science and the Theology of Nature* (Berkeley: University of California Press, 1982), pp. 113-26.

involved for an apologist who would undertake, from the vantage point—or perhaps the disadvantage point—of biblical studies, to speak 'in defence of the Christian religion'.[1]

1.   Further thoughts of Christopher Evans on resurrection may now be found in his monumental commentary on Luke; see C.F. Evans, *Saint Luke* (TPI New Testament Commentaries; London: SCM Press & Trinity Press International, 1990), pp. 885-928.

A NEW LOOK AT JOB 41.1-4 (ENGLISH 41.9-12)

J.C.L. Gibson

These four verses occur at a crucial point in the middle of Yahweh's second speech from the whirlwind. It is therefore doubly to be regretted that they are so enigmatic and have caused so much trouble to scribes, translators and commentators down the ages; for a great deal hangs on their interpretation. There is not even agreement that v. 4 (English v. 12) belongs with the other three. In this paper I side with the tiny minority which includes it in the passage, and in the case of vv. 1-3 (English vv. 9-11) with the rather larger minority which resists the temptation to emend and stays with the Masoretic Text. But I part company from that larger minority in the meaning I find in them.

My conclusions are at some variance with what I wrote on the verses in my little commentary of some years ago,[1] but I do not apologize for this; the book of Job has the disconcerting habit of making more of us change our minds more often than we care to admit. I have not, however, changed my mind on one very important issue affecting the passage, namely the identity of Leviathan. I argued strongly in my commentary[2] against the penchant of nearly all translators and scholars over the last several centuries for demythologizing Leviathan into a crocodile or (as the New and Revised English Bibles—and before them Herman Melville—would have it) a whale. If

---

1. *Job* (Daily Study Bible; Edinburgh: Saint Andrew Press, 1985). The two commentaries I mention by name are those of M.H. Pope, *Job* (AB; New York: Doubleday, 3rd edn, 1973) and M.H. Habel, *The Book of Job* (OTL; London: SCM Press, 1985).

2. Pages 249-54. For a more detailed discussion see my article, 'On Evil in the Book of Job', in *Ascribe to the Lord: Biblical and Other Studies in Memory of Peter C. Craigie* (ed. L. Eslinger and G. Taylor; Sheffield: JSOT Press, 1988), pp. 399-419.

verbal resonances are at all significant in a work of literature—and surely they are—it seems to me that the Leviathan who is in 41.2 (English 41.10) so menacing when 'roused' cannot be other than the Leviathan whom Job in his first desolate soliloquy (in 3.8) had wished could be 'roused' to undo his birth; and he is no crocodile or whale. (Let us call this resonance Echo 1.) It is not improbable that the poet is giving the Leviathan of Yahweh's second speech some of the lineaments of a crocodile or whale (in my view the first). But that does not affect the role he plays, which is identical with that played by the Leviathan who in the shape of a dragon or twisting serpent had to be crushed by Yahweh at the beginning of time (see Ps. 74.14) but will not (see Isa. 27.1) be finally finished off by him until time's end. Plainly put, that role is to be the embodiment of cosmic evil. Job is not, in the denouement of the book that bears his name, being mesmerized by the contemplation of a fantastic but still earthly monster into submitting to Yahweh's inscrutable providence. Rather, he is being brought up against the real cause of his sufferings, the existence in what is supposed to be Yahweh's good world of an evil power which not he but only Yahweh can control. By not picking up, or not properly picking up, an echo from one of its earlier chapters, most modern interpreters have allowed a book which at its close celebrates Yahweh's mastery over the forces of evil to run out instead in mystery.

But to the nitty-gritty. I set out below the Masoretic Text of Job 41.1-4 along with an apparatus of hard evidence for possibly changing it, that is to say, manuscript variants. I will mention later the softer evidence of some renderings found in the ancient versions and, where necessary, the even softer evidence of scholarly conjecture.

הֲגַם אֶל־מַרְאָיו יֻטָּל׃	1 הֵן־תֹּחַלְתֹּו נִכְזָבָה
וּמִי הוּא לְפָנַי יִתְיַצָּב׃	2 לֹא־אַכְזָר כִּי יְעוּרֶנּוּ
תַּחַת כָּל־הַשָּׁמַיִם לִי־הוּא׃	3 מִי הִקְדִּימַנִי וַאֲשַׁלֵּם
וּדְבַר־גְּבוּרֹות וְחִין עֶרְכֹּו׃	4 לֹא אַחֲרִישׁ בַּדָּיו

1.   Some MSS תחלתי; one MS תחלתך
2.   Some MSS יעירנו; some MSS יעירני; many MSS לפניו
3.   Oriental Qere לֹו

The הֵן, 'behold', of v. 1 signals, as it often does, a shift in topic or at any rate in emphasis. In the preceding verses (40.25-32 = English 41.1-8) Yahweh, in a series of bitingly sarcastic questions, had invited

Job to try to tame Leviathan or wheedle him into doing his bidding. Verse 1 sums up the hopelessness of such an attempt and its inevitable outcome, but by the use of a third-person suffix begins to broaden the lesson out; the suffix refers forward to the third-person subject of the following verb and may be rendered 'the hope of such a man. . . ' The changes in the suffix found in a number of manuscripts ('your [i.e. Job's] hope' and [oddly] '[a man's] hope in me [Yahweh]') look like glosses engendered by the unheralded 'his' which have found their way into the text from the margin; for neither accords grammatically with יָמֵל later in the verse. It is possible to emend the verb to suit, but an attractive resonance with Ps. 37.24 is thereby lost. (We will not count this as a numbered echo since it takes us outside the book of Job.) Likewise Symmachus's translation of אל by ὁ θεός, that is אֵל, 'God', although it raises the fascinating notion of Yahweh (or a 'divine being') being in danger from Leviathan, is probably simply due to his not understanding an awkward use of the preposition אֶל־, literally '*to* the sight of him'. But the phrase is perfectly acceptable if it is understood to contain the idea of approaching as well as seeing Leviathan. The only inescapable problem in the verse is the presence of the interrogative particle הֲ. A positive question is impossible, as can be seen from the Authorised Version, which has to insert a negative to make sense: 'shall *not* one be cast down. . . ?' The easiest way out is to omit the הֲ, and textually this is permissible as the previous word finishes with ה, that is to say, we have a case of dittography. I suggest the following paraphrase of v. 1: 'Let's think more about this. The expectation of such a man is bound to be frustrated. He only has to catch sight of him and get within range and he will be hurled headlong.'

The Masoretic Text has Yahweh at this point preaching a little sermon to Job. It is this traditional text of vv. 2 and 3 which is translated by the Authorised Version and, more recently, by the Revised Standard and New International Versions. The RSV reads:

> No-one is so fierce that he dares to stir him up.
> Who then is he that can stand before me?
> Who has given to me, that I should repay him?
> Whatever is under the whole of heaven is mine.

In common with the other two versions, it takes v. 4, which also has a first-person verb, as marking the resumption of the description of Leviathan:

> I will not keep silence concerning his limbs,
>> or his mighty strength, or his goodly frame.

St Paul, in loosely citing v. 3 in Rom. 11.35 (RSV, 'who has given a gift to him that he might be repaid?'), may be dependent on a Greek text allied to the Masoretic (the Septuagint is significantly different), but he has probably also been influenced by Elihu's words in 35.7, in the RSV

> If you are righteous, what do you give to him;
>> or what does he receive from your hand?

It should be noted finally that the Vulgate in v. 3 has a similar thrust to the three versions cited

> quis ante dedit mihi, ut reddam ei,
> Who has first given to me that I have to make restitution to him?

Looking at this line of tradition laid out, I cannot help suspecting that Paul has succeeded in angling it away from the original meaning. The notion that a good man, far less a sinner, could put God under an obligation to him, ridiculed by Elihu (and earlier by Eliphaz in 22.2-3), is a travesty of any stance adopted by Job and could therefore hardly have been the spur leading Yahweh to prick Job's pretensions. Paul, on the other hand, as he searched the Old Testament to back up his arguments in Romans, could well have been predisposed to read just such a notion into v. 3. Perhaps indeed he had access at the time to an early Hebrew text of a Masoretic type and for that very reason preferred it to the text of his usual Septuagint, translating it himself into Greek. I am led therefore to the conclusion that if the Masoretic Text is to be retained, it must be given a different interpretation to that which is usually associated with it.

Belonging as they do to the same tradition as the Vulgate, it is surprising that none of the versions mentioned has been attracted by its rendering of v. 4:

> non parcam ei et verbis potentibus et ad deprecandum compositis,

which is translated by Father Knox

> I give him no quarter, for all his boastful, all his flattering words.

The only English translation I know which moves in this direction is
the Jewish Publication Society's of 1917 (although cf. Moffatt); (this
version is also to my knowledge unique in adopting the Qere לוֹ, i.e.
'for him, as far as he is concerned'):

> Would I keep silence concerning his boastings, or his proud talk, or his
> fine array of words?

It is joined, however, by two recent commentaries, those of Pope and
Habel. Pope belongs to those who emend the Masoretic Text (see
later), but Habel accepts it, rendering:

> Is he not ferocious when roused?
>> But who can take their stand before my face?
> Whoever confronts me I requite,
>> For everything under the heavens is mine.
> Did I not silence his boasting,
>> His mighty word and his persuasive case?

Let us examine this rendering. The plural noun בַּדִּים may mean
either 'limbs (lit. parts)' as in the RSV or 'babbling, boasting' as in
Habel, and both meanings occur earlier in the book, the first in 18.13
of the gnawed limbs of a wicked man receiving his just deserts, but
the second more appositely for this passage in 11.3 where Zophar
chides Job, 'Should your babble silence men?' (RSV). Not only does
that verse have בַּדִּים in the sense which Habel gives it but it also has the
Hiphil of חרש in the rarer sense which he requires, that is, not 'to be
silent (about)' but 'to cause to be silent' (Echo 2). Habel is clearly on
stronger ground than the vast majority of authorities who have taken
v. 4 to be giving a physical description of Leviathan and have again,
it seems, failed to catch a resonance from earlier in the book. But does
he himself fully catch it? I do not think so. For the link between 41.4
and 11.3 to be a solid one, the 'babbling' or 'boasting' which Yahweh
is going to silence (the verb is imperfect) ought to be Job's and not
Leviathan's.

I believe it to be the same with the peculiar phrase חִין עֶרְכּוֹ. This
(taking חִין as a by-form of חֵן, 'grace') may be interpreted 'his comely
proportion' (AV), 'his graceful form' (NIV) or the like, or it may be
taken with Habel and the JPS version or, for that matter, with the
Vulgate (which neither Pope nor Habel mentions) to refer to the skill
with words of Yahweh's opponent. However, the occurrence of the
verb עָרַךְ, literally 'arrange, set in order', twice elsewhere in the book

book specifically of Job 'preparing' his case against God (13.18; 23.4) suggests not only that the second alternative is preferable but that Yahweh is thinking specifically of Job (Echo 3). Habel, in giving the imperfect verb a past meaning (by no means impossible in poetry) and making the silencing a silencing of Leviathan (though, it should in fairness be said, he wants Job to be secondarily implicated), is once more hearing an echo missed by the majority, but not hearing it accurately enough. Certainly Yahweh had, as Ps. 74.14 reminds us, slain the monster Leviathan in the past, and I have no wish to deny that one of the chief implications of Yahweh's second speech is that he is still able to defeat it; indeed I have already argued vehemently in favour of this. But we have no knowledge from the Old Testament (or from surrounding mythologies) of Leviathan (or his various counterparts) disputing in words with Yahweh (or his counterpart) and of this having to be dealt with before the monster was finally dispatched. In particular the passage which he cites from the Ugaritic Baal Cycle in which Prince Yam or 'Sea' sends messengers to El's court to demand the surrender of his arch-enemy Baal is not as supportive as he claims, its tone being one of hectoring contempt rather than of persuasion, even angry persuasion;[1] it simply does not fit with a word like 'grace', even if that word is being used by Yahweh with more than a touch of irony. From this enquiry into v. 4, therefore, I conclude that v. 4 most certainly ought to be included in the passage along with vv. 2 and 3 but equally that it must, via the 'anyone' of whom Yahweh is talking, be getting at Job, not at Leviathan; and consequently that אַחֲרִישׁ should be translated as a future.

---

1. In my *Canaanite Myths and Legends* (Edinburgh: T. & T. Clark, 1978), p. 42, I translate the passage as follows.

> The message of Yam, your lord,
> of your sire judge Nahar, is this:
> Give up, gods, him whom you protect,
> him whom you protect, o multitude,
> give up Baal and his lackeys,
> the son of Dagon that I may possess his gold

El immediately replies:

> Baal is your slave, o Yam,
> Baal is your slave, o Nahar,
> the son of Dagon is your prisoner.

Let us now turn to the majority of scholars who, as I have indicated, depart from the Masoretic Text of vv. 2 and 3 and resort to emendation. The first-person suffixes in 2(b), 'before me' and 3(a), literally 'has preceded me' and the first-person verb in 3(a), RSV '(that) I should repay' are changed to third-person forms, and the last two words in 3(b), literally 'it (is) to me' are variously tampered with. The Revised English Bible supports this solution:

> How fierce he is when he is roused!
> Who is there to stand up to him?
> Who has ever attacked him unscathed?
> Not a man under the wide heaven.

It goes on (v. 4): 'I will not pass over in silence his limbs. . . ' The Good News and Jerusalem Bibles are very similar. The effect of this interpretation is to remove the divine 'I' from the scene except as the distant speaker; there is in fact no little sermon. As an example of the many modern commentaries taking this line I cite Pope who, how-ever, like Habel, also takes in v. 4:

> Is he not fierce when one rouses him?
> Who could stand before him?
> Who could confront him unscathed,
> Under the whole heavens, who?
> Did I not silence his boasting. . . ?

In Pope's rendering, Yahweh does bring himself in with the briefest of lessons in v. 4, but otherwise it differs from the REB's only in the emendation chosen for the end of v. 3; and his translation of 4(a) comes up against the same objections already raised in the case of Habel's. I have not included Pope's translation of 4(b), which intro-duces an allusion to a very minor character in the Ugaritic tablets and involves him in further very conjectural emendation.

Of the changes of text in vv. 2 and 3, that of the suffix in 2(b) has considerable manuscript (and some versional) support, but not that of the suffix in 3(a). Along with the evidence (naturally not stressed) for a change of suffix the other way in 2(a) ('rouses *me*' for 'rouses him'), these disagreements do show that at least some in antiquity were uncertain whether it was Yahweh or Leviathan that was being opposed. The emendation of the verb in 3(a) has no manuscript support, but is based on the Septuagint:

τίς ἀντιστήσεταί μοι καὶ ὑπομενεῖ
Who shall stand against me and remain [sc. safe]?

This suggests a Hebrew וַיִּשְׁלָם (following a previous perfect verb); and there seems to be further support for the reading in 9.4 where וַיִּשְׁלָם is in fact rendered in the Septuagint by ὑπομενεῖ. The RSV in 9.4 translates: 'who has hardened himself against him [sc. God], and succeeded?' There is no ancient support for the emendations in 3(b) (e.g. REB לֹא הוּא; Pope מִי הוּא); the case for change there has to be made out on the syntactic grounds that תַּחַת far more often means 'under' than it does 'what is under'.

There is undoubtedly something to be said for these modern interpretations. The flow of Yahweh's speech is improved; Leviathan continues to be the centre of interest as he is both before and after the passage; and Yahweh keeps his distance and, as nearly always in both his speeches, leaves the reader to infer his meaning. On this kind of reasoning the Masoretic Text does begin to look like the work of pious scribes perturbed at the prominence being given to Leviathan and anxious to give Yahweh something to say on his own behalf. I am not convinced. For one thing the modernized text has more than a whiff of overkill about it. The previous passage with its sarcastic questions had surely sufficiently ridiculed the idea of Job attacking or wheeling and dealing with Leviathan. Did such a message need to be further laboured and applied to men in general?

But apart from that consideration, the textual and versional evidence is very eclectically used. Taken as a whole it supports by a considerable margin the distribution of the suffixes which we have in the Masoretic Text. Nor is the change to a third-person verb in 3(a) as attractive as it seems when the link between v. 3 and 9.4 is carefully looked at. The latter verse had Job at an earlier stage in his pilgrimage concluding that it would indeed be dangerous for him to set himself up against the all-powerful God who, as he thought, was so cruelly using him. But in the event Job went on, taking his flesh in his teeth and putting his life in his hands, to do what at first sight might seem to be something very like that; see 13.13-18 and especially the אֶל־פָּנָיו of v. 15 which Yahweh could well have been alluding to with the לְפָנַי of v. 2(b) here (cf. also 23.4) (Echo 4). A repetition of וַיִּשְׁלָם by Yahweh ought, then, to have been reminding Job of his former folly and hinting that it would have been safer for him to have remained in his fearful mood of 9.4. If because of a resonance with 9.4, וַיִּשְׁלָם has a claim to be considered the original text, it has by the same token to be accompanied (as indeed the Septuagint attests) by a first-person suffix on the previous verb. In other words, it is a possible emendation to the Masoretic Text but not to the majority emended text, where it would raise a quite inappropriate echo. (Another case, it seems, of scholarly hardness of hearing!) I am tempted to adopt it, but I am doubtful on two substantial grounds. In spite of the resonance with 9.4 there is no evidence for it in any Hebrew manuscript. But even more seriously, it makes us think in v. 3 of Job resisting Yahweh's power and suffering for it; not only is that a cruel observation to address to the man on the ash heap, worthier far of the friends (cf. Eliphaz in 15.20-26) than of Yahweh, but it is something that Job had never in fact done. He had no wish to defy God in terms of 9.4; what he wanted above all was, in terms of 13.13ff., to challenge God and per-suade him to change his mind, not at all, when one thinks of it, the same thing. I strongly suspect that in the Septuagint's rendering of v. 3 we are in touch with a mistranslation prompted by its own translation of 9.4 and not with a Hebrew text that ever existed. With regard, finally, to תַּחַת, the observation that it is more often a preposi-tion than a noun is true enough; but it blithely ignores an instance of a nominal use in 28.24 in the same well-known phrase as here and in a chapter that has more than a few similarities with the speeches of Yahweh: RSV 'he [God] sees everything under the heavens' (lit. 'what-is-under the whole heavens') (Echo 5).

My final conclusions may now be briefly stated. First, v. 4 with its first-person verb ought most definitely to be included in Yahweh's little sermon, and I find it difficult to understand why the Vulgate's early example has not been more often followed. Secondly, there is no justification for not keeping the Masoretic Text of all four verses apart from the deletion of one letter in v. 1 as a case of dittography.[1] Thirdly and most importantly, the interpretation of the passage ought to centre around the five verbal resonances[2] noted between it and

---

1.   The qal of עור in v. 2 is used with a causative force which it does not have elsewhere, but it is doubtful whether this is enough to make us change it, with a number of manuscripts, to a *hiphil*; in 3.8 the form used is *polel*.

2.   It has not been my intention in this study to commend, except tangentially, the search for verbal resonances as an exegetical tool or to berate traditional scholarship for not always being as alert to them as they ought. But interested readers may follow up both of these points in R. Alter's *The Art of Biblical Narrative*

previous passages in the book, viz. between v. 2 and 3.8 (Echo 1) and, taken together, 13.15 and 23.4 (Echo 4); between v. 3 and 28.24 (Echo 5); between v. 4 and 11.3 (Echo 2) and, taken together, 13.18 and (again) 23.4 (Echo 3).

The passage follows a section (40.25-32 = English 41.1-8) in which Yahweh had tauntingly called on Job to try either by force or (and this is particularly significant) by persuasion to bring Leviathan under control and see how he fared. In spelling out the disaster that will inevitably await him, v. 1 widens the scope of the passage to include any other mere mortal who supposes that he can free the world of the evil forces oppressing it. But the verses are still primarily for Job's ears, as the five listed resonances, when fully appreciated, make clear. Echo 1 would remind him of the black day when in a fit of depression he had been tempted to enlist Leviathan's help to cancel out the life that Yahweh had given him and when he had been fully aware of that creature's nefarious reputation; and Echo 5 would remind him of the one alone—and it was not Leviathan—who was in charge of all that took place under the heavens and at the same time of the many occasions on which he, Job, had accused him of not doing his job properly. Echo 2 would inform him that Yahweh was by now as thoroughly fed up with his constant talk as earlier Zophar and the other two friends had been. Above all, Echoes 3 and 4 would take him back to the two fraught occasions in ch. 13, when he had first steeled himself to dare all and defend his ways to Yahweh's face—'I have prepared my case'—and ch. 23, when more pessimistically but no less desperately he had renewed his ambition in spite of Yahweh's awful silence. The logic of the lesson Job is being given runs from the futility of any attempt he might make on his own to cut evil down to size, and achieve justice and recovery for himself (cf. the opening paragraph of Yahweh's second speech, 40.7-14), to the equal futility of the attempts he had already made—and at inordinate length—to bend Yahweh's will to his own, and, by fair means or foul, make Yahweh apologize to him for what he had gone through, and tell him to his face what a fine fellow he was. Such pride on Job's part had to be humbled and the

(London: Allen & Unwin, 1981), especially in ch. 1 where he uncovers several such echoes between Genesis chs. 37 and 38, two chapters which are usually thought to have nothing to do with each other.

torrent of self-centred entreaty and undeserved abuse which he had
directed at heaven had to be silenced.

I suggest the following translation of the passage:

1. I tell you the confidence of such a man is unfounded;
      he will be hurled headlong at the very sight of him.
2. Will he not be ferocious when anyone rouses him?
      Who then is he who is able to plead in my court?
3. Who has ever appeared before me and told me the verdict I must
      pronounce,
      me to whom everything under the heavens belongs?
4. Will I not silence his babbling,
      his forceful words and oh so fine arguments?

The irony of all this is that Yahweh, having reduced Job to silence,
almost immediately pronounces, and pronounces in public for all—
and especially the friends—to hear, the verdict he had so zealously
sought (42.7). But that was after Job had not only taken Yahweh's
rebuke on the chin but had grasped the more positive message of
Yahweh's second speech, namely that Yahweh could overcome the
pervasive evil in his creation and was even now, as Job was accusing
him of doing nothing, closing in for yet another encounter with his
age-long foe;[1] and after, having taken both messages to heart, he had
surrendered in mingled shame and joy. The lesson then for us who
read this excoriating book today is, yes, to watch our language in the
presence of God, but never to let our piety get in the way of our
urgency in prayer. We may go over the score, as Job went over the
score, and that will annoy and hurt God; but it will not prevent him
granting us our true heart's desire. We must, as Robert Davidson
would put it, have the 'courage to doubt', and say with Job 'let come
on me what may' (13.13) before heaven will consider us worthy of an
answer. Heaven will tell us that we have been playing with fire, but we
will know that the risk has been worth it.

1. It is significant that the second divine speech does not end with the verses we
have been studying but with an extended description of Leviathan, the purpose of
which can only have been to underline what a formidable threat he posed to Yahweh.
There was indeed none like him on earth (41.25 = English 41.33)—only in heaven!

COULD NOT THE UNIVERSE HAVE COME INTO EXISTENCE
200 YARDS TO THE LEFT? A THEMATIC STUDY OF JOB

Alastair G. Hunter

1. *The Structure of Job in Relation to its Themes*

Introduction
In the course of Alice's encounter with the White Knight[1] the subject
of the naming of things comes up. The White Knight (like many other
characters in the story) wishes to sing a song to our heroine, but
confusion arises when he attempts to identify the song: his precise distinctions between what the name of the song is called, what the name
really is, what the song is called and what the song really is leave
Alice 'completely bewildered'. In addressing the question of 'meaning'
in relation to the book of Job, much the same sense of bewilderment is
aroused. The name of the text is called 'The Book of Job' (but is it a
book at all, or is it a patchwork of ill-assorted and rather seriously
damaged reflections on a theme?) The name of the text is 'Job' (which
rather suggests that it is about this named individual; but then, most
commentators have read it not as 'the story of Job' but as a metaphysical debate about the problem of good and evil). So what is the text
called (to take up the next level of the White Knight's naming process)? Perhaps it could be called 'a dialogue in several stages, with
prologue and epilogue', if we interpret the problem of naming the text
as equivalent to that of *Formgeschichte* or identification of *genres*.
And as for what the text is—that is surely the famous hermeneutical
conundrum that what the text is is what you want it to be:[2] the answer
to the problem of innocent suffering; a type of the suffering of Christ;

---

1. Lewis Carroll, *Through the Looking Glass*, Chapter 8.
2. The list which follows is, of course, a sample, not a complete taxonomy!

a self-deconstructing exercise in postmodern literary criticism;[1] a verse-drama;[2] or a psychoanalytical study of human responses to stress.[3]

The primary subject of this study is the central sequence of dialogues which makes up the core of the book; namely, the opening soliloquy in ch. 3, the three cycles of debates with Eliphaz, Bildad and Zophar in chs. 4–27, the 'Quest for Wisdom' in ch. 28, and the final long soliloquy in chs. 29–31. Within this section (chs. 3–31) several themes[4] are addressed by the protagonists; namely:

1. *Themes relating directly to God*
   a. Job's demands that God give him a hearing, or vindicate him.
   b. Job's charge against God, of the vindictive use of divine power.
   c. Recognition of God as creator.
2. *Themes relating to general questions*
   d. Suffering, the innocent and the wicked [both in personal and general terms].
   e. Where is wisdom to be found?
3. *Themes reflecting feelings of despair*
   f. Life is short and brutal.
   g. Wish for death.
   h. The worthlessness of the adversaries'[5] advice.

These themes are developed variously by Job, Eliphaz *et al.*, and I shall examine this process in detail as it is worked out through the

1.   This may seem obscure: in fact, the analysis of structure in relation to theme in the book which is the main subject of this essay is intended as a case-study of the way that texts have inherent tendencies to fall apart and reshape themselves when they are freed from the straightjackets of objectivity, intention and referentiality of meaning.

2.   A. MacLeish, *J.B. a play in verse* (London: Secker & Warburg, 1959).

3.   As, for example, in *Job's Illness* by Jack Kahn (Oxford: Pergamon Press, 1975).

4.   Obviously the rather simple analysis which follows could be challenged on the grounds that it is *over*-simple. However, it is my belief that more detailed analyses, while appropriate at the level of the interpretation of shorter pericopes, tend to obscure what are the recognizable 'broad-brush' themes which form the fundamental architectural shape of the book.

5.   The use of this term is explained in the next paragraph.

cycle of dialogues, always keeping in mind the importance of connect-
ing the *structure* of the work with this thematic dimension.

One final preliminary note is in order. Although the traditional
description of Job's 'sparring partners' is *friends*, the use of this
English word to render the Hebrew conveys a nuance which is inappropriate.[1] The idea is much more that of 'a neighbour', 'an associate', 'one who lives in the same community', 'a relative'. And the
relationship between Job and the three is, I believe (and hope to
demonstrate in this essay), an adversarial one rather than one of
friendship in the sense of solacing or comforting—there is nothing
comfortable about what the three have to say, nor should they be
criticized for this. The formal structure is that of a contest in which
rival contenders offer their differing views in the setting of a riddle:
'Is it possible to be innocent and not to prosper?' Indeed, given the
clear links that Job has with Wisdom literature more generally, it may
not be inappropriate to identify the central issue as primarily an intellectual rather than a moral one. The idea that Eliphaz and the others
are 'friends' or 'comforters' thus raises quite the wrong expectations:
we are not looking at a pastoral case study. This does not mean that
the formal nature of the debate is the last word: having identified this
structural level, there is no reason not to explore any number of ways
of reading the text (as I have already made clear in the opening paragraph). Nor would I wish to claim my structural analysis as the only
one possible; what I am concerned to clarify is that, given the sort of
structure I here identify, the term we use to refer to Job's 'partners in
dialogue' is not unimportant. I shall therefore identify them in what
follows as his adversaries, by which I specifically intend the nuance
appropriate to the adversarial character of legal contests.

Commentary on the Themes
1. *The opening soliloquy and the first cycle of dialogues.* The opening
soliloquy is entirely devoted to a moving expression of the death-wish
theme, one of four themes which Job addresses in the first stages of
the dialogue (chs. 6–7), the others being the charge that God is

---

1.   The Hebrew term is *rêa'*; it is in fact not used directly of the three characters
within the dialogue section proper. Elihu adopts the term in 32.2, and it recurs in the
narrative epilogue in 42.7, 10.

vindictive, the brutishness of life, and the hopelessness of the adversaries' advice. It is not irrelevant to note that these are all strikingly negative in tone; and the distrubution of their further appearances is significant. The death-wish theme is abandoned after ch. 10 and that of the brutishness of life after ch. 17. The complaint that the adversaries' advice is worthless (a fairly minor theme) recurs, with diminishing emphasis, in Job's first replies to Eliphaz and Zophar, his second response to Eliphaz and his second to Bildad. Thereafter it disappears except for a return in 26.1-4. Although this is usually read as an ironic reply to Bildad, I offer below an alternative understanding of this passage which will form part of my structural/thematic analysis. The remaining theme (God's vindictiveness) is likewise given considerable coverage in the first cycle, less in the second, and none in the third, although it does reappear in 30.1-19, as part of Job's final soliloquy. This is something of a special case, however, and does not affect the basic observation that there is a clear development from the first to the third cycle; and that, in particular, Job's opening soliloquy and his first response to Eliphaz explore broadly negative themes which are departed from by the middle of the second cycle.

Moving on to chs. 9–10 (the reply to Bildad's first speech), Job begins by introducing the two remaining themes which are addressed directly to God: recognition of God as creator, and the demand for a hearing. The former is a relatively insignificant motif within the dialogues, only clearly appearing in chs. 9 and 26; it is worth listing separately, nevertheless, because it plays a dominant role in the speeches of Elihu (chs. 32–37) and in Yahweh's reply to Job (chs. 38–41). We might also note, without attempting to attach any importance to the observation, that Job's two meditations on this theme come in response to Bildad. The other new theme is one of the two major central themes of the dialogues, recurring in chs. 12–14, 16–17, 19, 22, 23–24 and in Job's closing appeal in chs. 29–31.

With regard to the development of the dialogue, the opening speeches of both Eliphaz and Bildad are entirely devoted to the general subject of the justice of God: an affirmation of the received wisdom that only the wicked suffer. But we ought to recognize that this point is not made at all in *personal* terms at this stage; rather it is in the form of a general statement of self-evident truth. Job's speeches, on the other hand, are graded. Chapter 3 consists entirely of the death wish, and the reply to Eliphaz in chs. 6–7 is couched in purely negative terms, but covers four themes. In chs. 9–10, however, a new note is sounded. It seems that Bildad has prompted a change of tone, although not a direct *response*: there is no meeting of minds. The new themes addressed to God suggest a more positive approach, although this note is not sustained; for the remainder of the speech returns to the death wish and the charge that God is vindictive, producing as it were a falling off as Job returns to the mood of chs. 6–7. This is, however, the last we hear of the death wish.

The third stage of the cycle (chs. 11–14) displays some fascinating structural features. Zophar breaks ranks, as it were, by abandoning the 'party line' and opening with a reflection on the contrast between wisdom and folly, and the ineluctable truth that only God has wisdom (e.g. 11.5-6a, 7-9), in terms which powerfully anticipate ch. 28.[1] He then proceeds to personalize the claim that only the wicked suffer by charging Job directly with the responsibility for examining his own conscience. As if recognizing this initiative, Job returns in like terms, taking Zophar's second point first by protesting his innocence, and then offering some thoughts of his own on the theme of God and wisdom. This is the first time that Job has responded directly to another participant in the dialogue, and this is the catalyst for further developments. Thus, although Job's first response to Zophar ends, like his replies to the other two, on a negative note, the general effect is of an oscillation between negative and more positive reflections, rather than a simple downward path. Thus ends the first cycle. It began with a death wish and ends with a diatribe, but in between we have seen interesting developments in Job's responses, and (curiously) evidence of a 'special relationship' between Zophar and Job.

2. *The second cycle of dialogues.* In the second cycle of dialogues Job's adversaries (perhaps they had held a briefing meeting!) present what appears to be a solid front on the theme of deserved suffering with which they dominated the first. Moreover, as if he has picked up a tip or two from Zophar, Eliphaz begins his second speech (15.1-16) with a direct personal criticism of Job—'Are you the only man who was ever born? Do you know better than God? Are you exempt from

1.   This theme, like that of God the creator, does not dominate the dialogues; but (especially in ch. 28) has a profound significance for the hermeneutic of the book as a whole.

the rules of righteousness that apply to everyone else?' Midway through the chapter, however, he returns to the general theory, and this is sustained also by Bildad and Zophar. Job's first two responses (chs. 16–17 and 19), like their equivalents in the first cycle, give no indication that he is responding to, or wishes to respond to anything his opponents have to say. As in the first cycle, negative themes appear; but now in a more desultory manner. The brutishness of life is addressed only once (a mere three verses, compared with 23 in the first cycle). Job's negative evaluation of his adversaries' advice appears twice, but is given only eight verses (compared with 26). It should also be noted that Job's responses to Eliphaz and to Bildad in this second cycle end on a more positive note—an expression of Job's challenge to God and demand for more vindication.

Once again, however, we find a striking change when Job answers Zophar. Just as Job responded directly to Zophar in the first cycle, so also in ch. 21 the whole content of Job's speech is a treatment of the theme which he has (with exception of six verses at the beginning of ch. 12) studiously avoided: the theme of the innocent, the wicked and the place of suffering. His argument, not surprisingly, is directly counter to that of Zophar: but it is a clear encounter, not (as in earlier replies to Eliphaz and Bildad) a simple avoidance of the issue. The proportion given to this question (34 verses out of 101, 33.66%) indicates a continuing development: in the third cycle Job gives the theme 58 out of 79 verses (73.42%) and in the final soliloquy 59 out of 96 (61.46%).

3. *Interlude: the story so far.* To sum up our observations thus far, we note the following patterns:

1. A general consensus among Job's adversaries that the important issue is the question of God's justice, mostly addressed in general terms, but on two occasions directed against Job personally. Only Zophar (11.1-12) varies this pattern.
2. Clear movement in Job's thinking:
    a. negative expression of a death wish in ch. 3;
    b. various negative themes in chs. 6–7;
    c. a downward path, from positive to negative, in chs. 9–10;
    d. an oscillation pattern between positive and negative in chs. 12–14;

    e. return, but with diminishing emphasis, to the negative
themes in chs. 16–17, 19; but in each case a concluding
positive theme—appeal to God;

    f. the cycle ends, in ch. 21, with Job addressing for the first
time at any length the adversaries' chosen theme.

3. A tendency for Job's reflections to be dissociated from those
of Eliphaz and Bildad—his 'replies' are not replies in the
sense of a response to what they say; rather they represent a
further stage of Job's *own* consideration of his situation. But
this is dramatically in contrast with the fact that Job makes a
direct and genuine *reply* to each of Zophar's speeches. Is this
significant? We may at least suggest that the different pattern
of the second cycle (see 2.e) is related to the special function
of Zophar; it will be of particular interest, then, to see what
happens in the third cycle.

4. The third cycle of dialogues. We must recognize at the outset that
the crucial third cycle is not complete—lacking as it does any contribution from Zophar. But perhaps this might have been expected—
given that we have already identified the third adversary as having a
distinctive function. In fact, I shall propose that part of the reason for
the truncation of this last cycle is that Job now responds directly to
Eliphaz and Bildad; the dialogue no longer needs Zophar as catalyst.
The cycle is also strange in that chs. 26 and 27 are thought by many
commentators to contain material which would have sounded better
from the lips of one of the adversaries—the absent Zophar, for
example? However plausible such claims may be, and however attractive the possibility of reconstructing a perfect cycle, I shall argue that
this is too superficial an approach. Not only the well-known critical
principle of *lectio difficilior*, but also the deeper levels of meaning of
the third cycle suggest that the apparent difficulties have profound
hermeneutical importance.

Following on my remarks about Zophar's role as catalyst, it is of
note that in his third speech (22.12-30) Eliphaz takes up a major Joban
theme—the challenge to God. This is the first time that any of his
adversaries has addressed a theme which was first introduced by Job,
and the first time also that a response is made by them to Job's arguments. Eliphaz makes clear his view that Job's demands of God are
both futile and evidence of his sinful hubris (22.12-15, 27, 29).

Together with the fact that in chs. 23–24 and 26–27 (with the possible exception of 26.1-4) Job deals only with *positive* themes, this seems to answer in the affirmative the question I indicated above: does the Zophar intervention at the end of each of the first two cycles prepare the way for a change of mood in the following cycle? For what now ensues is a close relationship between Job, Eliphaz and Bildad: at last a genuine debate has taken off—though surprisingly that debate reflects mostly an acceptance by Job of the agenda laid down by his adversaries. This is *not* the result one would expect from a traditional reading of the book—and it does not imply that Job simply agrees with the others. But the recognition of this development opens up possibilities for the understanding of Job's last response to Eliphaz and Bildad which take account of (rather than being at odds with) the structural patterns to which we referred in the opening paragraph of this section.

With these comments in mind, let us turn to Job's third-cycle speeches. Chapter 23 begins, quite predictably, with a stout defence of his repeated demands to be heard, and when heard, justified. But there then follows a passage (23.8-17) which is surely one of the cruxes of the whole cycle of dialogues, a passage which resists any attempt at classification along the lines of the themes which we have so far used, and yet which seems to allude to several of them. It is also a passage in which we surely detect a movement in Job's thinking in the direction of, if not acceptance, at least a sense of his own inadequacy. Since the passage has a number of puzzling features I will begin by giving my own translation:

> Behold, I go forward but he is not there,
> > and back, but I do not recognize him.
> He is at work on my left hand, but I do not perceive him,
> > he conceals himself on my right hand so that I cannot see him.
> Yet he knows my way:
> He has tried me like gold,
> > and like gold I shall come forth.
>
> My foot clings to his path,
> > I have kept to his way and will never wander;
> His lips command:
> I will never depart from his instructions to me,
> I have treasured up the words of his mouth.

> For he is single-minded: who can gainsay him?
>> What he desired, he has done.
> He will certainly carry out what he has ordered for me:
>> many such plans are in his mind!
> Therefore I am disturbed by his presence,
>> when I consider, I am afraid of him;
> for El has numbed my brain,
>> Shaddai has troubled me.
>
> Yet I have not been silenced by darkness
>> though he has covered me in gloom.

The opening theme of this speech—the unsuccessful search for God on all sides—has one very striking parallel in Psalm 139, where the writer speaks memorably of the impossibility of *escaping* God's presence:

> Thou dost beset me behind and before,
>> and layest thy hand upon me. . .
>
> Whither shall I go from thy Spirit?
>> Or whither shall I flee from thy presence?
> If I ascend to heaven, thou art there!
>> If I make my bed in Sheol, thou art there!
> If I take the wings of the morning
>> and dwell in the uttermost parts of the sea,
> even there thy hand shall lead me,
>> and thy right hand shall hold me (Ps. 139.5, 7-10).

The reversal is ironic: the psalmist who (like Jonah) longs to flee from God finds that God is unavoidably present; Job, who passionately desires a confrontation with God, finds that the deity remains hidden (though undoubtedly present). But there are further connections with Psalm 139. Verses 11-12 ('If I say, "Let only darkness cover me, / and the light about me be night," / even the darkness is not dark to thee, / the night is bright as the day; / for darkness is as light with thee') also represent an intriguing reversal: Job concludes by insisting that even the darkness with which God surrounds him cannot silence him; the psalmist recognizes that his or her attempts at obfuscation cannot confuse God! Again, vv. 2-4 address the theme of Job 23.10-11, and vv. 13-18 that of Job 23.12-14. The remaining theme of Job's speech (his sense of awe and terror in the presence of God [vv. 15-16]) finds a response in v. 6 of the psalm—and also, interestingly, in

Job's concluding confession (42.3). The psalm concludes (vv. 19-24) with a plea that the wicked might receive their just deserts, and that Job might be vindicated: the themes precisely of Job 24 and of 23.1-7.

The point of drawing out these parallels with Psalm 139 is not to suggest any direct influence one way or another, but to indicate the nature of this crucial passage in Job. It belongs with those personal/ liturgical reflections which recur throughout the Psalter and which suggest a coming to terms with the nature of God and humanity, good and evil, *in the context of the cult.*[1] This seems a surprising note: we are not accustomed to think of Job in such terms. But it is undoubtedly a true note, and has importance for the way that the remainder of the book is shaped (or rather, in the way that his thoughts are expressed), for it is at pains to demonstrate the fitness of Job's attitude to God: awe, obedience, the need to be purified, steadfastness of purpose and the recognition of God's power.

After such a sharp change of emphasis it is not perhaps surprising to find in ch. 24 an apparently confused passage on the theme of the wicked, the oppressed, and the indifference of God. Confused because it is not clear whether Job is here continuing his earlier charge (in ch. 21) that the wicked prosper (thus, seemingly, vv. 13-23[2]), deploring the callousness of God in the face of the cry of the oppressed (thus vv. 1-12), or whether he has come to endorse the 'party line' (v. 24). So incoherent is this chapter that many commentators have proposed significant amendments to the text, or have wondered whether an earlier, more radical statement (justifying Job's concluding challenge in v. 25) has been tampered with. Reading meaning from such disarray is difficult; unless of course we take the confusion to be the point;[3] Job's earlier certainties are now under attack, and this is to be dramatically reinforced in the last stage of the

---

1.   Robert Davidson has an interesting discussion of this point with reference to Psalm 73 in his *The Courage to Doubt* (London: SCM Press, 1983), pp. 33ff.

2.   Although different translations interpret this passage in different ways: thus NEB treats it as a statement supporting the traditional case, as does the AV and NIV; RSV takes the opposite view.

3.   The claim that the confusion of the text is the point is admittedly post-modern. Such a text has, with a real vengeance, deconstructed both authorial intention and readerly control, leaving the interpreter with the difficult task of sailing safely between the Scylla of radical textual emendation and the Charybdis of incoherence.

dialogue proper (chs. 26-27). It is a feature of the book of Job that, like its principal protagonist, its readers are not infrequently reduced to silence (or speechlessness)—a case of the medium being the message?

Job's last reply to Bildad presents us with real problems. In the first place there is the matter of 26.1-4, which is commonly interpreted as a sarcastic riposte to Bildad (hence the RSV's exclamation marks). But the text is ambiguous:

> How have you helped him who has no power?
>> You have saved the arm without strength.
> How have you counselled him who has no wisdom?
>> You have provided insight in abundance.
> With whom have you uttered words,
>> and whose breath comes forth from you?

I believe that these lines may well indicate not a bitter comment but the beginnings of a recognition that there is wisdom other than what Job himself possesses. He is clearly not quite sure of its provenance; but (perhaps reluctantly) is forced to admit its value. This may be surprising (we have after all been trained to expect nothing but antagonism between Job and the others); but it is strangely in tune with what follows. For 26.5-14 consists of a celebration of God's creative powers of impeccable orthodoxy (compare, for example, Elihu in ch. 37 and Yahweh in ch. 38), and a disquisition on the fate of the wicked (ch. 27) which is in substantial agreement with the line put forward by Eliphaz and company. But there remains a personal note which reminds us of the Job with whom we are familiar. However much he may have been swayed by the intransigence of his adversaries, they cannot be allowed to carry their case against Job personally. *He* is not unrighteous. This is most powerfully insisted upon in 27.2-6, in words which carry, even in English translation, a vivid sense of the passion with which they are imbued. The passage begins with a telling echo of 23.16:

> As El lives, who has taken away my right,
>> and Shaddai, who has made my soul bitter. . .

and concludes in tones of ringing defiance:

>> till I die I will not put away my integrity from me.
> I hold fast my righteousness, and will not let it go;
>> my heart does not reproach me for any of my days.

These are not the words of the self-pitying, somewhat cringing figure of the first cycle. They are spoken by a man who has now seen the full paradox of his situation: I *am* innocent,[1] I have no regrets. Yet justice must be done and must be seen to be done—to this extent at least the case argued by Eliphaz, Bildad and Zophar carries weight. Hence the passion with which the denunciation of the wicked is made in vv. 7-23. If nothing else, the arguments of the adversaries have forced Job (and his readers!) to confront the paradox squarely: innocence may be affirmed, justice must be done; how can these be reconciled? It is a classic example of an unanswerable question, to which the only constructive response must be: surely the question is wrong.[2] I shall return to this matter in the concluding section of the paper, when I have commented on the remaining passages: the poem on wisdom in ch. 28, and Job's closing speeches in chs. 29–31.

5. *The poem to wisdom and the closing soliloquy.* I do not wish to comment at length on chs. 28 and 29–31. Chapter 28 has been so often and so readily dismissed as a jarring intrusion into Job's private grief that it must seem capricious to insist that it belongs in context and has a purposeful presence there. Nevertheless I would make this claim, bearing in mind the intellectual nature of the debate and the fact of Job's functioning within the Wisdom tradition. For it turns the spotlight, *at precisely the appropriate moment*, on the underlying principle of the whole debate: the belief that a rational dialogue can succeed in resolving the dilemma which faces both Job and his friends; the belief, in short, that wisdom—*hakam*—is within the grasp of human intelligence. In truth, however, only 'God understands the way to it, / and he knows its place' (28.23); furthermore, picking up a traditional motif of the Wisdom literature, but applying it with peculiar pertinence to Job's situation, we find:

1. *ṣaddîq*—a profoundly religious conception—is the pertinent term. Note the intensity of the phrase at the beginning of v. 6: *bᵉṣidqātî hehᵉzaqtî.*
2. The notorious philosophical conundrum, 'How do you respond to the question, "Have you stopped beating your wife? Answer Yes or No"', is a trivial example. Iain Banks, in *Walking on Glass* (London: Macmillan, 1985), p. 217, uses another such riddle as one motif of his novel: 'What happens when an unstoppable force meets an immovable object?', and in true riddling fashion resolves the puzzle by recording the 'answer' on the back of a matchbox! (Those interested in the answer must read the book; I do not have the right to give away the author's secrets!)

> Behold, the fear of the Lord, that is wisdom;
>   and to depart from evil is understanding (28.28).

Compare the two key passages in the third cycle, specifically 23.15-16 ('Therefore I am disturbed by his presence, / when I consider, I am afraid of him; / for El has numbed my brain, / Shaddai has troubled me') and 27.3-4 ('as long as my breath is in me, / and the spirit of God is in my nostrils; / my lips will not speak falsehood, / and my tongue will not utter deceit'). Although, as we have seen, Job has acknowledged the necessity of facing up to the adversaries' arguments, at the very points where he does so he demonstrates that he satisfies the conditions for true wisdom and understanding. At the stage the dialogue has reached, these are surely highly relevant connections, and significant indications of the way forward to a resolution within the final chapters of the book.

The dialogues end, as they begin, with a soliloquy. But where the opening soliloquy was wholly despairing, in the end Job defends his personal integrity at some length (ch. 29 and most of 31), attributes his sorry state once again to God (30.1-19), and makes a final dramatic appeal to be heard (30.20-31 and 31.35-37). It seems reasonable to accept a small re-ordering of the text of ch. 31, to replace vv. 35-37 at the end, as Job's final words; but even if we leave the text as it stands, the contrast between Job's (virtual) last words ('like a prince I would approach him') and his first words ('Let the day perish wherein I was born') could hardly be stronger. And this is clearly demonstrated by the distribution of themes which moves from a heavily negative cluster at the beginning to this note of confident challenge at the end. The one reversion to a theme from earlier sections (the vindictiveness of God in 30.1-19) is a necessary element of Job's 'summing-up': the challenge is to God because it is God who must be held responsible for the situation of crisis in which Job finds himself.

2. *On Asking the Right Question*

In his recent book, *Cosmopolis*,[1] Stephen Toulmin characterizes one of the principal themes of the Leibniz–Clarke correspondence[2] (the

1.   New York: Free Press/Macmillan, 1990, p. 126.
2.   *The Leibniz–Clarke Correspondence* (ed. H.G. Alexander; Manchester: Manchester University Press, 1956).

nature of space and time) by means of the hypothetical question which serves as the title of this essay. The debate in question is a fascinating one, in which Clarke defends Newton's idea of space as a *sensorium*, as some kind of absolute 'substance', against Leibniz's insistence on the relativity of both space and time. And because the subject is one on which there can be no last word, the questions it prompts are endless—and endlessly frustrating. To give something of the flavour of the debate, I quote one paragraph from Clarke's third letter, and one from Leibniz's response (his fourth letter).[1]

Thus Clarke:

> If space was nothing but the order of things coexisting; it would follow, that if God should remove in a straight line the whole material world entire, with any swiftness whatsoever; yet it would always continue in the same place: and that nothing would receive any shock upon the sudden stopping of that motion. And if time was nothing but the order of succession of created things; it would follow, that if God had created the world sooner than he did, yet it would not have been created at all the sooner. Further: space and time are quantities; which situation and order are not.

To which Leibniz replies:

> It is like a fiction, (that is) an impossible one, to suppose that God might have created the world some millions of years sooner. They who run into such kind of fictions, can give no answer to one that should argue for the eternity of the world. For since God does nothing without reason, and no reason can be given why he did not create the world sooner; it will follow, either that he has created nothing at all, or that he created the world before any assignable time, that I, that the world is eternal. But when once it has been shown, that the beginning, whenever it was, is always the same thing; the question, why it was not otherwise ordered, becomes needless and insignificance.

There is, to a modern ear, a wonderful sense of logic and reason gone mad in such debates, not dissimilar to the mediaeval debate about the number of angels which could balance on the head of a pin. Perhaps the closest modern analogy is to be found in that most prophetic of Victorian works, *Alice in Wonderland* and *Through the Looking Glass*, where Carroll's application of logic to fantasy at one and the same time mercilessly exposes the limitations of rationalism and with marvellous prescience anticipates most of the major issues of literary

---

1. *Correspondence*, pp. 32, 38-39.

theory and theology in the late twentieth century. We cannot dwell on the matter now, but Lewis Carroll still awaits an adequate intellectual study of his seminal 'Alice' work. It is hard to understand why the century which gave *Peanuts* serious theological treatment has yet to come to grips with *Alice* (a much more substantial and deserving case).

What lies behind this seemingly random tour of the outer edges of rationalism is a quite serious purpose: to reflect upon the importance of what questions are asked, and how they are phrased, when deeply life-threatening issues are under discussion. The importance of getting the question right is of course no new emphasis. Plato's application of the Socratic technique, which depends so much on persuading victims (not, I think, an unfair term to use) to arrive at the 'right' answer by means of leading questions, is a well known, if somewhat devious device. And Collingwood more recently stressed the importance for historical investigation of asking questions which were appropriate to the kind of information which is sought,[1] and which you have some hope of answering. 'How long is a piece of string', 'What colour are God's eyes' and 'Where did the universe begin' are clearly (are they not?) inadmissable questions. What is more difficult is to recognize such questions when we enter areas of passionate and vital concern to our individual well-being. Is it meaningful, for example, to ask of one's partner, 'Do you *really* love me?'? Even an affirmative answer to this question can offer the questioner little comfort. In the first place, it is the kind of enquiry which can hardly seriously expect the answer 'no'; yet it is not rhetorical, for it seeks reassurance in a situation of genuine doubt. So the affirmation might be patronising: in order to keep him/her happy I'll say what I'm expected to say. Worse, however—the 'yes' might be devious, even within the compass of a (partially) honest reply. For example: I'm having affairs with several other people, but my relationship with you is one which I want to preserve; so I 'really' love you, and I don't 'really' care about the others.

The theological enterprise is at once fascinating and frustrating precisely because the questions it raises are existentially urgent, but at the same time apparently unanswerable. This is why theological systems so often degenerate into dogmatism, because the human mind

---

1.   See, e.g., *The Idea of History* (Oxford: Oxford University Press, 1946), pp. 269-82.

(like nature) 'abhors a vacuum', and readily propounds formulae which serve to close the gap between the known and the unknowable. Leibniz's response to the Clarke/Newton advocacy of the vacuum[1] is a fascinating instance of the way theological presuppositions are called upon to counter the apparent results of scientific enquiry: an interesting reminder that even empirical scientists are not free of metaphysical dogmas in their pursuit of understanding of the universe. (The whole objective/subjective Cartesian dichotomy upon which so much scientific enquiry depended is, of course, a metaphysical assumption, not an observed phenomenon.)

The book of Job, which is the focus of our particular attention, has prompted many volumes of speculation in the realm of urgent questions lacking persuasive answers. Indeed, even a glance at the secondary literature on the subject arouses feelings not unlike those prompted by the Leibniz–Clarke correspondence. There exists a bewildering array of literary, psychological, christological, sociological and pious discussions of the book, most of which seek to understand how the problem of suffering—with which Job manifestly deals—can be resolved in the world of a good God and a just universe. Quite clearly, no one has yet successfully squared that particular circle;[2] equally clearly no one ever will, for it belongs to the

1. Another of the themes of the correspondence referred to above is a disagreement between Clarke (following Newton) who accepted the experimental evidence for the existence of a vacuum, and Leibniz, who denied it—although one of his reasons might strike a modern reader as rather quaint: 'the more matter there is, the more God has occasion to exercise his wisdom and power. Which is one reason, among others, why I maintain that there is no vacuum at all' (*Correspondence*, p. 16).

2. The quasi-mathematical enterprise here alluded to is rather appropriate in the light of the Leibniz–Clarke correspondence, for it refers to the misconceived attempt by many amateur rationalists to express the area of a circle in terms of purely rational numbers (that is, numbers which can be expressed as fractions). Unfortunately the number *pi* which underlies all the measures of the circle is resolutely irrational (that is, its decimal expression consists of an infinite string of digits after the point which never resolves itself into a repeating pattern). That mathematicians have chosen to describe some numbers as *rational* and others as *irrational* is purely serendipitous for our discussion, though logical enough given the alternative meaning of rational as 'capable of being expressed as a ratio'. The whole business is a salutary reminder that our emotional response to the words we experience is often more significant than we would like to admit: circle-squarers are the flat-earthers of the mathematical world, and neither is as mad as strict logic might suggest. The world *is* flat for many practical purposes, and if you stop short of infinity you *can* square the circle.

realm of competing absolutes: the absolutely good versus the absolutely just. It is our Wonderlandish fate to be part of an era which has enthroned the principle of logical precision in all things, forgetting that our whole being is formed of materials which respond to logical argument—if they respond at all—only in the most faltering and fitful manner. It is tempting to ask, therefore, whether we have not been seduced into putting quite the wrong question to the book of Job. For the 'problem' of suffering (as distinct from the physical, mental and spiritual anguish of suffering, all of which are perfectly real) is something of a contrived conundrum, depending as it does on speculative assumptions about the nature of God and the universe. That the universe as we know it ought to be 'meaningful' within the rationalist terms of modernist thinking, and that we are capable of comprehending even *that* form of meaning, are axioms of quite startling audacity. Could it be—as with Leibniz, Clarke and Newton—that there is something wrong with the questions we habitually put; that there is another way to read the dialogues of Job without getting ourselves tangled in the ineluctable net of rationalist discourse?

Job himself is much given to asking questions (many of them rhetorical), and much of the irony of the book lies in his being suddenly faced with a response to these questions—and that from a God who demolishes Job's case by means of equally rhetorical language. I have attempted to show in the first part of this essay that the very structure of the book is arguably designed to undermine Job's own starting point and to lead him (and us as readers) into a new perception of the relationships involved.[1] But what of 'the question', the 'problem of suffering'? What in the end is the contribution of Job to this long-standing riddle? I believe that just as the cycle of dialogues both structurally and in terms of content succeeds in subverting Job's initial set of priorities, so the book as a whole may be read as a dramatic undermining of the propriety of asking such questions in the

---

1.   See my earlier remarks in *Christianity and Other Faiths in Britain* (London: SCM Press, 1985), pp. 134-39. I would stand by much of what I then wrote, although it will be clear to those who check the matter further that I have in the present study concentrated more on the way that the dialogues are structurally contrived than on the reader's direct responses. It is still, I think, appropriate to read from the book a sense of alienation from Job's verbose exercises in self-justification, while at the same time recognizing 'his own' growing self-awareness—a process which (as I then argued) is further developed in the remaining chapters.

first place. It might even be understood humourously, or satirically;[1] I would prefer to describe the process as one of deconstruction, although I admit that a certain wry humour is to be found in the fact that the epilogue quietly unstitches everything that Job has earlier argued by restoring to him twice as much as he had before as a 'reward' for his righteousness! But surely the clearest *intellectual* implication of our study of Job is that the question as traditionally put is simply misconceived. It leads either to paradox or to incoherence; a result which in any other field of rational inquiry would immediately prompt the response, 'You're asking the wrong sort of question'. It seems to us obviously meaningless to put the question which is the title of this essay; for the meaning of 'place' is only defined within creation, and therefore the term cannot sensibly be used in discussion of the *nature* of creation. Similarly, the defining of God's nature is not an abstract exercise which can be carried out in isolation from our position as thinking life-forms within a universe about which we postulate certain general truths (including the observation that individuals who appear to us to be 'innocent' also appear to us to 'suffer'). The theodicy question is thus subject to the same *intellectual* objections as the Clarke/Leibniz question: it presumes a knowledge of God which is in fact dependent upon the definition of terms like 'justice' and 'innocence' which appear in the question. This, in the end, is why the drama of Job renders the hero speechless, and is precisely the point of his response in 42.3.

> Therefore I have uttered what I did not understand,
> > things too wonderful for me, which I did not know.

But of course Job is far more than an intellectual exercise (though it is undoubtedly at least that). It is a spiritual odyssey and a psychological journey into self-knowledge. I have suggested above[2] that the former works out—perhaps surprisingly—in terms of a cultic experience not dissimilar to that of the psalmists. As to the latter, there is room here only to hint at what might be at work. Jack Kahn's *Job's Illness* has already provided a major contribution to this approach; I would wish

---

1.   W. Whedbee, 'The Comedy of Job', in Y.T. Radday and A. Brenner (eds.), *On Humour and the Comic in the Hebrew Bible* (Sheffield: Almond Press, 1990), pp. 217-49. The article first appeared in *Semeia* 7 (1977).
2.   In the discussion of 23.8-17.

only to add a further dimension (perhaps best described as 'literary-psychological') in terms of a phrase familiar to Scots: the self-righteousness of the unco guid. Burns's *Holy Willie's Prayer*, and Hogg's *Confessions of a Justified Sinner*, will serve as potent symbols of what I mean: the alienation of the individual whose self-awareness is in terms of his or her personal probity in a world of otherwise mediocre individuals. It is an alienation born of arrogance masquerading as piety—something which is as contemporary as it is ancient. Might not the drama of Job as a whole be interpreted as a journey from a peculiarly solipsistic notion of righteousness to an integrated, balanced view of one's role as servant of God in relationship to others. The drama begins by describing an almost impossibly idyllic scene (one may suspect here some ironic hyperbole) which is rapidly destroyed by various calamities as a result of which Job is left alone, suffering, but protesting his innocence. In a dramatic sense, we then follow through the dialogues the process by which a man, whose instincts are to proclaim that everyone (including God) is wrong but him, is brought to a quite different sense of his status (see Part 1 of this essay). It is only when Job abandons his isolation and slowly discovers how to relate to those who challenge him that he can find some meaning in his situation. The last sections of the book (Elihu, 32–37, and Yahweh, 38–41) signal a significant reversal: Job is now the thoughtful listener, rather than the stalwart debater. His final confession completes the process—he is now reconciled not only to God but to his fellows (note his prayers for his adversaries in 42.8-10)—and this is spelled out in graphic terms by the extravagant restoration of his fortunes in the epilogue.

These final comments are, of course, sketchy in the extreme. But they do have one virtue, that of taking the prologue and epilogue seriously as vital elements of the whole work. And what does that work describe? A psychological journey from solitary righteousness (1.1) to a proper understanding of religion as a celebration of the community of men and women and God together (42.10-11). In other words, the ultimate question of the book of Job is not, 'How do we reconcile the justice of God with the suffering of humanity?'; it is rather, 'How do we find ourselves as individuals in relationship with others within the community of faith?'

Whether or not he would agree with my analysis of Job, I am happy to make this contribution to Robert Davidson's Festschrift in recognition of his own dedication as teacher and scholar to the search for identity within community.

THE TWO THEOLOGICAL VERSIONS OF THE PASSOVER PERICOPE IN EXODUS

William Johnstone

On a number of occasions[1] I have sought to argue that passages in the book of Exodus, especially in the Sinai pericope in Exodus 19–40, have passed through two final processes of theological redaction which I have termed the 'D-version' (because of its intimate relationship to Deuteronomy and the wider Deuteronomistic History) and the 'P-edition' (retaining the traditional label for the latest 'document' of the Pentateuch, recognized here, however, not merely as 'source' but also as redaction, rather as the Chronicler is both 'source' and 'redaction' in relation to the Deuteronomistic History[2]). In this article[3] I should like to apply this hypothesis to the Passover pericope in Exodus, especially Exodus 12–13. A study of how a religious institution—Passover—has been cast into literary form in two successive redactions—the D-version and the P-edition—would, if substantiated,

---

1. 'Reactivating the Chronicles Analogy in Pentateuchal Studies, with Special Reference to the Sinai Pericope in Exodus', *ZAW* 99 (1987), pp. 16-37; 'The Decalogue and the Redaction of the Sinai Pericope in Exodus', *ZAW* 100 (1988), pp. 361-85; *Exodus* (Old Testament Guides; Sheffield: JSOT Press, 1990), esp. pp. 73-86.

2. On this as on other topics it is impossible within the confines of this article to give other than eclectic reference to the scholarly literature. The question of 'source' vs. 'redaction' is discussed with special reference to Exodus by W.H. Schmidt (author of the Biblischer Kommentar *Exodus*, now in course of preparation) in 'Plädoyer für die Quellenscheidung', *BZ* ns 32 (1988), pp. 1-14. Interestingly enough, even such a doughty defender of 'sources' as Schmidt concedes ('Plädoyer', p. 13) that a redaction especially interested in the Mosaic traditions and standing in close relationship to Deut. and DtrH exists in Exodus and that the question of its extent remains open.

3. The substance of this article was read as the Presidential Address to The Society for Old Testament Study, London, 3 January 1990.

offer an inner-biblical example relevant to the major concern of this collection of essays: tradition, both verbal and practical, provides the framework within which an understanding of contemporary life is sought; in the process, tradition itself is not merely transmitted but transformed. It is a pleasure to offer this study as a mark of esteem to a versatile scholar and churchman who has not only contributed greatly over four decades as lecturer and examiner to the life of the institution where I work, but has also sought in a distinctive way to present and apply the theology of the Old Testament in contemporary terms.

It may be helpful, first, to recapitulate briefly the argument so far. The book of Deuteronomy, more broadly, the Deuteronomistic History, provides a text parallel to material in the book of Exodus which enables a pre-P Deuteronomistic text to be recovered in the book of Exodus which was subsequently re-edited by the P-writer. The matter may be put statistically. There are 719 verses in Exodus 19–40. The material on the Tabernacle (Exod. 25.1–31.17; 34.29–40.38, i.e., 463 verses) I am willing with many others to ascribe to P. I should assign a further 35 or so verses in chs. 19, 24 and 32 to P (approximately 19.10-15, 18, 20-25; 24.1-2, 9-11, 14-17; 32.25-29, 35; 33.18, 20-23; 34.2, 3), giving some 498 verses all told. Of the remaining 221 verses, approximately 116 are taken up by the Decalogue and the Book of the Covenant (Exod. 20.1-17, 22.1–23.19), which are likely to have had an independent history. There thus remain only 105 verses which are neither P nor Decalogue nor B. What is the affiliation of these verses? Almost one third of them have verbal correspondences, in some cases identity, with material in Deuteronomy (especially the 'back-bone' of the material, Exod. 24.12, 18; 31.18; 32.7-10, 15, 20; 34.1, 4, 28 // Deut. 9.7–10.11) and/or the Deuteronomistic History (for the coda of the Book of the Covenant in Exod. 23.20-33 cf. the coda to the conquest narrative in Judg. 2.1-5; for the golden calf in Exod. 32.4 cf. 1 Kgs 12.28). Many of the remaining verses, like 19.3-9, 20.18-21, 24.3-8 and those in chs. 32–34, are strongly marked with Deuteronomic/Deuteronomistic phraseology. I have also argued that both the Decalogue and the Book of the Covenant have passed through Deuteronomistic redaction.

A good illustration, among many, of how a text of Exodus which has been re-edited by P, can be reconstructed on the basis of parallels in Deuteronomy is supplied by Exod. 34.1-4 // Deut. 10.1-3:

Exod. 34.1, 4	Deut. 10.1-3
1 ויאמר יהוה אל משה	1 בעת ההוא אמר יהוה אלי
פסל לך שני לחת אבנים כראשנים	פסל לך שני לוחת אבנים כראשנים
	ועלה אלי ההרה
	ועשית לך ארון עץ:
וכתבתי על הלחת	2 ואכתב על הלחת
את הדברים	את הדברים
אשר היו על הלחת הראשנים אשר שברת:	אשר היו על הלחת הראשנים אשר שברת
	ושמתם בארון:
	3 ואעש ארון עצי שטים
4 ויפסל שני לחת אבנים כראשנים. . . .	ואפסל שני לחת אבנים כראשנים
ויעל אל הר. . . .בידו שני לחת אבנים:	ואעל ההרה ושני הלחת בידי:

After due allowance is made for the fact that Exodus is couched as third-person narrative and Deuteronomy as first-person reminiscence, there is word-for-word correspondence between the outer frameworks of these two texts. I should suggest that the explanation for this identity is that both come from the same source (as one would argue in the case of Samuel–Kings // Chronicles—or Jeremiah 52, or Isaiah 36–39 // Kings), viz., D. On this hypothesis the reason for the suppression of the remaining D material in Exod. 34.1-4 becomes clear: it concerns the ark of the covenant. Since P has already given the specifications for the ark of the testimony in Exod. 25.10-22 and is about to record the construction of it in accordance with these specifications in 37.1-9, it is superfluous to mention it once more here. This suppressed material has been replaced by matter reflecting P's preoccupation with ritual purity and hierarchy. Deut. 10.1-3, however, permits the recovery of the pre-P text that once stood in Exod. 34.1-4.

The interplay between the two final recensions of the book of Exodus thus illustrated preserves an element of the dialectic and paradox which are an essential feature of biblical interpretation. The recognition of these two synchronic redactions in diachronic tension is not simply a matter of the interpreter's preference and presupposition, but is the identification of an element that is objectively present in the text and only an interpretation that recognizes at least that degree of complexity can begin to claim to be inductively and phenomenologically describing the text as it stands.[1]

1.   As the somewhat polemical tone of that last paragraph hints, this approach has to maintain itself against alternatives on either side. On the one hand, there is synchronic, 'final form', interpretation, of which J.I. Durham's *Exodus* (WBC; Waco, TX: Word Books, 1987) is a recent example. His view is that Exodus is a 'one-track book. . . theologically single-minded', predicated on the theology of the Presence of Yahweh (*Exodus*, p. xxiii). The dangers here, in my opinion, of under-description are not unconnected with understating the evidently composite character of the book of Exodus. On the other hand, my approach has recently been explicitly criticized as insufficiently differentiated by, especially, C. Dohmen of the 'Münster school' of Pentateuchal criticism, in F.-L. Hossfeld (ed.), *Vom Sinai zum Horeb* (Würzburg: Echter, 1989). Dohmen remarks that by my approach the complexity of the text is 'eher verschleiert denn erklärt' (*Sinai*, p. 28 n. 37). My response would be that it is difficult enough already, even with the help of the control of the D/DtrH material, to establish with tolerable certainty the penultimate, pre-P version of the D-school, let alone repose any confidence in more far-reaching hypotheses about origins and developments. Dohmen's ingenious analysis is, in my view, beyond verification and he should not be surprised if few follow him. Within the Sinai pericope he finds seven redactional stages: J, E, Je, three Deuteronomic and P. The J account of the theophanic encounter between Yahweh and Moses on the mountain (a couple of verses in ch. 19 [20, 25a] and parts of half-a-dozen in 34 [1a*a*, 2*, 4a*, 6a*a**, 8a, 10a]) is veiled in wordless mystery (Moses goes up the mountain, comes back down and makes a promissory covenant). E adds that the theophany was at least accompanied by God's speech, though the content is not recounted (Exod. 19.19). Je introduces the tablets (Exod. 24.12*; 31.18*; 32.19) but they are blank: they are the public attestation of the occurrence of the theophany; the phrase *luḥot 'eben* is a plural of *Gattung* and not a plural of number. The original D text (<Je) also has blank tablets, though it now understands them in the sense of a genuine numerical plural (*luḥot 'ᵃbanim*). D, in the interests of the prohibition of images in the second commandment, introduces the inscription on the tablets of the Decalogue as the basis for the covenant. Meantime in Exodus, Exod. 34.10-26 contains the legal corpus of the *Privilegrecht* (Je), written (v. 27), but not on the tablets. A late D editor is, therefore, responsible for Exod. 34.1b, which understands that Moses wrote the *Privilegrecht* on the tablets. That the tablets are 'two' is first stated in Deut. 9.10, which derives from R[P]. The competition between Decalogue (introduced into Exod. 20 for the first time by P) and *Privilegrecht* is finally resolved in P in the ambiguities of Exod. 34.28.

Quite apart from the highly speculative nature of this reconstruction, it is precisely Dohmen's failure to use the Deuteronomy parallels as control which makes him fail to see that, for example, Exod. 34.28b corresponds directly with Deut. 10.4a and that the subject of 'he wrote' is Yahweh, thus undercutting much of his argument.

Nonetheless, on the biblical principle of interpretation, *'iš lᵉpi 'okᵉlo* ('each

I turn now to apply this hypothesis to the first part of Exodus, especially to the Passover pericope in chs. 12–13. The D legislation for the observance of the Passover in Deut. 16.1-8 must provide one of the most critical—even, at first sight, insuperable—hurdles for the theory that there is a Deuteronomic/Deuteronomistic text in Exodus 12–13, underlying the final P-edition. The idiosyncratic features of the Passover legislation in Deut. 16.1-8, as opposed to other liturgical calendars in the Hebrew Bible including Exodus 12–13 (material conventionally attributed to B in Exod. 23.14-17 and 34.18-24; and to P in Exod. 12.1-14, 43-49; Lev. 23.5; Num. 9.1-14; 28.16; 33.3; cf. Josh. 5.10-11; Ezek. 45.21; Ezra 6.19-22), scarcely need emphasizing: in D the Passover lasts not just for one night but for one night plus seven days, thus annexing to itself the Festival of Unleavened Bread; the rite is observed not in homes throughout the land but in the one sanctuary in the one place which Yahweh will choose; the rite thus resolutely associated with the cultus of the central sanctuary is given the sacrificial terminology, *zebaḥ*, and follows sacrificial practice—the victim is not only a kid or lamb of the small cattle but may also be chosen from the large and is boiled, not roasted. If, as I should be disposed to believe, Josiah's Passover carried out this Deuteronomic legislation (2 Kgs 23.3, 21-23; 2 Chron. 35.1-19), then the JPSA translation of 2 Kgs 23.22-23 correctly conveys the revolutionary, indeed unique, character of the Deuteronomic observance:

> Now the passover sacrifice had not been offered in that manner in the days of the chieftains who ruled Israel, or during the days of the kings of Israel and the kings of Judah. Only in the eighteenth year of King Josiah was such a passover sacrifice offered in that manner to the LORD in Jerusalem.[1]

according to his capacity'), slightly whimsically derived from this very section of Exodus (12.4; cf. 16.18) as the original title of this paper, I should resolutely defend the right of a Durham and a Dohmen to pursue their contrasting methods of interpretation, however unsatisfactory I find them both to be.

1.   The question of the pre-Josianic history of the development of the institution of Passover need not be pursued here (see, e.g., J. Van Seters, 'The Place of the Yahwist in the History of Passover and Massot', *ZAW* 95 [1983], pp. 167-82, for some discussion and bibliographical leads). I should be inclined to the view that there is such a history but it may be that, in the light of the discussion in the text below, the necessary sources for tracing that history are lacking in the Hebrew Bible: if Exod. 12–13 is a reworking by P of Deuteronomic/Deuteronomistic material and B has passed through Deuteronomistic redaction, then Deut. 16.1-8 may be the earliest

That translation points up the challenge of whether the D-legislation in Deut. 16.1-8, with its revolutionary observance of the Passover, enables a similarly revolutionary Deuteronomic text to be recovered in Exodus 12–13, which has subsequently undergone substantial modification at the hands of the P-editor. At first sight, the recovery of such a text seems a forlorn hope. I have few grounds for dissenting from the prevailing view that Exodus 12, even read with the best will in the world, shows little sign of D. I should indeed regard the legislation on Passover in Exod. 12.1-13, 21-28, 43-50 (and on unleavened bread, vv. 14-20) as an almost purely P composition[1] (though it may itself have undergone development—e.g. v. 19 repeats v. 15): for example, the prominence of Aaron beside Moses in vv. 1, 28, 43, 50; the dating by the Babylonian calendar, vv. 2, 18; the reference to Israel as an *'edah*, vv. 3, 6, 19, 47; v. 12b uses the same vocabulary as Num. 33.4b; for the requirement to observe on pain of death, vv. 15, 19, cf. Exod. 31.14, Lev. 7.20. The P (or, at least, non-D) character of much of Exodus 12 is, I think, fairly non-controversial. We shall, however, return to Exodus 12 below.

But what, then, of Exodus 13? I should like to present an argument that Exod. 13.3-7[2] contains an original Deuteronomic/ Deuteronomistic text attested by Deut. 16.1-8 in which the Passover has been suppressed by P—because it has already been dealt with in quite other

literary source. The fact that that source itself may be composite may bespeak complex prehistory not only of the literary formulation but of the institution itself. But for the latter we are dependent upon educated guesses about inherent probabilities and the plausibilities arising from anthropological parallels (such as are adduced by, e.g., J.B. Segal, *The Hebrew Passover* [The School of African & Oriental Studies; London Oriental Series, 12; London: Oxford University Press, 1963]; J. Henninger, *Les fêtes de printemps chez les sémites et la pâque israélite* [Paris: Gabalda, 1975]).

1. Cf., e.g., Van Seters, 'Yahwist', pp. 172-75. F. Kohata (*Jahwist und Priesterschrift in Exodus 3–14* [BZAW, 166; 1986], pp. 267 n. 31) provides a convenient account of the attributions which have been proposed for Exod. 12.21-28 running all the way from N to P.

2. M. Caloz ('Exode, xiii, 3-16 et son rapport au Deutéronome', *RB* 65 [1968], pp. 5-62) subjects the passage to analysis assuming the correctness of the attribution of materials in the Tetrateuch to sources proposed in O. Eissfeldt, *Hexateuch-Synopse* (Leipzig, 1922) ('Exode', p. 9)—which, to a significant degree, is the very point at issue.

terms by P in Exodus 12—just as the ark was suppressed in Exod. 34.1-4.

Once again it may be helpful to lay out the two texts to reveal where the parallels occur:

<table>
<tr><td align="center">Exod. 13.3-7</td><td align="center">Deut. 16.1-8</td></tr>
<tr><td align="right">3 ויאמר משה אל העם</td><td align="right">1</td></tr>
<tr><td align="right">זכור את</td><td align="right">שמור את</td></tr>
<tr><td align="right"></td><td align="right">חדש האביב ועשית פסח ליהוה אלהיך</td></tr>
<tr><td align="right">היום הזה אשר</td><td align="right"></td></tr>
<tr><td align="right"></td><td align="right">כי בחדש האביב</td></tr>
<tr><td align="right">יצאתם ממצרים מבית עבדים כי בחזק יד</td><td align="right">הוציאך יהוה אלהיך ממצרים לילה</td></tr>
<tr><td align="right">הוציא יהוה אתכם מזה</td><td align="right"></td></tr>
<tr><td align="right"></td><td align="right">2 וזבחת פסח ליהוה אלהיך צאן ובקר</td></tr>
<tr><td align="right"></td><td align="right">במקום אשר יבחר יהוה לשכן שמו שם</td></tr>
<tr><td align="right">ולא יאכל חמץ</td><td align="right">3 לא תאכל עליו חמץ</td></tr>
<tr><td align="right">4 היום אתם יצאים בחדש האביב</td><td align="right"></td></tr>
<tr><td align="right">5 והיה כי יביאך יהוה אל ארץ</td><td align="right"></td></tr>
<tr><td align="right">הכנעני . . .</td><td align="right"></td></tr>
<tr><td align="right">ארץ זבת חלב ודבש ועבדת את העבדה</td><td align="right"></td></tr>
<tr><td align="right">הזאת בחדש הזה</td><td align="right"></td></tr>
<tr><td align="right">6 שבעת ימים תאכל מצות</td><td align="right">שבעת ימים תאכל עליו מצות</td></tr>
<tr><td align="right"></td><td align="right">לחם עני כי בחפזון יצאת מארץ מצרים</td></tr>
<tr><td align="right"></td><td align="right">. . .</td></tr>
<tr><td align="right"></td><td align="right">8 ששת ימים תאכל מצות</td></tr>
<tr><td align="right">וביום השביעי חג ליהוה</td><td align="right">וביום השביעי עצרת ליהוה</td></tr>
<tr><td align="right"></td><td align="right">אלהיך לא תעשה מלאכה</td></tr>
<tr><td align="right">7 מצות יאכל את שבעת הימים</td><td align="right"></td></tr>
<tr><td align="right">ולא יראה לך חמץ</td><td align="right"></td></tr>
<tr><td align="right">ולא יראה לך שאר בכל גבלך</td><td align="right">4 ולא יראה לך שאר בכל גבלך . . .</td></tr>
</table>

Is Exod 13.3-7 basically a Deuteronomic text which has been re-edited by P? There are a number of unevennesses in Exod. 13.3-7 which provide the *prima facie* case that it has at least undergone editorial adjustment:

1. The addressees are masculine plural in vv. 3-4 but masculine singular in vv. 5-7 (and thereafter).
2. Verse 3b is a legislative snatch abruptly introduced and equally abruptly abandoned.
3. Verse 4, 'today you are going out in the month of Abib', is

lame: its five words provide two definitions of time which are not co-ordinate with one another.

4. According to v. 6, only the seventh day is a *ḥag*, a pilgrimage festival; there is no such festival elsewhere in the Hebrew Bible.

5. Verse 7a has unusual syntax: the feminine plural subject is followed by a masculine singular verb[1]; the adverbial accusative of time, 'for the seven days', is introduced by the *nota accusativi, 'et*.[2]

6. There is repetition in v. 7b.

While it may thus be recognized that this passage has undergone editorial adjustment, can a basically Deuteronomic/Deuteronomistic text within it be recognized? It is certainly strongly marked with Deuteronomic phraseology: v. 3—'house of slaves' (cf. Exod. 20.2); 'strength of hand' as applied to Yahweh (frequent in Deuteronomy, e.g., 3.24; 4.34; 5.15; 6.21); v. 5—the list of the pre-Israelite population (cf. Exod. 23.23). There are verbal reminiscences of the legislation of Deuteronomy 16 in the specifically legislative material in vv. 3b, 6-7 (cf. Deut. 16.3a, 4a, 8).

Can it even be argued that the Deuteronomic text of Deut. 16.1-8 provides materials for the restoration of an underlying Deuteronomic text in Exod. 13.3-7 which has been subsequently modified by the P-editor?

The text is, I submit, explicable from this point of view. Since P has already given his legislation for the Passover in Exodus 12, the Passover has been rigorously excised from this passage and the text has now been transformed from one on Passover into one on the Festival of Unleavened Bread. This is arguable on grounds of parallels and of differences.

1. Parallels. Apart from close correspondence in Exod. 13.3 // Deut. 16.1, there are four almost exact parallels: Exod. 13.3 // Deut 16.3; Exod. 13.6 // Deut. 16.3; Exod. 13.6 // Deut. 16.8; Exod. 13.7 // Deut. 16.4.

2. The main differences are accountable on the assumption that P is deliberately reusing D-material for its own purposes:

---

1. GKC 121.b regards the construction as an impersonal passive with preceding object. One notes a similar construction in Exod. 12.16, 48 (P).

2. But cf. Lev. 25.22; Deut. 9.25; BDB notes the construction as 'very rare'.

a. *pesaḥ* of Deut. 16.1, 2, has been suppressed—P has dealt with it in Exodus 12.

b. The 'over it (sc. *pesaḥ*)' has consequently been omitted in Exod. 13.3, 6.

c. The whole of Deut. 16.2 has been suppressed, since it insists on the centralization and culticization of the Festival.

d. For similar reasons most of Deut. 16.4 and all of Deut. 16.5-7 has been omitted. The omission of this material has facilitated the transposition of Deut. 16.8.

e. The plural address in Exod. 13.3-4 matches the plural P has already used in Exodus 12. The singular address of Deuteronomy 16 is resumed in Exod. 13.5-7.

f. In Exod. 13.3b a new title referring to unleavened bread has been constructed in place of the suppressed Passover. The verbal form has been changed into the impersonal passive (the singular address of the D-form would not in any case suit P's plural address). It is, however, singularly inadequate as a title for the Festival of Unleavened Bread (cf. Exod. 23.15 // 34.18, for the appropriate form of the legislation, *'et ḥag hammaṣṣot tišmor*).

g. In Exod. 13.6 *ᶜaṣeret* has been replaced by the anomalous *ḥag*. In the P conception, Passover cannot have a seventh day to be solemn assembly: *ᶜaṣeret* in P is otherwise used of the eighth day of Tabernacles (e.g. Lev. 23.36).

h. The inconsequential Exod. 13.4 represents the turning into plural address of remnants of Deut. 16.1.

i. Exod. 13.5a is pure Deuteronomic and may have belonged to the underlying D-version (although it could be P-reuse of Deuteronomic clichés). *ᶜabodah*, however, in v. 5b looks like P (Num. 4.23, etc.).

j. Exod. 13.7a is an adaptation of Deut. 16.8a, with, again, the adjustment of the direct address of D's singular verb into P's impersonal passive of legislation.

k. Exod. 13.7b*a* appears to be a doublet reusing *ḥameṣ* from the new title in v. 3b.

The correctness of the hypothesis that an original D-version of the Passover has been suppressed in Exodus 13 by P in preference for his own version in Exodus 12 can be confirmed when we return to consider the latter chapter. Two series of observations on the legislation for the Passover in Exodus 12 can now be made.

1. The general P-character of the material in Exodus 12 has already been conceded. But, if this is the P legislation on the Passover, how does it relate to the earlier D legislation (whether that legislation be found only in Deuteronomy 16 or in Exodus 13 as well)? It is presumably intended to correct and, to a degree, to supersede D's practice. That this is so is indicated by the fact that there are indeed verbal citations and material reminiscences, but made in such a way as to make clear that the relationship between P and D is mainly one of polemical correction of D by P. The polemical element centres, naturally, on the P-conception of Passover as a *domestic* rite, with its victim taken from the small cattle, roasted whole over the spit, as opposed to D's sanctuary rite, where the immolation of the victim is formally linked to the sacrificial system of the cultus in terminology and in practice. The elements, which P found objectionable, are those listed particularly in Deut. 16.2, 5-7; thus P in Exodus 12 emphasizes the domestic, non-cultic nature of the observance throughout and provides aetiology for the observance and for the term itself in v. 13; it specifies the choice of the victim from the small cattle, v. 3; it synchronizes the slaughter as *ben ha^{c}arbayim* (v. 6), rather than D's *ba^{c}ereb k^{e}bo' hašemeš* (Deut. 16.6); it uses the not-specifically-cultic verb *šaḥaṭ* for the slaughter of the victim, not *zabaḥ*, vv. 6, 21; it prohibits the boiling of the victim, v. 9; so far from returning to their tents in the morning, Israel are forbidden to leave their houses all night, v. 22b. The pilgrimage Festival of Unleavened Bread is distinguished from Passover, vv. 14-20.

Besides these polemical corrections, there are, however, verbal and material reminiscences: the eating in haste, *b^{e}hippazon* (although Deut. 16.3 speaks of *leaving* in haste) (v. 11b); v. 12*abc* resembles 13.15*abc*; v. 15a resembles material in 13.6 and v. 25a resembles 13.5, although the plural verb characteristic of P is used (v. 25b introduces the P expression $^{ca}bodah$; cf. v. 26b); v. 26a appears to introduce the D motif of instruction of the son, except that here again the plural is used, and the verb is *'amar* not D's *ša'al*; v. 27a*a* retains the Deuteronomic phrase (including *zebaḥ* of the Passover!) but the remainder with the domestic aetiology must be P. These polemical

corrections and verbal and material reminiscences may suggest that
still more of the material in the D-legislation for Passover in
Deuteronomy 16 was originally present in the D-version of the
Passover which lay before P in Exod. 13.3-7 and stimulated his revision: specifically, at least Deut. 16.3b*ab*, 4b, 7. A plausible reconstruction of the original D-text of Exod. 13.3-7, based both on the
parallels to Deut. 16.1-8 in Exod. 13.3-7 and on the polemical corrections by P in Exodus 12, is thus as follows:

ויאמר משה אל העם שמור את חדש האביב ועשית פסח ליהוה אלהיך
כי בחדש האביב הוציאך יהוה אלהיך ממצרים לילה:
והיה כי יביאך יהוה אלהיך אל ארץ הכנעני . . . ארץ זבת חלב ודבש
וזבחת פסח ליהוה אלהיך:
לא תאכל עליו חמץ שבעת ימים תאכל עליו מצות
ולא יראה לך שאר בכל גבלך שבעת ימים:
ששת ימים תאכל מצות וביום השביעי עצרת ליהוה אלהיך:

2. If the legislation on Passover and unleavened bread in Exodus
12.1-28, 43-50 thus belongs to P, then it is subsequent to the D-version. If it is omitted as an insertion subsequent to the D-version and
based upon it, then the remaining material should close up faultlessly.
In my view, Exod. 12.29-36 does indeed continue directly from Exod.
11.1-8 as the execution of the threatened tenth plague.[1] As in the other
nine plague scenes, so here in the tenth there is no break in the pre-P
version between the threat to Pharaoh and the Egyptians and the
carrying out of that threat.

The inclusion of the P-material in Exodus 12, on the contrary,
introduces elements of incoherence and inconcinnity into the narrative. According to the P scenario, Israel is saved from the tenth plague
because they are celebrating Passover in their houses. But why should
Israel have been thought to have been under any threat from the tenth
plague, when, like the other nine, it was meant to impress *Egypt* and
to force them to let Israel go unscathed? Why should it have been necessary for Israel to take special precautions against a plague from
which they had already been promised immunity (Exod. 11.7: the
verb *hiplah* has already been used in connection with the fourth and
fifth plagues in Exod. 8.18; 9.4, without implying any action on

---

1. So, many (with variations) from J.F.L. George (1835, cited by
J.W. Rogerson, *Old Testament Criticism in the Nineteenth Century: England and
Germany* [London: SPCK, 1984], p. 67) to Van Seters, 'Yahwist'.

Israel's part)? There is the further inconcinnity between the selection of a *yearling* ram/kid as victim (Exod. 12.5) and the *firstborn* of Israel for which it was meant to be the means of protection.[1] Contrariwise, this inconcinnity is removed when the intrusive P material in Exod. 12.43-51 is removed and the tenth plague of the death of the firstborn of Egypt is brought into immediate relation, not with the Passover, but with the offering of the firstborn of Israel in Exod. 13.1-2. In the light of these considerations I should argue that before P there was no material in Exodus 12 on the Passover; the Passover legislation was confined to ch. 13.

To summarize thus far: the D-version had no Passover material in Exodus 12. Rather, its Passover regulations were to be found in ch. 13 in reformulation of the material on unleavened bread. The P-edition has suppressed this Passover in ch. 13 and, instead, has inserted its regulations on the Passover in ch. 12 with the incorporation of vast new materials of its own and polemical re-use of fragments of D-material. What is the significance of these phenomenological observations for the understanding of the Passover in the D-version and in the P-edition, respectively?

In order to understand the significance of the Passover pericope in the D-version, one has, I believe, to widen the area of discussion significantly beyond Exodus 12-13. Before we can consider its significance we must establish its extent. A basic clue is provided here by the Deuteronomic chronology. Why does the D-writer define the Passover as lasting for one night plus seven days? What does he envisage as happening during the octave (or, should one say, the heptad?) of the Festival?

D and P have radically differing views of the chronology of events which took place following the exodus—and of the related question, the itinerary which the Israelites followed.[2] In the final edition of the itinerary in Exod. 12.37-42; 13.17–19.2 we have an abbreviated form

---

1. The (inconsistent) classical view is expressed by M. Noth, *A History of Pentateuchal Traditions* (Englewood Cliffs, NJ: Prentice–Hall, 1972), p. 67: the Passover is derived from an indigenous rite against 'the Destroyer', the object of whose attack was the fertility of man and beast, especially the firstborn 'because they were so highly valued'. Cf. Heb. 11.28.

2. For a standard account, cf. G.I. Davies, *The Way of the Wilderness: A Geographical Study of the Wilderness Itineraries in the Old Testament* (Cambridge, 1979).

of the P-route itemized in Num. 33.1-15: it takes Israel six weeks or more to march from the Red Sea to Sinai, from the wilderness of Shur to the wilderness of Sin and the wilderness of Sinai via the stopping places of Marah, Elim, Massah, Meribah and Rephidim (cf., e.g., Exod. 16.1; 19.1). By contrast, Deuteronomy knows nothing of any such itinerary *before* Horeb: Deut. 1.6 begins the review of events with Israel already at Horeb (cf. Deut. 4.34-35, which passes immediately from plagues and exodus to Horeb). Incidents which Exod. 15.22–19.2 portrays as taking place *before* Sinai, Deuteronomy presents as occurring *after* Horeb. Thus in Deut. 1.9-18 Moses appoints judges to help him rule the people *after* the instruction to depart from Horeb (so Num. 11.16-30); the parallel appointment in Exod. 18.13-26 takes place *before* Sinai. In Deut. 9.22 the enraging of Yahweh at Massah takes place *after* Horeb between Taberah and Kibroth-hattaavah, the post-Horeb location of which is confirmed in Num. 11.3, 34; Massah, however, is located *before* Sinai in Exod. 17.7. For Deuteronomy, Meribah is 'Meribath-kadesh' (Deut. 32.51; 33.2), which, however, is located eleven days *after* Horeb (cf. Deut. 1.2), whereas in Exod. 17.7 again Meribah is placed *before* Sinai. This variation between D and P in the chronology and itinerary of the journey leading up to Horeb/Sinai corresponds to their divergent overall conceptions: for D, Kadesh-barnea is the starting point for 38 years' wandering in the wilderness (Deut. 2.14); for P, it is reached only towards the end of the 40 years' wandering (Num. 33.36-38).

What effect has this divergence between the D and P conceptions of chronology and itinerary had on the formation of the Exodus narrative of the route from Red Sea to Horeb/Sinai, especially in Exod. 15.22–19.2? I should suggest that we have a situation similar to that in Exodus 12–13: the P editor, using materials available to him in the earlier D-version (in this case actually in Num. 11–21) has radically recast that version according to his own conceptions. In the D-version of Exodus there was *no* material in *this* location between Exod. 15.22 and 17.16 and in 18.13-26: the D-version had virtually only Exod. 18.1-12, the account of the rendezvous at the mountain of God in fulfilment of the promise in Exod. 3.12. This does not mean that some of the remaining material in Exod. 15.22–19.2 is not strongly marked with D characteristics (especially in Exod. 17–18) or that all the material therein is the creation of P. Rather, P as editor has drawn on D material already lying to hand in Numbers 11–21 and has transposed and refashioned it for his own purposes (the clearest example is Exod. 17.6, where Yahweh stands on the rock on Horeb—the D-term for P's 'Sinai'—which Israel is not to reach until ch. 19!). This provides an example of why redaction criticism is essential. It is totally misleading, as it is in ch. 12, to try to divide Exod. 15.22–19.2 into 'sources', as on the old literary criticism. One must work here with the concept of redaction: there was scarcely any D-'source' material present *in this context* in the D-version of Exodus; yet D-material has been re-used here from elsewhere in the P-edition of these chapters.

What impact, then, do these findings have on our understanding of the D-concept of the octave of the Passover? I should suggest that the following is a possible reconstruction of D-chronology of the one night plus seven days period of the Festival. After the night of the escape from Egypt, Israel passes in three days directly from Red Sea to Horeb: compare the speed implied by Exod. 19.4, 'I have carried you on eagles' wings and brought you to myself'; compare, too, Moses' request of Pharaoh that he lead Israel on a three-day journey into wilderness (Exod. 3.18; 5.3; 8.23; [15.22 is a context edited by P]) to hold a *ḥag*, a pilgrimage-festival (Exod. 5.1; 10.9) with flocks and herds, to *sacrifice* (*zbḥ*) to Yahweh (cf. the Deuteronomic concept of the Passover). For three days they prepare themselves at Horeb (although Exod. 19.10-11, 15-16 is now in a P-edited context); on the third of these, that is, the sixth day of the Festival, Yahweh reveals the Decalogue directly in the sight and hearing of the people (Exod. 20); Moses writes the remainder of the revelation, the Book of the Covenant, overnight and on the following day (Exod. 24.4), that is, the seventh of the Festival, the covenant is formally concluded. That is why in Deut. 16.8 the last day of the Festival of Passover is called an *caseret*, a 'solemn assembly'. The Passover pericope in the D-version of Exodus thus runs forward to Exod. 24.8 (Exod. 24.12 begins the next section of the D-presentation, Moses' forty days and nights on the mountain).

Where, then, does the D-version of the Exodus Passover begin? The Passover pericope in the D-version also has strong links with the Exodus narrative preceding ch. 12. To appreciate this we have once more to return to Deuteronomy, to the legislation on the Passover. It is striking that, in Deuteronomy, the legislation on the Passover in Deut. 16.1-8 is immediately preceded in Deut. 15.19-23 by the legislation on the presentation of firstlings, precisely the institution which provides the envelope around the Passover in Exod. 13.1-2, 11-16. Not only so; firstlings–Passover in Deuteronomy are immediately preceded by the legislation on the release of Hebrew slaves (Deut. 15.12-18). In this sequence, the release of Hebrew slaves–firstlings–Passover which reflects the D-legislation, it seems to me, we have the fundamental clue for understanding not only the extent of the D-version of the Passover pericope in Exodus but also its theology.[1]

The relevance of the three sections of Deut. 15.12–16.8 in providing structural elements which give coherence to the narrative in Exodus 1–15 is, I should submit, readily apparent.

1. The legislation on the freeing of Hebrew slaves in Deut. 15.13 (*ki* t^e*šalle*^{e}*hennu hopši me*^{c}*immak lo' t*^{e}*šalle*^{e}*hennu reqam*) provides two key thematic terms for the Exodus narrative, the verb *šillaḥ*, 'release', and the adverb *reqam* coupled with the negative *lo'*, 'not empty-handed'. The verb *šillaḥ*[2] recurs in every chapter from Exodus 3–14, 40 times in all (Exod. 3.20; 4.21, 23 (2×); 5.1, 2 (2×); 6.1, 11; 7.2, 14, 16, 26, 27; 8.4, 16, 17, 24, 25, 28, 35; 9.1, 2, 7, 13, 17, 28, 35; 10.3, 4, 7, 10, 20, 27; 11.1 (2×), 10; 12.33; 13.15, 17; 14.5 [some of these re-used in P-contexts]). But the all-pervasive theme is not just the freeing of the Hebrew slaves: they are not to be freed empty-handed. Thus, although *reqam* occurs only once in Exodus 1–15 (at 3.21), that occurrence is highly significant inasmuch as it is in the context of the first occurrence of *šillaḥ*:

> I will stretch out my hand and smite the Egyptians with all the miraculous deeds which I shall perform among them. Then they will release you. I will give this people favour in the eyes of the Egyptians so that, when you go, you will not go empty-handed.

1.   For diverging studies of how DtrH is modelled on D as the casting of law into narrative, see G. Brauli, 'Die Abfolge der Gesetze im Deuteronomium 12–26 und der Dekalog', *BETL* 68 (1985), pp. 252-72; 'Zur Abfolge. . . Deuteronomium 16,18–21.23: Weitere Beobachtungen', *Bib* 69 (1988), pp. 63-91. The suggestion of C. Carmichael (*Law and Narrative in the Bible* [Ithaca, NY: Cornell University Press, 1985], as in his earlier *The Ten Commandments* [Oxford Centre for Postgraduate Studies, 1983]) that the laws are formulated in response to issues raised in the narratives seems to me to be precisely the opposite of the actual process so far, at least, as Exodus is concerned.

2.   Other verbs 'to release', e.g., *g'l, grš, hwṣy', hwšy', ḥṣyl, pdh*, might have been used.

The phrase 'give favour in the eyes of the Egyptians' recurs in 12.36 (cf. 11.2-3) in the context of 'spoiling the Egyptians', so that, in my view, the traditional interpretation whereby the spoiling of the Egyptians is understood as compensation for the years of the slave's work in accordance with the Deuteronomic law in Deut. 15.13-14 is fully justified.[1]

2. An even more fundamental idea is provided by the legislation on firstlings. The true focus of the D-version of Exodus 13 is not Passover but the dedication of the firstborn. The pre-eminence of the offering of firstlings is made clear in Exod. 13.1-2, where it is communicated as direct word of God. The instruction for the ensuing one-night-plus-seven-day Passover is reduced in status as Moses' own instruction. This dedication of the firstborn in connection with Passover is another of the revolutionary features of the Deuteronomic reformation. It was not simply the Passover that was centralized; the centralization of the cult, that is to say the abolition of the local sanctuaries, also involved centralization of the offering of the firstlings. These could now no longer be offered as in B on the eighth day after birth at the local sanctuary; D, accordingly, has to make provision for their offering yearly in connection with the Passover. This revolutionary step provides the occasion for no-doubt revolutionary theological reflection. The word b^ekor, 'firstborn', is equally a thematic term of Exodus 1–15 (4.22, 23; 11.5 [4×]; 12.29 [4×]; 13.2, 13, 15 [4×] [12.12 is re-use by P] are the relevant occurrences). The first occurrence in the context of 4.21-23, with the key word *šillaḥ* also occurring three times, thus sets the scene for the whole D Passover pericope:

> Yahweh said to Moses, 'When you go back to Egypt, all the wonders which I have put in your power you will work in Pharaoh's presence. But I will harden his heart and he will not release the people. You will say to Pharaoh, "This is what Yahweh has said: 'Israel is my son, my firstborn. I have said to you, "Release my son so that he may serve me." But you have refused to release him. Therefore I am about to slay your son, your firstborn'"'.'

These words contain all the ingredients of the following D-narrative down to Exodus 13: the focus is the dedication of Israel to Yahweh as

---

1. Cf. D. Daube, *The Exodus Pattern in the Bible* (London: Faber & Faber, 1963), pp. 22-23, 50-54.

Yahweh's son in the person of their firstborn sons dedicated in association with the Passover. In contrast to the illogicality of the P-edition where the plague narrative culminates in the Passover, the concept of Israel as Yahweh's firstborn in the D-version provides the logic for the culminating tenth plague and the link with the whole plague cycle: if Egypt will not let Israel, Yahweh's firstborn, go free, then they will be forced to release them at the cost of their firstborn. The concept of Israel as Yahweh's son is, of course, Deuteronomic (Deut. 14.1).

This cycle of ideas may explain the enigmatic narrative in Exod. 4.24-26, the incident in the wayside inn when Yahweh attempts to kill Moses, which immediately follows the passage I have just cited. It is at the cost of the dedication of his firstborn son through circumcision that Moses is saved. It is fitting that the leader of the people who are dedicated as Yahweh's firstborn by the dedication of their firstborn should himself be dedicated by the dedication of his firstborn.[1]

3. On this argument the whole span of Exod. 1.1–24.8 in so far as it is Deuteronomistic must be taken together as the D Passover pericope. Under the heading of Passover, understood in the revolutionary sense of a one-night-plus-seven-day Festival, and interpreted in the light of the equally revolutionary association with it of the dedication of the firstlings, the D-writer has linked together the themes of the Hebrews as Yahweh's sons, redeemed from slavery, dedicated as his firstborn and bound in a relationship to him of awe, which is sealed in the formal tie of covenant. The Passover on this conception is Israel's annual sacramental actualization and participation in these truths; it is not merely an apotropaic rite lest Israel suffer the same fate as the Egyptians nor is it merely a celebration of liberation.

One may well ask what the gains are of recovering this D-layer in Exodus 1–24. I should suggest there are at least three. (1) There are phenomena here which have to be explained. There are varieties of witness to what the Passover was, the interrelationship of which has to be clarified. The biblical text is in contradiction about the extent and character of the Passover. The canon has at times, and certainly here, a curiously jagged, dialectical, character, which cannot be ignored. (2) This D-layer in Exodus provides the narrative accompaniment to the law of Deut. 15.12–16.8, and especially of 16.1-8, which other-

---

1.   B.P. Robinson ('Zipporah to the Rescue: A Contextual Study of Exodus iv 24-6', *VT* 36 [1986], pp. 447-61) associates the blood with that of Passover.

wise hangs suspended in the air without rationale. The Deuteronomic legislation in Deut. 15.12–16.8 is reproduced in narrative form in the D-version of Exodus 1–24 (as, one suspects, much of the Deuteronomistic History reproduces in narrative form other parts of the D law code, e.g., Deut. 17 on the judges period and the monarchy). (3) Even if all this analysis were entirely false, it may still have brought into clearer focus one aspect of the narrative—the importance of the concept of Israel as Yahweh's firstborn, which otherwise tends to be lost in the presentation of the Passover in the final form of the text. There are cases when the danger is that the final form of the text in its obliterative power is *less* than the sum of its parts, if these parts are not given due weight in and for themselves.

The significance of the Passover for the P-edition is the significance of the Passover in the familiar 'final form' of the text, of the text 'as it stands'. As such, it is probably superfluous to try to say anything further on it. However, the recovery of the prior edition of the text in the D-version does enable a number of distinctive features of the P-edition to be highlighted.

For P, the Passover pericope ends at Exod. 15.21. In P, the Passover is much more restricted; it is a festival in its own right with its own significance, rather than, as in the D-version, an all-encompassing framework within which all manner of institutions and affirmations are gathered. The emphasis is now on the celebration of and sharing in the act of freeing by Yahweh and of sparing his own people, not on the obligations thereby imposed on Israel which culminate in the terms of the Book of the Covenant. The P-writer has driven a wedge between the act of God affirmed at Passover and the covenant obligations imposed on Israel by inserting the pre-Sinai cycle of rebellion and murmuring in the wilderness in Exod. 15.22–19.2.

Whereas D envisages the possibility of unitary, harmonious existence through obedience—Yahweh's unbroken relationship to Israel his firstborn son who is dedicated and bound to him in the blood-tie of the covenant, which, although it has passed through the trauma of the golden calf incident, can be remade on the same terms by God's mercy despite Israel's unfaithfulness—the P-writer is profoundly pessimistic about the realizability of covenant obedience in life as it presently is. In the wilderness, the metaphorical, all-encompassing wilderness of this world, there is a profound alienation between God and his people. The revelation of the unattainable covenant response required must now culminate in the atonement cultus in Leviticus. The route to dedication is no longer through the holistic concept of 'a kingdom of priests and a holy nation' (Exod. 19.6; cf. Deut. 14.1-2) but is envisaged in terms of hierarchy: the commonality are rigorously excluded at the foot of the mountain.

D's concept of Passover has, therefore, to be revised by P: no longer is it the holistic celebration of the whole people with access to the temple cultus for the slaying of their victims and participation in the feast. The offering of firstlings disappears from view as an annual focus of dedication of Israel as Yahweh's firstborn expressed through the dedication of their own firstborn: in Numbers 18 it is submerged as part of the emoluments of the priesthood (offered monthly, Num. 18.16?). The domestic Passover is separated from the temple Festival of Unleavened Bread. The two poles of worship—intimacy and objectivity, accessibility and inaccessibility—are now institutionally separated. P recreates religious intimacy in his development of the Passover as a household rite; this is not the cloying intimacy of personal, individualized spirituality but the robust intimacy which affirms the unity of the family and solidarity with the neighbour. But the other pole of religion, the sense of awe at the unattainable mystery of the otherness of God, is now institutionalized in the rites of the temple with its hierarchy of holiness, which are detached from Passover and attached to Unleavened Bread and the other pilgrimage Festivals. P has radically polarized the practicable domestic aspects of religion and the unattainable holiness expressed through the temple cult.

FROM EVIDENCE TO EDIFICE:
FOUR FALLACIES ABOUT THE SABBATH

Heather A. McKay

Introduction

Everyone 'knows about' the biblical sabbath, and their 'knowledge' regularly includes the following assertions about the sabbath and the religious practices that took place on it:

1. Sabbath was a 'cornerstone of religious practice' in ancient Israel.[1]
2. Sabbath was a day of worship for Jews in Old Testament times.[2]
3. Jews worshipped in synagogues on the sabbath in New Testament times.[3]

---

1. D.A. Glatt and J.H. Tigay, 'Sabbath', in *Harper's Bible Dictionary* (San Francisco: Harper & Row, 1985), p. 888; J. Morgenstern, *The Interpreter's Dictionary of the Bible*, IV (New York: Abingdon Press, 1962), pp. 137-39.
2. W. Rordorf, *Sunday: The History of the Day of Rest and Worship in the Earliest Centuries of the Christian Church* (London: SCM Press, 1968), pp. 53-54; G.F. Hasel, 'The Sabbath in the Pentateuch', in *The Sabbath in Scripture and History* (ed. K.A. Strand; Washington, DC: Review and Herald Publishing Corporation, 1982), pp. 21-43, esp. p. 33; R.E. Clements, *God and Temple* (Oxford: Basil Blackwell, 1965), p. 130; N.-E.A. Andreasen, *The Old Testament Sabbath: A Tradition-Historical Investigation* (SBLDS, 7; Missoula, MT: SBL, 1972), pp. 251-54; M. Greenberg, 'Sabbath', *EncJud*, XIV (Jerusalem: Keter, 1972), p. 560; *Concise Dictionary of the Bible* (ed. S. Neill, J. Goodwin and A. Dowle; London: Lutterworth, 1967), p. 273, but note the opposite conclusion on p. 332.
3. D.E. Gowan, *Bridge between the Testaments* (Allison Park, PA: Pickwick Publications, 1984), pp. 158, 279-80; R. Posner, 'Synagogue', *EncJud*, XV, p. 582; H.H. Rowley, *Worship in Ancient Israel* (London: SPCK, 1967), pp. 227-28.

4. Jesus of Nazareth attended regular worship in synagogues on the sabbath.[1]

But these assertions are assumptions which beg various questions, and therefore do not merit our assent. If accepted uncritically, they help to construct a sabbath edifice in the mind, filling the gaps between pieces of genuine knowledge for the sake of cosmetic completeness. A fresh scrutiny of the textual evidence available will improve our understanding of the sabbath, and allow the four assertions to be replaced by more reliable statements. Thereafter, if gaps remain in our edifice, then at least they can be seen for what they are.

Background

Sabbath observance is plainly and frequently enjoined in the Hebrew Bible.[2] There is no lack of clarity about the command to do no work on the sabbath. The biblical sabbath was a weekly day of rest, observed by Jewish communities, at least from the postexilic period,[3] and on that basis, we can look at the four assertions that this paper contends are fallacies.

1. *The Sabbath was a Cornerstone of Religious Practice in Ancient Israel*

The Hebrew Bible describes a sabbath of rest for the ordinary people, and, for the priests, a day, among other days, on which they carried out religious duties. In *historical reality*, the groups could show their reverence for the sabbath day by special behaviour, and in the *texts* this behaviour could be described.[4] Comparing the behaviour prescribed for different holy days is a way of assessing their relative importance, and should allow us to see if the sabbath was so important in religious practice as to merit the name 'cornerstone'. The most suitable recurring holy day for comparison with the sabbath is New

1. D.A. Carson, 'Jesus and the Sabbath in the Four Gospels', in *From Sabbath to Lord's Day: A Biblical, Historical and Theological Investigation* (ed. D.A. Carson; Grand Rapids: Zondervan, 1982), pp. 57-97, esp p. 71.
2. Exod. 20.10; 31.14, 15; 35.2; Lev. 16.29, 31; 23.3; Deut. 5.13, 14; Jer. 17.22, 24.
3. Andreasen, *Old Testament Sabbath*, pp. 235-36.
4. With the caveat that the writers of a text have power over what it says, and may be biased in their descriptions to a greater or lesser degree.

Moon, so we will now look at how these two days are dealt with in the texts of the Hebrew Bible.

A study of the two days shows that the sabbath is treated with extreme reverence in certain texts of the Hebrew Bible,[1] but New Moon has greater status than the sabbath in other texts. The picture is far from straightforward, however, because there are anomalies in the way New Moon is referred to in the texts. For example, in 1 Samuel 20, New Moon is portrayed as an important religious occasion, from which absenting oneself was a serious matter. Yet this is the only passage to speak of New Moon in this way. On the other hand, we know that New Moon was widely recognized as a holy day, for it occurs, linked with one or more other holy days, in 17 places in the Hebrew Bible. The frequent pairing of the days, New Moon and sabbath, has led several scholars to look for similarities between the two days, but they have found little stipulation for worship of any kind on the sabbath as opposed to the trumpet-blowing and sacrificing of New Moon.[2]

The cultic calendars of Leviticus, Numbers and Ezekiel (see Tables 1–3) deal with holy days and the practices required on them, but do not present identical sets of instructions. Two out of the three show New Moon to be more important than the sabbath. This indicates that we are dealing with changes of perspective, or of practice.

Table 1: Numbers 28–29

Daily	2 lambs
Sabbath	twofold daily offering
New Moon	2 bulls, 1 ram, 7 lambs and 1 goat
Passover	exactly as New Moon and do no work
Firstfruits	exactly as Passover

---

1. The manna incident in Exod. 16; the disgust about trade in Neh. 13.15-22 and Jer. 17; the power of the sabbath to overcome handicaps to acceptability by God in Isa. 56.

2. H.-J. Kraus, *Worship in Israel* (Oxford: Basil Blackwell, 1966), pp. 76-80; G.F. Hasel and W.G.C. Murdoch, 'The Sabbath in the Prophetic and Historical Literature of the Old Testament', in Strand (ed.), *The Sabbath in Scripture and History*, p. 45; S. Kubo, 'The Sabbath in the Intertestamental Period', in Strand (ed.), *The Sabbath in Scripture and History*, p. 57; A.S. Herbert, *Worship in Ancient Israel* (Ecumenical Studies in Worship, 5; London: Lutterworth, 1959), pp. 45-46.

1st day of 7th month	as above but blow trumpets and only kill 1 bull
10th day	as 1st day and also afflict oneself
15th day	do no work, keep a feast for seven days and make an offering
(?Booths)	13 bulls, 2 rams, 14 lambs and 1 goat
2nd day of 7	12 bulls, 2 rams, 14 lambs and 1 goat, decreasing by 1 bull daily till the 7th day, then
8th day	1 bull, 1 ram, 7 lambs and 1 goat

Table 2: Ezekiel 45–46

1st day of 1st month	1 bull
Passover	1 bull, then 7 bulls, 7 rams and 1 goat for 7 days
15th day of 7th month	the same as Passover
Sabbath	6 lambs and 1 ram
New Moon	1 bull, 6 lambs and 1 ram
Appointed feasts	general instructions
Daily	1 lamb

Table 3: Leviticus 23

Appointed feasts	general heading
Sabbath	no mention of sacrifice
Appointed feasts	general heading
Passover	unspecified offering by fire for 7 days
First fruits	1 lamb
Weeks	7 lambs, 1 bull, 2 rams, 1 goat, 2 lambs
Day of Solemn Rest	blow trumpets, do no work, make an offering by fire
(1st of 7th month)	
Day of Atonement	unspecified offering by fire
Booths	unspecified offerings by fire

In Numbers, the New Moon offering is much greater than the sabbath offering, by many factors of extravagance, indicating that New Moon was almost as important to the authors as the three pilgrim feasts, and much more important than the sabbath. The sabbath has, in fact, no peculiar listing of sacrifices, but merely an implicit double dose of the daily offering.

The listings in Ezekiel show the sabbath and New Moon as days of similar importance, although New Moon has a clear edge over sabbath, in amounts of livestock slaughtered. The sabbath, however, has much more importance than a weekday, which was not the case in the Numbers material. The sabbath is here more important than a weekday but not as important as New Moon.

The material in Leviticus contains two references to the sabbath,[1] which look as if they have been added to an existing cultic sequence. The first describes the sabbath as the day of solemn and holy rest and interrupts the preamble to the cultic calendar, which then repeats itself and carries on.

> The Lord said to Moses, 'Say to the people of Israel, The appointed feasts of the Lord which you shall proclaim as holy convocations, my appointed feasts, are these. Six days shall work be done; but on the seventh day is a sabbath of solemn rest, a holy convocation; you shall do no work; it is a sabbath to the Lord in all your dwellings. These are the appointed feasts of the Lord, the holy convocations, which you shall proclaim at the time appointed for them.'

The second tucks the sabbath into the middle of a reprise of general directions for holy days almost at the end of the calendar, right in the middle of the lists of offerings, apparently in parenthesis to the word, 'day':

> These are the appointed feasts of the Lord, which you shall proclaim as times of holy convocation, for presenting to the Lord offerings by fire, burnt offerings and cereal offerings, sacrifices and drink offerings, each on its proper day; besides the sabbaths of the Lord, and besides your gifts, and besides all your votive offerings, and besides all your freewill offerings, which you give to the Lord.

Sabbaths are suddenly part of the list of lesser offerings!

Surprise at the intrusion of the sabbath in this sequence of feasts is not new. Baumgarten quotes the rabbinic question, 'What place has the sabbath in the chapter dealing with festivals?'[2] We can see that the rabbi who asked that question must have considered the sabbath to be

1. Lev. 23.3, 38.
2. J.M. Baumgarten, 'The Counting of the Sabbath', *VT* 16 (1966), pp. 277-86, esp. p. 278.

other than a feast day. Also the two pieces about the sabbath jar badly
with the rest of the material and seem like additions to the text. But
why should the sabbath intrude into a list of feast days? We are
impelled to envisage a group in whose interests it would be to make
the insertion, a sabbath-honouring group, editing Leviticus. To them
the sabbath was so important that it had to appear, and New Moon was
of zero importance, for it is certainly not given a place in this particular list. When we remember the many couplings of the days, New
Moon and the sabbath, in the Hebrew Bible, the absence of New Moon
here is more significant. New Moon has been effectively eliminated
from the proceedings; but although the sabbath is included, it is without a sacrifice prescription.

We can see a gradation of the importance of the sabbath in the three
texts. The Numbers material values New Moon a great deal more
highly than the sabbath, and the book of Ezekiel follows suit, although
not to the same extent. The sabbath there is also more important than
a weekday. The editors of the Leviticus text revered the sabbath
greatly as a holy day, but not as a feast day with sacrifices, and placed
the sabbath rather ruthlessly in amongst the feast days, like an outsider
being ushered to the head of a queue.

It would require great subtlety of exegesis to try to uncover the
idiolects of changing or rival factions writing in the Hebrew Bible and
that is an enterprise quite beyond the scope of this paper, but it is
possible to assess the effect of time on the esteem with which New
Moon was regarded by looking at a text from a much later time.
Philo, in the early first century CE, makes it plain that New Moon was
still a very important holy day for Jews. To be sure, he makes a
definite and pejorative contrast between the celebration of the day of
the New Moon by 'some states', and the 'sacred seventh day' of the
Jewish nation,[1] but he elsewhere devotes a large section of apologetic
material to the propriety of Jews celebrating the day of the New
Moon.[2] However abstruse and lengthy Philo's justifications might
seem to us, they show that at his time New Moon had still some
importance—although secondary to the sabbath. The New Moon faded
very slowly from the religious consciousness of the Jews, and is

1. Philo, *Dec.* 96.
2. Philo, *Spec. Leg.* 2.140-44.

mentioned once in the New Testament exhortations to Christians on resisting the criticisms of Jews.[1]

We can also assess the effect of time on the esteem in which the sabbath was held by looking at texts from the later Persian period, and comparing their attitudes to the sabbath with those of the Hebrew Bible. And we find, complementing the waning in importance of the New Moon feast day, the waxing of the status of the sabbath in the Apocryphal and Deutero-canonical writings.

In some of these texts the sabbath day seems to have acquired a rather different character from the other six days, in that it is no longer merely one of them set aside for rest, but is also a day with some intrinsic quality of holiness, which empowers the sabbath to affect other days and people's behaviour on them; the sabbath's power extends through *time*. This can be seen in the book of Judith where the sabbath, *and also the day preceding it*, are days when the pious widow, in the midst of her mourning rites, is free of the requirement to fast.[2]

In *Jubilees* there is an increase in the *thrall* of the sabbath as evidenced by the widening of application of the death penalty for breaking, defiling or polluting the sabbath, even by such acts as marital relations or planning the next day's journey.[3] The sabbath was able to curb more aspects of life than work only.

And, later still, Philo makes a somewhat illogical extension of sabbath rest to *plants* (since they could only be involved in a passive sense or at the most complicitly!), by recommending that his readers spare even the plant kingdom from involvement with work on the sabbath by refraining from plucking fruit from the resting trees.[4]

All these texts, by their attitude to, and reverence for, the sabbath, show that this particular holy day was in the ascendant as the Jews moved into the Common Era. The fact that its importance was increasing at that time points backwards in time to a point when its status was less. The assumption that the sabbath was always the dominant holy day is a fallacy, and the conclusion can be made that the sabbath became the most important holy day in Israel during the last two centuries BCE.

1. Col. 2.16.
2. Jdt. 8.6.
3. *Jub.* 50; cf. *Damascus Covenant* cols. 10, 11.
4. Philo, *Vit. Mos.* 2.21-22.

2. The Sabbath was a Day of Worship for Jews in Old Testament Times

This statement is misleading, for the texts describe the sabbath as a day of rest only, without mentioning any worship for the common people. The priests worshipped in the temple on the sabbath, but that was no more than their everyday practice.

There are no grounds for statements such as, 'God instituted the sabbath for His people' to be 'celebrated as a day of joyful assembling before God' in which 'their devotions, praises and thanksgivings... flow from grateful and appreciative hearts'.[1] Sustaining that view is only possible if no attempt is made to distinguish between those texts which speak of sabbath observance and those which speak of sabbath worship.[2]

Worship, in my view, is a purposive activity, whereby people of similar beliefs assemble to carry out similar rites and rituals in order to pay homage, with adoration and awe, to a particular, named deity. Worship may include psalms, prayers and blessings, or sacrificing.[3] Instructions for, or descriptions of, these types of activity in the texts will be here regarded as evidences of worship either expected or carried out by the Israelite community.

Psalms were sung in the temple every day, so it is impossible to consider psalm-singing to be a form of worship peculiar to the sabbath, especially since only one psalm, Psalm 92, has as its title 'Song for the Sabbath Day', and no other psalm refers to the sabbath at all.[4] This makes a less than impressive contrast with the 52 sabbath psalms referred to at Qumran.[5] However, supposing in spite of that

1. H.H.P. Dressler, 'The Sabbath in the Old Testament', in Carson (ed.), *From Sabbath to Lord's Day*, p. 35.

2. See Rordorf, *Sunday*, p. 43, and W. Harrelson, 'The Religion of Israel', in *A Companion to the Bible* (ed. H.H. Rowley; Edinburgh: T. & T. Clark, 2nd edn, 1963), p. 347, for examples of this.

3. Reading of sacred texts, from the point of view of learning them or understanding them, is not considered to be worship in this paper, unless the aspect of addressing the deity by the reading is made explicit.

4. For the view that the titles of psalms were assigned at a date after their composition, when conclusions were drawn about their suitability for use in worship, see W.O.E. Oesterley, *The Psalms* (London: SPCK, 1959), p. 18; C.A. Briggs and E.G. Briggs, *The Book of Psalms* (ICC; Edinburgh: T. & T. Clark, 1907), p. 283.

5. J.A. Sanders, *Discoveries in the Judean Desert of Jordan. IV. The Psalms*

that psalm-singing were a regular feature of worship on holy days (including the sabbath), the texts do not reveal who was involved in the singing. There is evidence in Chronicles and Nehemiah that there were teams of temple singers,[1] but whether others could listen, or join in, is never made explicit in the biblical sources. All we can be certain of is that temple officials sang psalms as part of their performance of worship; nothing in the texts points to participation by the common people.

Another common form of worship, prayer, is similarly not referred to as part of worship on the sabbath, but is rather a personal activity which can take place anywhere, not excluding a holy site: for example, Hannah's prayer at the shrine in Shiloh,[2] which took place on Elkanah's annual visit to worship and sacrifice there. But this instance of prayer tells us nothing about activities on the sabbath. And references to prayer in the temple are never connected to the sabbath.

We might look to details about sacrifices to fill out the content of worship. But when we do that we find that only priests were actually involved in sacrificing[3] and it is nowhere stated that the people were present at the sacrifice session.[4] Haran endorses this perception when he says that priestly 'ritual takes place in the arcana of the house of God, unseen by the people as a whole'.[5]

A thorough reading of the Old Testament has revealed no details of worship behaviour, as defined above, on the sabbath, by the ordinary people, as opposed to the priests who operated in the temple cult. Hence it can be stated that the sabbath was not a day of worship for the ordinary Jewish believer in Old Testament times.

Scroll of Cave 11 (Oxford: Clarendon Press, 1972), pp. 91-92. This reinforces my previous conclusion that there was significant development of sabbath worship through the last centuries BCE.

1.   1 Chron. 6.31-33; 9.33; Neh. 7.1, 44; 11.22.
2.   1 Sam. 1, 2.
3.   See especially Lev. 1–6.
4.   Ezek. 45–46, especially 46.2-10, but note that this describes a vision of the future restored temple.
5.   M. Haran, *Temples and Temple-Service in Ancient Israel* (Oxford: Clarendon Press, 1978), p. 224.

3. *Jews Assembled for Worship on the Sabbath in New Testament Times*[1]
In this assertion, the hidden pitfalls lie in assuming that:

1. Any sabbath assembly of Jews would be for worship.
2. Any assembly would be held in a particular, purpose-built building.
3. The practices recorded in the New Testament were long-standing ones.

Evidence will be presented to show that, in New Testament times, Jews met together for varied activities on the sabbath, that the name for the location, whether social or physical, was far from univocal, and that development of the institution through time has to be taken into consideration before any definite conclusions can be drawn.

Since sabbath worship, to take place at all, would require a locus, and the developed form of Jewish worship that has continued until today takes place in buildings called synagogues, then it would seem possible that clarifications might be found by researches into early synagogues and/or the assemblies that met in them.

That previously long-held beliefs about synagogues have been recently opened to question can be seen in the critical re-assessment of the evidence for early synagogues by Gutmann, Chiat, and Grabbe.[2] They review the evidence for synagogues during the period of the Second Temple. Grabbe is convinced of the reality of synagogues in the Diaspora from the second century BCE, accepting equation of the terms προσευχή and συναγωγή,[3] but finds the archaeological evidence for synagogues in Palestine to be slender before the first

---

1. After I had completed this article, my attention was drawn to the excellent article of H.C. Kee, 'The Transformation of the Synagogue after 70 CE: Its Import for Early Christianity', *NTS* 36 (1990), pp. 1-24, which covers much common ground and reaches many similar conclusions.

2. J. Gutmann, 'Synagogue Origins: Theories and Facts', in *Ancient Synagogues: The State of Research* (ed. J. Gutmann; Missoula, MT: Scholars Press, 1981), pp. 1-6; M. Chiat, 'First-Century Synagogue Architecture: Methodological Problems', in Gutmann (ed.), *Ancient Synagogues*, pp. 49-60; *idem, Handbook of Synagogue Architecture* (Brown Judaic Studies, 29; Chico, CA: Scholars Press, 1982); L.L. Grabbe, 'Synagogues in Pre-70 Palestine: A Re-Assessment', *JTS* ns 39 (1988), pp. 401-10.

3. Grabbe, 'Synagogues', pp. 402-403.

century of the Common Era, a time when the literary evidence of the New Testament becomes pertinent. Gutmann and Chiat take the stance that there are no certain first-century synagogue remains in Palestine.

I do not accept equation of the terms προσευχή and συναγωγή, following a close scrutiny of Philo's and Josephus's writings (see below). Thus architectural evidence for the existence of προσευχαί is not here regarded as evidence for the existence of synagogues. The strongest evidence for synagogues is the literary evidence of Josephus and the New Testament.

One piece of architectural evidence demands our consideration, however, and that is the Theodotus inscription,[1] which is usually referred to as providing proof of the existence of a synagogue in Jerusalem in the first century CE.[2] At the same time this existence of a synagogue is taken to be proof of weekly worship services close to the temple. But a closer reading shows that several assumptions have to be made to reach that conclusion. Reading the text of the inscription without assumptions points to rather a different conclusion.

> Theodotus, son of Quettonos (Vettenos), priest and archisynagogus, son of an archisynagogus, grandson of an archisynagogus, built this synagogue for the reading of the law and for the teaching of the Commandments, and the hostel and the chambers and water fittings for the accommodation of those who [coming] from abroad have need of it, of which [synagogue] the foundations were laid by his fathers and by the Elders and Simonides.

The inscription commemorates a man who ruled the synagogue following his father and grandfather, and who had built this synagogue, a building in which the reading of the law took place and the teaching of the commandments. The first two generations in the family did not 'build' this synagogue, although they 'ruled' it. They were responsible for the foundations, but they could hardly rule over those. So they were rulers of the *gathering*, and their grandson was the one who provided or completed the *building*.[3]

1. Chiat, *Handbook*, pp. 201-202.
2. The original dating was on palaeographic grounds, but according to Kee ('Transformation', pp. 7-8) not convincing; a date at the end of the second century is to be preferred.
3. Cf. Lk. 7.5 for a literary reference to someone building a synagogue, in this case a Roman centurion, apparently not a member of the synagogue.

No mention is made of the day or days on which the law would be read; daily is just as likely as weekly. But important enough to merit even more space in the inscription is the hospitality suite, with 'water fittings' for the accommodation of travellers. The stone which bears the inscription was part of a building which acted as a place for withdrawal from daily life, to read and study Torah. No doubt Jews who were travelling needed a place to rest on the sabbath—and what better place than a hostel–synagogue complex? But in this inscription, there is no mention of any practices that we have included in the term 'worship'.

It needs to be pointed out, however, that literary and archaeological evidence should be considered separately, and that the information the two types of source supply cannot be conflated willy-nilly. This is especially important because the same word συναγωγή can be used to mean the assembly of people or the building in which they met. All references to happenings in a synagogue cannot be assumed to be references to a building, or to describe activities in a building. In this paper, descriptions of doors, entering, seats, or of arson, threatened or perpetrated, will be regarded as literary evidence of a building in the mind of an author writing about assemblies of Jews.

Philo of Alexandria would seem a likely source of literary evidence for synagogues and sabbath worship, but a search through Philo's literary corpus to find details of sabbath worship in synagogues yields little in the way of evidence. For while he often refers to the many and ubiquitous προσευχαί[1] of Alexandria and Rome,[2] where the Jews met weekly to read and study their laws, and which were, at times, the focus of the community's hostility to Jews,[3] and also uses another word for what appears to be the same institution—προσευκτήρια, places of prayer, which he describes as being similar to the philosophical schools of the Greeks, in providing 'edification and betterment in moral principle and conduct'[4]—he does not use the term 'synagogue' in any descriptions of usual Jewish sabbath activities.[5] The sabbath day

---

1. Translated as 'prayer-houses', 'houses of prayer' or 'meeting-houses'.
2. Philo, *Leg. Gai.* 138, 157.
3. Philo, *Leg. Gai.* 132-38; *Flacc.* 41-50.
4. Philo, *Vit. Mos.* 2.216.
5. The Loeb translation gives 'synagogue' as a translation of προσευχή, in the English version of *Flacc.* 45, 47, and *Leg. Gai.* 346, and 'synagogues' for συναγώγια in *Leg. Gai.* 311.

meetings he does describe were not primarily concerned with worship
as I have defined it, for he states that 'each seventh day there stand
wide open in every city thousands of schools of good sense. . . in
which the *scholars* sit. . . with full attention'.[1]

To help his readers form a clearer picture of what happened at the
sabbath assemblies, Philo says that those present sat 'together in a
respectful and orderly manner' and heard 'the laws read so that none
should be in ignorance of them'. They sat in silence except for adding
something to signify approval of what was read. A priest or elder who
was present read and expounded the holy laws to them.[2] It is apparent
that, in Alexandria at the time of Philo, the sabbath had become a day
of gathering for study and contemplation as well as a day of rest; but a
parallel development as a day of worship was not necessarily a part of
this process of change. The Jews came to a building called a
προσευχή where they could sit, to receive and exchange instruction,
but not explicitly to offer homage.

Sabbath activities that match our definition of worship can first be
discovered in Philo's description of the *daily* religious life of the
Therapeutae, who, as well as reading the holy Scriptures and seeking
'wisdom from their ancestral philosophy by taking it as an allegory',
also *composed 'hymns and psalms to God'*. But their *sabbath* meetings
are described in terms indistinguishable from those of the Jews in the
προσευχαί. Philo describes how they assemble together on the
seventh day, sitting

> in order according to their age in the proper attitude, with their hands
> inside the robe, the right hand between the breast and chin and the left
> withdrawn along the flank. Then the senior among them. . . gives a well
> reasoned and wise discourse [which] passes through the hearing and into
> the soul. . . they sit still and listen showing their approval merely by
> their looks and nods.[3]

However, their sanctuary, which he does not refer to by any name,
takes us into the realm of descriptions of synagogues, for he describes
it as having a double enclosure, with the women separate but within
earshot. This is rather like the popular image of the synagogue building of the Jews at the beginning of the Christian era, but here in Philo

1. Philo, *Spec. Leg.* 2.59-64 (my emphasis).
2. Philo, *Hyp.* 7.9-13.
3. Philo, *Vit. Cont.* 27-33.

it is attributed solely to the Therapeutae.

Similar to his description of the sabbath of the Therapeutae is his account of the Essenes who went on the sabbath to 'sacred spots' which—he says—'they call synagogues. There, arranged in rows according to their ages, the younger below the elder, they sit decorously as befits the occasion with attentive ears.'[1] They listened to the books read aloud and discourses, often using allegorical means of interpretation (not unlike the practice of the Therapeutae). Evidently, the word synagogue is not his word; rather, he describes *their institution* by the name *they* give it—synagogue. And this is the only occasion that Philo uses the word 'synagogue' to mean either an assembly of Jews or a building in which they met.

Further evidence of the lack of rigidity with which the names for religious meetings and religious meeting-places were applied is provided by Philo's use of yet another term for the meetings of the Jews, συναγώγια (gatherings). One usage occurs in his account of the permission, given by Augustus, for Jews to come together in *gatherings*, which were 'schools of temperance and justice', and which opened their doors to outsiders.[2] This agrees with his description of Jews congregating in προσευχαί in Alexandria. But, in the other account of these *gatherings*, he describes the Jews as appearing in public in the usual posture of 'right hand tucked inside and the left hand held close to the flank under the cloak' and assembling to read and expound their holy books and ancestral philosophy.[3] This is uncannily like the description he elsewhere gives of the Therapeutae.

We may conclude that the name for the gatherings of Jews on the sabbath and/or the name for the building in which they gathered were not applied unequivocally when Philo was writing, and similarly that the practices on the sabbath day were still varied. For he used four different names for the sabbath assembly (προσευχή, προσευκτήριον, συναγωγή, συναγώγιον), of which only προσευχή and συναγωγή refer definitely to buildings; and he also provided differing descriptions of what happened at the gatherings on the sabbath.

Philo's writings show that Jews assembled on the sabbath, not to worship, but to study and discuss Torah. There was uniformity

1. Philo, *Omn. Prob. Lib.* 81-83.
2. Philo, *Leg. Gai.* 311-12.
3. Philo, *Somn.* 123-28.

neither of practice, nor of the name for the gathering. Where a building is indicated, for example, if it were burned down by an angry mob, it is most frequently called a προσευχή.

A similar picture of sabbath activities can be culled from the late first century CE writings of Josephus. Speaking generally, Josephus says that on the sabbath Jews abstained from work and gathered to listen to the law and know it thoroughly, thus sharing Philo's perception of the Jews' sabbath activities,[1] but placing them mainly in gatherings or buildings called συναγωγαί.

Elsewhere he paints a more vivid picture of activities in the synagogue, by describing an incident at the synagogue in Caesarea where the Jews were being harassed by the local people. They, having found out that Jews regarded blood as offensive, deliberately slaughtered birds outside the entrance to the synagogue on the sabbath, when the Jews were assembling there. There was a scuffle, after which the Jews 'snatched up their copy of the Law and withdrew to Narbata'.[2]

He also writes of 'the synagogue of the Jews' at Dora, into which zealous young citizens brought an image of Tiberius, in flagrant disavowal of the rights granted to Jews by Roman law.[3] He makes it plain that the introduction of the statue stopped the place being a synagogue, and implies that its acceptability to Jews as a place of assembly was what made it into a synagogue.

But he also refers to the prayer house (προσευχή) at Tiberias as providing a large meeting-place in a similar context to the descriptions of prayer-houses in Philo.[4] This is the longest piece of writing available which describes Jews assembling in a communal building, and so it merits close scrutiny. He writes that on the sabbath 'there was a general assembly in the Prayer-house, a huge building, capable of accommodating a large crowd'. A heated political discussion, at which Josephus was not present, took place, 'and a riot would inevitably have ensued, had not the arrival of the sixth hour, at which it is our custom on the sabbath to take our midday meal, broken off the meeting'. Arriving at 7 am the next morning Josephus 'found the people already assembling in the Prayer-house, although they had no

1. Josephus, *Ant.* 16.40-46; *Apion* 2.177.
2. Josephus, *War* 2.284-92.
3. Josephus, *Ant.* 19.301.
4. Josephus, *Life* 272-303.

idea why they were being convened'. After being sent off on a spurious errand by the local leaders, Josephus returned to this meeting to defend himself against the verbal attacks of his opponents. On the next morning—Monday—another meeting, a public fast, was called. Josephus put on sword and breastplate 'as little conspicuous as possible' and went to it. He says that they were 'proceeding with the ordinary service and engaged in prayer when Jesus [a local leader] rose and began to question me about the furniture and uncoined silver which had been confiscated', asking their whereabouts. Josephus states that he expected to be murdered, then swords were drawn on both sides, but he escaped.

Josephus's descriptions, therefore, provide corroborative evidence for all the activities described by Philo, for προσευχαί and συναγώγια, but he attributes them, in the main, to buildings and/or groups called synagogues. But we have to remember that the multi-faceted session at Tiberias, incorporating a complex mixture of religion and politics, and including prayer, eating, celebration of a public fast, discussion and physical violence, took place in a προσευχή, and that the prayers of the 'ordinary service' held there were on the Monday of a public fast.

Thus there are signs that, in contrast with the writings of Philo, in the works of Josephus the word 'synagogue' was in the process of acquiring a more fixed meaning, and both the building and the institution represented the forerunner of the modern synagogue, but with the addition of political and belligerent behaviour. There is no sign of any worship service having taken place on the sabbath.

Hence we may conclude that Jews, at the end of the first century CE, did many things at their meetings in prayer-house or synagogue on every day of the week, not all of them religious or pacific. Jews travelling to Jerusalem lodged in a synagogue close to the temple. In other towns and cities Jews studied together on the sabbath but communal worship on the sabbath is not described at all.

4. *Jesus Attended Regular Sabbath Worship in Synagogues*
If sabbath synagogue worship was not a regular feature of Jewish religious life as it was known to Philo and Josephus, it seems probable that it could not have been known to Jesus either. But to explain the apparent disagreement of this proposal with the Gospels, one would need to acknowledge that the Gospel accounts which imply or recount

Jesus' attendance at sabbath worship are written with hindsight, and, in this case, that makes the vision of Jesus' world less clear. A parallel shift of perspective can be more easily detected between descriptions of Paul's preaching activities in the Epistles and in Acts.

A careful study of the relevant New Testament material shows that there is no occurrence of the word 'synagogue' in the letters of Paul, or anywhere in the Pauline corpus. Since Paul was a contemporary of Philo and Jesus this lack is worth noticing, especially as the word 'synagogue' occurs in the Gospels and Acts 65 times, 15 of the occurrences in Acts relating to visits Paul made to synagogues while travelling in the Diaspora. Paul's letters refer only to visits to churches in people's houses,[1] and to lodging with friends.[2] It looks as if the writer of Acts is describing Paul's activities in terms that were intelligible to him and his readers, and that included the synagogue building as the natural religious talking-shop in any community where Jews lived.

One major problem in dealing with the descriptions of synagogues found in the Gospels and Acts is the fact that readers seeking a historical perspective have to work within at least two time zones: that of the events described, and that of the writers/editors. It is perfectly possible that the authors present the image of the synagogue that they themselves knew, rather than a historical picture of how things were in Jesus' or Paul's day.[3]

In the book of Acts, the term 'synagogue' often means a building in which Jews met together on the sabbath to read Scripture and listen to teaching. For example, in 15.21, James says 'from early generations Moses has had in every city those who preach him, for he is read every sabbath in the synagogues', thus confirming the procedures that we have understood from Philo for προσευχαί and Josephus for synagogues.[4]

But other activities also took place in the synagogue, namely teaching, preaching, reading, almsgiving, praying, scourging, sitting, beating, disputing, speaking and imprisoning. So, just as described by

1. Rom. 16.5; 1 Cor. 16.19.
2. 1 Cor. 16.6-8.
3. The difference in the profile of synagogues between the writings of Paul (no occurrences) and the narrative about Paul in Acts (15 out of 25 total occurrences of the word) is another example of this difficulty.
4. But note also the reference to a προσευχή in Acts 16.13, which does not, however, clearly indicate a building.

Josephus, the building was not used purely as a quiet place of study!

In the Gospels we have the problem that all four have their own hidden agendas. All four paint a slightly different picture of Jesus' activities in, and comments on, the synagogue.

In John's Gospel, there are only two references to Jesus teaching in synagogues,[1] much fewer than in the Synoptics, but then there are three references to the fact that those who believe in Jesus as Christ are to be expelled from the synagogue.[2] This would point to John's community knowing of a conflict with the synagogue, and John's Jesus warns his readers of this. The two time zones, and two attitudes to the synagogue, can be clearly seen.

Mark's Jesus teaches three times in the synagogue in Galilee on the sabbath, heals in the synagogue on the sabbath, knows of rulers of the synagogue, and of best seats in the synagogue, and gives a warning to his followers of dangers of being beaten in the synagogue.[3] The synagogues warned against appear to be buildings in which disciplinary beating takes place against Christians, but the synagogue ruler Jairus falls at Jesus' feet and asks for his help. Again the two points of view are apparent.

Matthew's and Luke's Jesus shares the characteristics of Mark's, but in Luke Jesus teaches in the synagogues of Judaea as well as Galilee, reads and expounds Scriptures, Torah and prophets in the synagogue on the sabbath, and gives two warnings of danger from the synagogue authorities.[4]

So what we learn of the synagogues at the time of the writing of the Gospels and Acts, although from the point of view of threatened Christians, exactly matches the picture already painted by Philo (for προσευχαί) and Josephus (for συναγωγαί and προσευχαί), a picture of the synagogue as a place where Jews met to deal with *all* matters that were of concern to them as a community.[5] They met and argued about political matters, about innovative teaching and explanation of the Torah, they disciplined their peers for religious shortcomings, but they did not have communal worship on the sabbath. The

1. Jn 6.59; 18.20.
2. Jn 9.22; 12.42; 16.2.
3. Mk 1.21; 3.2; 5.22-38; 6.2; 12.39; 13.9.
4. Lk. 4.44; 12.11; 21.12.
5. Acts 6.9; 9.2, 20; 13.5, 14, 15, 43; 14.1; 15.21; 17.1, 10, 17; 18.4, 7, 8, 17, 19, 26; 19.8; 22.19; 24.12; 26.11.

only text which shows a definite change towards the synagogue practice of later Judaism is Lk. 4.17, where Jesus is given the book of
Isaiah to read. This is the only Gospel text to include Scriptures other
than Torah in any description of synagogue practice on the sabbath,
and the only text in the Gospel where Jesus is described as reading in a
synagogue on the sabbath. This detail is missing from the Markan and
Matthaean parallels, and the only parallel is in Acts, where the reading
of the law and the prophets is described for the synagogue in Antioch,
and implied for Jerusalem, on the sabbath.[1]

The time between the writings of Paul and Philo, on the one hand,
and the writing of the Gospels and Acts, on the other, would seem to
have marked a crucial stage in the development of either synagogue
buildings, or of the application of that name to extant buildings; and,
if Luke paints a faithful picture of the synagogues of his day when
writing Acts, he would seem also to have seen an expansion of the
synagogue's religion-centred activities over against the political ones.
The writings of Josephus belong to the same period of change, but,
perhaps because of his career interests, refer to political activities
more than to religious wrangles. The evidence that we have indicates
that synagogues did not become the religious institutions that they
have often been assumed to be until the end of the first century CE, at
the earliest.

The fallacy in our fourth statement will now be apparent. No one
worshipped in synagogues on the sabbath in first-century Palestine, so
Jesus could not have attended a service there on the sabbath.

One New Testament text that seems at first sight promising in our
search for synagogue worship is Mt. 6.5, in which Matthew's Jesus
gives advice about prayer.

> And when you pray, you must not be like the hypocrites; for they love to
> stand and pray in the synagogues and at the street corners, that they may
> be seen by men.

This does not make clear, as has been assumed,[2] that prayer was a
commonplace action in synagogues, and may even point to the reverse

---

1. ¯ Acts 13.15, 27.
2. P.A. Micklem, *St Matthew* (London: Methuen, 1917), p. 54; F.V. Filson,
A Commentary on the Gospel according to St Matthew (London: A. & C. Black,
1960), p. 94.

conclusion, that is, that praying did not normally take place in the synagogue. For what is it that is noticeable about the hypocrites in this saying? It is not their standing as they pray that is remarkable, for in Mark, Jesus refers to 'whenever you stand praying',[1] so the stance seems normal enough. No, it is the location that draws the eye. The three other New Testament references to praying in a religious building describe the location as the temple.[2] So it looks as if praying in a synagogue was just as ostentatious and odd as praying at a street corner, and not at all the normal practice of the true worshipper. Jesus could only encourage his disciples to be good Jews, after all, not good Christians!

It looks as if the name 'synagogue' and the forms of worship which are often conjured up in our mind's eye were not exclusively attached to the sabbath assemblies of the Jews till after 70 CE and at the time of the writing of the Gospels. Josephus describes one morning service with prayer in a προσευχή—but that is on a Monday of a public fast. Evidence from the Gospels shows the synagogues to be places of study of Scripture, and of religious disputation and discipline, but not of organized services of worship on the sabbath.

Thus we conclude that Jesus carried out the normal activities of Jews in the synagogue, reading and listening to Torah, disputing and determined arguing. He did not attend sabbath services of worship, for there were none at that time.

The Edifice from the Evidence

Our four original assumptions are fallacious and should be replaced by these more modest assertions.

1. The sabbath became the most important holy day in Israel during the last two centuries BCE.
2. The sabbath was not a day of worship for the ordinary Jewish believer in Old Testament times.
3. Jews could carry out many activities in the synagogue or prayer-house on every day of the week. They studied there on the sabbath in first-century Palestine, but worship is not described.

1. Mk 11.25.
2. Lk. 1.10; 18.10; Acts 22.17.

4. Jesus carried out the normal activities of Jews in the synagogue, reading and listening to Torah, disputing and determined arguing. He did not attend sabbath services of
worship, for there were none at that time.

We can be very clear about the sabbath as a day of rest, meeting,
listening, reading and expounding Scriptures for first-century
Judaism. But the addition of the worship aspect must be a later
phenomenon, with hints of its beginnings in the book of Acts.

Before that time there is a much more equivocal picture, and the
clearest evidence in favour of the traditional understanding of the
sabbath comes from the community at Qumran, or from the Essenes
and Therapeutae. The development of synagogue worship seems to
have been accelerated at the time of—and perhaps by the emergence
of—the early Christian groups. Perhaps the existence of rival factions
sharpened distinctions and hardened patterns and praxis. Certainly the
intensity of the descriptions of synagogues and controversy over them
in the Gospels would suggest that they were a great focus of attention
in the community at that time.

But in trying to chart the development of sabbath worship we must
bear in mind that description of prayer in the synagogue is reserved to
the Gospel of Matthew, and even there it is at best ambiguous; and
descriptions of singing hymns to God belong only to the daily habits
of Philo's Therapeutae and the Qumran community, or Paul when in
prison overnight![1]

In the absence of any evidence for weekly Jewish worship on the
sabbath, we are forced to conclude that our knowledge of exactly
when and where, and under whose auspices, the gathering of the Jews
on the sabbath took on the role of worship as opposed to study
remains opaque.

---

1. Acts 16.25.

THE END OF TIME: A BIBLICAL THEME IN MESSIAEN'S *QUARTET*

Iain G. Matheson

Can music engage with the Bible in any way other than the mere setting of its texts and stories? Thousands of musical works are linked to the Bible by their text; Handel's *Messiah*, Walton's *Belshazzar's Feast*, Britten's *Noye's Fludde*, Stravinsky's *Symphony of Psalms*—however complex or simple the musical language, the connection with the Bible is a straightforward verbal or narrative one. At this level the Bible is nothing more (or less) than a word-book, a source of texts for the composer. It is used in the same way as any other literary source, including the sacred texts of other religious traditions. It is set by composers who may or may not profess a Judaeo-Christian faith; Stravinsky, Bach, Ives on the one hand, Stockhausen, Tippett, Verdi on the other. That they should happen to take their text from the Bible rather than any other source-book is a matter of cultural conditioning, having no intrinsic connection with any music which results. At this level the link of Bible and music is fortuitous and contingent.

Compared to the vast repository of music connected to the Bible at this superficial level, there are few works concerned to respond to the Bible in any deeper theological way, even by composers who might happily acknowledge the influence of the Bible and of faith in their lives. Such a lack might suggest that explicit musical engagement with the Bible in any other than a verbal way is difficult if not impossible; the examination of this suspicion is the subject of the present paper.

Olivier Messiaen is a Roman Catholic who more than any other contemporary composer has attempted to address specific biblical and theological concerns in his music. Most appropriately for the present study, almost all of his works written with explicit theological interest are instrumental; no words appear except in title and prefaces. Of 59 works noted in Sherlaw Johnson's catalogue, 20 have titles expressive of biblical, theological or liturgical themes; only four of these involve any word-setting. By contrast there are eight pieces for organ, five for orchestra, two for piano(s) and one for clarinet quartet— the *Quartet for the End of Time*, written in Stalag 8A prison camp in 1941.

The *Quartet* is based on Rev. 10.1-7:

> I saw a mighty angel coming down from heaven, wrapped in cloud, with a rainbow round his head. His face was like the sun, his feet like pillars of fire. He planted his right foot on the sea, his left on the land and, standing on the sea and the earth, he raised his hand to heaven and swore by Him who lives for ever and ever, saying: There shall be no more time; but on the day the seventh angel sounds the trumpet, the hidden purpose of God will have been fulfilled.

Messiaen's interpretation of this text is twofold. First there is the literal (verbal or narrative) use, spelled out in the *Quartet's* title and the titles of its movements, which roughly outline the events of the text. It is not too whimsical to suggest that Messiaen's decision to use this particular text rather than any other may well have been prompted by the prisoner-of-war conditions in which he found himself, in which time might indeed have seemed literally endless, and the Apocalypse close at hand.

However, if this were all, the *Quartet* would be nothing more than a sound-picture, albeit non-verbal; a setting of a biblical narrative, of the kind discussed at the outset, unfolding in some programmatic way the events surrounding the announcement of the end of time; like a Strauss tone-poem whose form is to some extent determined by the unspoken narrative it intends to depict. It is his second interpretation which Messiaen himself emphasizes as more important; the text is the starting point for a work which articulates his philosophical views regarding different sorts of musical time. Messiaen assures his audience that 'I did not in any sense want to comment upon the Apocalypse. My only wish was to articulate my desire for the dissolution of time' (Golea).

The text on which the *Quartet* is based is a culmination of the Bible's concern with time as a theological issue from its opening verse to its last book. The Bible presents humans made in the image of God as creatures who are aware of time, history and their own impending death (in this they are distinct from the animals). But the Bible's point is not that time is a pre-existent thing into which God places his creation; instead, time itself is created as part of the whole. God does not create in order to fill up time, but gives the creation time to be alive. Tillich's infamous 'God does not exist—he is', whatever else it obscures, emphasizes that God does not need to occupy time and in fact does not; time is a prerequisite for creaturely existence but not for eternal being. Time is outside God and depends on him, just as musical time depends on the composer (see below).

God's action is perceived by his creatures to take place in historical time, because humanity has no direct sensory awareness of eternity and ontology. Theologians have tried to express the time-less and change-less nature of God's action in the theology of the sacraments, in which a creative event is continually remade in the experience of those who have made it part of their history. This is what Bultmann calls 'eschatological event'—at once past and present, capable of becoming present again and again. The work of God is not tied to the moment of its occurrence in time, precisely because it never did occur 'in time'.

Language fails when it tries to express the unity of past–present– future in God. Plato puts it this way:

> 'was' and 'will be' are created species of time which we in our careless- ness mistakenly apply to eternal being. For we say that it was, is and will be; but in truth 'is' applies to it, while 'was' and 'will be' are properly said of becoming in time (*Timaeus* 37E6-38A6).

Traditionally the nearest theology approaches an expression of this is the doctrine of eternal life; adopted and baptized, people are invited and enabled to participate in the life of God, the unity of identity and change. Clearly eternal life involves a good deal more than time, but one aspect of it is 'the end of time' and the step into eternity towards which Messiaen's selected text points.

Music appears well-placed to respond to the Bible's presentation of time as a theological issue. Music is the art form most obviously concerned with the passage of time; rhythm, tempo, time signature, pulse. The movement and irreversibility of time is the specific 'subject' of all music, made explicit in Messiaen's title. Sound is essentially fleeting and elusive; the listener who passes out of earshot for a moment has lost something irretrievable (at least until the next performance, when, however, the music will be different in crucial ways). Unchanging sounds quickly become either unnoticeable or intolerable.

The discussion of time both in theology and in music is made all the more confusing because no common vocabulary exists. 'Real time', 'ontological time', Heidegger's 'public time', Suvchinsky's 'chrono-metric time'—the relationship of these and others is hard to establish. Traditional music time is a subjective measurement of pure duration, measured objectively by the clock. The underlying principle of musical time is change; memory is important in the perception of this. It is memory which tells how a thing was compared to how it is, and what it retains of its former state. Composers stress different proportions of 'objective' and 'subjective' time, so that not only the duration but the quality of sound become significant; a musical moment may be great or trivial as well as long or short, subjectively significant although (when measured by the clock) objectively brief. This musical manipulation of time is close to Tillich's understanding of kairos and chronos; and such manipulation is basic to Messiaen's *Quartet*.

From the composer's standpoint, time has another, added importance. As well as anticipating the planned effect on the audience of objective and subjective time, the composer occupies a separate world of what may be called architectural time; that is, the composer may take hours to write music which, objectively, takes only minutes or seconds to perform—his time as much as God's is outside the time he creates. Like God, the composer constructs a different kind of time from that which he himself occupies, and until the work is finished (that is, performed and heard creatively) not even the composer can fully participate in its new musical time-world, since it does not yet exist. (The roles of performer and audience are thus crucial in bringing musical time into being.)

The 'dissolution of time' which Messiaen seeks implies a new sort of rhythmic music, one which for Messiaen 'eschews repetition, barlines and equal divisions, and ultimately takes its inspiration from the movements of nature, movements which are free and unequal in length'—in other words the very opposite of what is traditionally understood as 'rhythm'. Messiaen develops various rhythmic techniques in the *Quartet* to articulate this very particular understanding of musical time, and his vision of 'the end of time' clearing the way for the beginning of a new type of musical time. Surprisingly, Messiaen does not make any special use of silence as a particular type of musical time, even though this has been held to be a poetic quality of the end of time—the hymnwriter's 'silence of eternity'.

The work is laid out in eight movements; Messiaen explains that seven is the number of days of the time of God's creation, plus one pointing towards eternity.

1. Liturgie de Cristal
2. Vocalise pour l'Ange qui annonce la fin du Temps
3. Abîme des oiseaux
4. Intermède
5. Louange à l'Eternité de Jésus
6. Danse de la fureur, pour les sept trompettes
7. Fouillis d'arcs-en-ciel, pour l'Ange qui annonce la fin du Temps
8. Louange à l'Immortalité de Jésus

In this brief analysis only those aspects of the *Quartet* which relate to time and rhythm will be considered.

The work contains two rhythmic innovations which have been important in the history of twentieth-century music. Both occur right away in the first movement, as well as later. The cello and piano in 'Liturgie de Cristal' each follow an isorhythmic pattern (that is, a rhythmic sequence overlaid on a melodic shape, each recurring continuously but independently of one another); the cello has a five-note melodic shape over a rhythmic ostinato of fifteen values, while the piano plays a twenty-nine chord sequence over a rhythm of seventeen values. Such use of 'talea' and 'color' is a common organizing principle in many mediaeval compositions, a fact which Messiaen acknowledges, although he claims not to have known any such works when he wrote the *Quartet*. Messiaen's innovation is to combine two such isorhythms, multiplying enormously the complexity of patterns which must occur before the two instruments return to their starting point. This results in a dissociation of rhythm from melody and harmony (which together had assumed increasing dominance throughout the eighteenth and nineteenth centuries) and so emphasizes the autonomy of music's time over other formal matters. The *Quartet* is the first work of Messiaen's second period to use more than two instruments, and is thus particularly suited to the development of polyrhythms in this way. By their nature isorhythms have an inevitability about them; their progress is non-developmental and conforms to pre-compositional decisions about patterns. The effect of this in the subjective-objective perception of the audience is to create a sense of stasis, even while knowing that clock time must be passing at its usual rate; and thus a tension is created between two sound-worlds. Because of Messiaen's use of two isorhythms, it would take long hours for the patterns to resolve themselves completely (which Messiaen allows to happen in some other works); Messiaen instead brings the movement to quite arbitrary end with a chirrup on the violin which, with the clarinet, has been accompanying the severe intellectual discipline of cello and piano with relatively undisciplined bursts of birdsong. Right away, time is brought to an 'untimely' end by the birds— Messiaen's symbol of eternity and freedom (see below).

The second innovation here is the use of 'non-retrograde' rhythm; the rhythm of the cello part is non-retrogradable, that is to say palindromic. It consists of a three-note rhythm [A] and a longer twelve-note pattern [B], each reflected around their mid-point:

When this is combined with Messiaen's five-note melodic shape, the following pattern emerges:

By the use of this technique at various points throughout the *Quartet*, Messiaen aims to create rhythms which 'contribute to an elongation of time'—the direction of time is addressed, and its irreversibility questioned.

A rhythmic aspect of this movement (and later ones) which is perhaps more obvious to the performer than to the audience, is that Messiaen uses traditional notation to represent rhythms which have no correspondence to the given time signature. He quotes in illustration a fragment 'as it was conceived by the composer':

and the same 'written in a false metre, with exact accentuation':

and comments: 'If the performers observe the indicated accents well, the listeners hears the *true* rhythm' (my italics). This shows the conflict between Messiaen's rhythmic ideas and traditional means of notating rhythm; and his belief that there is a 'true' rhythm which is heard rather than seen.

The third movement depicts 'the abyss of time, its sadness and weariness' contrasted with the birds who are 'the opposite of time; they are our desire for light, for the stars and for the things of heaven'. (Messiaen does not go into detail here—though he does so in many later works—as to the songs of which birds have been transcribed.) Contained within the birdsong are examples of note-lengths modified by adding and subtracting semiquavers, a technique which becomes important elsewhere in the *Quartet*:

and snippets of non-retrograde rhythm incorporated into the flow of music:

In the fourth movement Messiaen deliberately contradicts his own revolutionary understanding of rhythm, by developing a very traditional rhythmic pattern for violin, clarinet and cello in unison. This roughly balances awareness of subjective and objective time: the audience's perception of the music advances at about the same rate as the clock (an example of 'chronometric time').

The purpose of this vigorous and highly forward-moving 'Intermède' is to prepare the way for 'Louange à l'Eternité de Jesus', the first of two melodic movements for stringed instrument and piano, marked 'Infiniment lent, extatique'. The two movements 5 and 8 are related by their texture, their tonal centre (E major—prior to this the *Quartet*

has established no clear tonality), their theological idea—first homage to Jesus the eternal Word, then homage to Jesus the man risen to immortality—and above all by their extreme slowness. Messiaen again questions the idea of musical progress by prescribing a tempo of 44 semiquavers per minute, so that the shortest note lasts 1.36 seconds. Subjectively the movement seems even slower; the audience is made aware that forward motion has been almost entirely removed.

It is worth noting at this point—it will become significant later—that both movements 5 and 8 had already appeared in other works by Messiaen; the fifth in *Fetes des belles eaux* written for the Paris Exhibition of 1937; and the eighth as the second part of *Dyptique* (1930)—in both cases with no theological idea attached to them.

The sixth movement is another furious dance, this time for all four instruments in unison. It again makes use of non-retrograde rhythm; from letter F to H in the score each bar is a self-contained non-retrograde unit.

In this movement Messiaen systematically uses the added value procedures begun in 'Abîme des oiseaux' to form groups of 5, 7, 11 and 13 semiquavers; saying laconically 'one recalls our predilection for these numbers'.

The effect once again is to 'stretch' time (that is, to augment the more traditional note values of crotchet, dotted crotchet, minim and dotted minim—4, 6, 8 and 12 semiquavers respectively) and slow it down.

The seventh movement has two themes, one new, the other derived from the second movement. One way in which Messiaen combines them is to present the pitches of one in the rhythm of the other, so that once again rhythm is declared to be independent of melody and harmony.

The *Quartet* as a whole contributes to a general 'slowing-down' of music which had been in progress since tonality ceased to be a main structural principle for many composers. Using serial and non-tonal procedures, it is hard to maintain the subjective perception of movement amidst densely chromatic harmony and melody; most compositions written consistently with such techniques consist of a succession of more-or-less static blocks of sound, whatever the specified tempo of each. To this extent the *Quartet* achieves its aim of ending the listener's expectation that musical time will always be progressive and developmental.

Messiaen succeeds in writing a work which focuses the audience's attention on time and rhythm, almost to the exclusion of other aspects of music; but whether he is equally successful in establishing the link which exists in his own mind between time as a musical concern and also as a theological one, is another matter. The Bible is quite clearly Messiaen's starting point—his 'inspiration'—for the *Quartet*, and he wants performers and audience to be aware of this; but the only means he has to guarantee this is the use of titles which create certain expectations for players and listeners. The titles of movements force their thoughts in a certain direction, and the title of the whole work is an unavoidable clue to the composer's intentions; any audience would have received the work quite differently if it had simply been called 'Clarinet Quartet'. By composing a non-vocal piece, Messiaen *seems* to avoid the simplistic word-setting link between Bible and music; but in fact he is driven to use words to make his intentions clear, and they crucially influence the way the music is played and heard.

This may or may not be important for anyone's appreciation of the music; but it certainly indicates that any direct link there might be between a piece of music and the Bible can only exist for the composer; the music itself cannot communicate the link except by extra-musical means, using words of association; and with the use of words the composer ceases to compose and becomes an author. Stravinsky's assertion, 'My music does not express anything' is vindicated; music cannot express anything other than itself. It is its own language, which need not and cannot be translated, and into which no other language can be translated. The problem of demonstrating a link between the Bible and music is part of the wider problem of programme music. Because music refers only to itself, it is incapable of containing or expressing any extra-musical idea—especially in a biblical one, which necessarily points beyond itself. To impose any programme on music is at best contingent and arbitrary. (This 'at best' may be very good indeed, as for instance in the case of Debussy and many other impressionist composers; but even in that visually-inspired music there is no intrinsic connection of music and image; the audience obediently 'visualizes' what it is told—verbally—the music depicts.)

To be sure, the *Quartet* is highly 'expressive' and 'evocative' in the way music is customarily presumed to be. But its expression and evocation captures the idea of timelessness *more* powerfully than words, not less, hinting at meanings beyond the expressive capacity of words. To surround music with words is to reduce it, not clarify it; as Schumann knew when, asked to explain his latest piano piece, he simply played it over again. In the preface to the score, Messiaen himself falls into the trap of using highly visual and descriptive language of the *Quartet*, as though he thought it meant something: the language of the work, he says, is 'essentially ethereal; it is spiritual and universal. The modes harmonically and melodically realize ubiquitous tonality and they approach the listener from the eternity of outer space and infinity.' Elsewhere he describes his music as 'music which lulls to sleep and which sings, which is of new blood, speaking gestures, and unknown fragrance, an unsleeping bird, music of stained-glass church windows, a whirl of complementary colours, a theological rainbow'. In subjecting music to descriptive words, analysts and critics have created the false impression that this is actually meaningful; whereas it never was even in tonal music, and is certainly meaningless when the tonal illusion of musical narrative is removed. The difficulty of finding words about music is equal to or greater than the difficulty of finding words about God, for in both cases words fail to express the unity of past–present–future. Again in the preface, Messiaen effectively admits that the biblical basis of the work, however crucial to himself as composer, is not important for other: 'Do not be preoccupied with all this [descriptive analysis] when you perform; simply play the score, the notes and the exact values, the marked nuances'.

Messiaen's use of the Bible here and elsewhere is intentional rather than fortuitous, to the extent that much of his music might well never had existed had he not been a Christian steeped in the Bible and theology. On the other hand, it is difficult for anyone except Messiaen (and perhaps for him also) to say that this is definitely the case: it may be that his music would have found some quite different starting point. As has been said, the fifth and eighth movements of the *Quartet* appeared in earlier works with no theological ideas related to them. This means either that the music nevertheless did have such a link, which Messiaen chose at that time to keep to himself or more likely that the music as originally conceived had no theological connection, and possibly no extra-musical source at all. The notion of music's 'inspiration' is too big to be gone into here, other than to say that it is one which exists as much in listeners' fantasy as in composers' reality. The search for an aetiology to explain the origin of any work of music is undertaken most often after a work is composed; there is no reason why any extra-musical event or object need be invoked to explain music's existence. In the present case, given the evidence of fifth and eighth movements, it is quite possible that Messiaen composed a series of independent movements on different occasions, and used the opportunity of his imprisonment to group them all under one heading which emphasized their common concern with musical time; given his theological background, it is not surprising that this should be expressed in a text from the Bible, but another text such as Shakespeare's 'But wherefore do not you a mightier way/Make war upon this bloody tyrant Time?' (Sonnet 16) would have served equally well.

It is perfectly easy to impose extraneous programmes on music, especially tonal music with its inbuilt dramatic form of tension and resolution. Sonata form, for instance, corresponds neatly to an (Augustinian) outline of creation–fall–redemption:

Exposition:	First subject—God creates the world
	Second subject (in related key)—Satan confounds the harmony of Eden
Development:	The cosmic struggle between God and Satan
Recapitulation:	First subject—God-in-Christ reconciles the world with God
	Second subject (now in tonic key)—Satan is overruled, and humanity is again able to live at peace with God

or almost any biblical narrative shape:

Exposition:	First subject—the loving father
	Second subject—the prodigal
Development:	Adventures of the prodigal
Recapitulation:	Reconciliation of father and son—the feast

Such programmes are entirely possible. Some are indeed sanctioned by the composer and are in that sense the 'real programme'. Nevertheless they are not intrinsic to the music, which can as well be listened to in purely musical terms without awareness of any extra-musical associations. (Western philosophical and religious traditions have encouraged people to seek meaning in everything, and it is not therefore surprising that Western listeners instinctively feel that music is—or should be—'about' something. This is in sharp contrast to such music as that of John Cage, a Zen-inspired composer who has commented 'I do not object to being engaged in a meaningless activity'.) Many composers have announced programmes for their works, and in some cases explained them in enormous detail—Berlioz's *Symphonie Fantastique*, for example—while others have acknowledged such precompositional programmes but chosen to keep them mysterious—Rachmaninov's *Etudes-Tableaux*; yet others have claimed religious or theosophic origins for their music—as in the work of Alexander Scriabin—in which the notional programme of the music is a positive hindrance to any listener who is aware of it, while to those who remain blissfully unaware of it, their appreciation of the music is unclouded. Finally, no doubt many works which are known only as 'abstract' music had connections in the minds of their composers with private events which have remained entirely private.

Messiaen's *Quartet* can be considered as 'biblical' in a much more general way; not because it is linked in the composer's mind with a biblical text, or because biblical words are used in titles, but because all music (and all art) is intrinsically theological. It is concerned with the same matters as the Bible—space, time, transcendence, meaning—whether or not any given work has any verbal links with the Bible, whether or not it is the work of a Judaeo-Christian composer. Indeed, to the extent that both Bible and music relate to transcendent realities, music can be said to be more biblical than the Bible. The Bible points its audience towards transcendent reality—God—by depicting the Word in words; it is itself a secondary text. Music, on the other hand depicts *itself*—ontologically it is its own primary text and reality, pointing its audience towards nothing but itself; an absolute to which nothing can or need be added. Whether it is in fact possible to do what the Bible attempts, that is to represent God in an objective way, is a question beyond the scope of the present paper; it is certainly not possible to represent or describe music in any language other than music itself.

The ability to create is part of the image of God who creates. God's creative art may be broken down into four parts, each of which finds a human echo:

1. God's creation is a work of love, in which, through sharing himself, God prepares the way for the communion of creator and creature; and in which God places his purpose at risk (though his being cannot be so placed) to be accepted or rejected. In the same way, music is a work of love; the composer enters a relationship with performers and audience, looking for a response, choosing to put him/herself at risk, for the sake of both audience and work.

2. God's creation is a work of freedom, brought about by nothing but God's decision to create. God is free-for-us, when he might otherwise have been free-from-us. In creation God brings something new into being, responsibly and intentionally. Music is similarly free; through the given categories of created existence it enables human choice for composer, performer and audience, exercised positively and responsibly; it makes freedom possible by bringing the new into being.

3. God's creation is open-ended; it is potential, and people as recipients of God's grace are invited to play a crucial part in its achievement. Music shares this open-endedness, leaving performer and audience a part to play in bringing the work to life and receiving it creatively. The composer is not isolated but depends on a response; his creation, so long as it remains with him, is incomplete.

4. God's creation is relational, just as God is in his Being. God the maker is freely immanent in his continuing involvement with all he has made. God is not content to remain within the community of the Trinity, but goes out to community with his creatures. In the same way, music is the basis of communication in the continuing chain of relationships between composer, performer and audience, to which a new link is added each time the work is performed. Music is thus a collective rather than an individual art.

These categories overlap in every direction; but they are helpful to clarify the nature of human creativity in the image of God.

Music, like God's actions seen in history, has its meaning in an unrepeatable cosmic event which is capable of recapitulation in the lives of those who participate in it by performing and hearing. In this it has a profoundly sacramental role, offering a revelation of the sublime. Music and faith are complementary aspects of transcendence, pointing to the deepest reality, 'that than which no greater can be thought' (Anselm). In an age of secularism and individualism, neither music nor faith can reach very great heights; and in an age which rejects overt expressions of faith, it is understandable that music can tend to become a substitute. Whether this is finally possible is a matter for debate. There can be no doubt, however, that in its power of revelation and of ecstasy, music often enters the realm of the holy; Messiaen's *Quartet* itself is ample demonstration of this.

Alongside its declared subject, the end of time, Messiaen's *Quartet* deals with the beginning of time; in it, and in all music, the composer shares with God the work of origination. Despite its emphasis on God as creator, the Bible nowhere attributes to God the Orpheus-like creation of music, or depicts him bestowing the gift of music on his creatures (as opposed to song—Ps. 40.3; but song in the Bible is primarily a verbal gift). Its interest is largely in the responsive role of the listener, hearing the Word (rather than the music) of God. The source of music is to be found, if at all, in Jubal, Adam's great-great-great-great-great-grandson (Gen. 4.21). When music is mentioned in the Bible, it is usually functional—most often liturgical—rather than revelatory. This is true even of the music of heaven (e.g. Rev. 14.2-3) which is a vehicle for words about God rather than of value in its own right. Why the Bible should give this relatively humble place to music is by no means clear. It may well be that the writers did not wish to obscure the transcendent reality of God by declaring the transcendence of music, and so they attempted to reduce music to a useful role. In fact, as Heidegger persuasively argues, this cannot be done, since the 'purpose' of music (and all art) is to have no purpose but to make its audience aware of what usually passes unnoticed under a mask of utility; the thing-itself cannot be seen because its usefulness obscures its being.

The human ability to make music is prior to the creation of a historical Bible; far from music being subsequent to the Bible, the Bible is itself generated by people who were already able to express themselves musically (and in visual art). The role of the artist is to create opportunities for creative response, and the audience's role is to complete music (and the Bible) by receiving it (for music on paper is not music until it is played and heard, and theology on paper is not the word of God until the word is spoken and lived); and these roles are rooted in the God-given capacity for freedom, expressed as choice. In theology as in music it is the free response of those who hear which accomplishes or denies the work of the creator; and this capacity for freedom, which underlies human accountability to God, is present in people as part of the image of God (alongside the capacity for love) before the writing of the Bible. The Bible's own account of the matter is that humanity's discovery and use of its own freedom is a necessary precondition of any action whatsoever which is not directly attributable to God (most clearly shown in Gen. 3.1-13; also Josh. 24.22; 1 Chron. 21.11-12; Prov. 1.29-31; etc.); and while such actions include both music-making and the writing of the Bible, the former is certainly earlier, perhaps necessarily so. Without the experience of music-making as a positive expression of freedom, people might well have not imagined the possibility of written text, or even the concept of language; though whether this imaginative leap should in any case be thought of as progress from a pre-literary (but musical) world, is a matter which lies beyond the scope of the present paper. Finally it is a question of chickens or eggs—the Bible as pretext of music, or music as pretext of the Bible?—with the balance of the argument in favour of the later; but beyond this lies the elusive question—how did the concept of music originate at all?

BIBLIOGRAPHY

All quotations are taken from *Technique de mon language musicale* unless otherwise indicated.

Bell, C., *Olivier Messiaen* (Twayne Publishers, 1984).
Golea, A., *Recontres avec Olivier Messiaen* (Geneva-Paris: Slatkine, 1984).
Griffiths, P., *Messiaen and the Music of Time* (London: Faber & Faber, 1985).
Johnson, R.S., *Messiaen* (London: Dent, 1975).
Messiaen, O., *Technique de mon language musicale* (trans. J. Satterfield; Paris: Alphonse Leduc, 1944).
—*Quartet pour la fin du temps* (Paris: Durand, 1957).
Nicols, R., *Messiaen* (Oxford: Oxford University Press, 1975).

STORY-PATTERNING IN GENESIS

George G. Nicol

The narratives of Genesis divide readily into three major sections, the Primaeval History, the Patriarchal Narratives (concerned with Abraham, Isaac and Jacob), and the Joseph Story, corresponding to chs. 1–11, 12–36 and 37–50 respectively. The first section is concerned with primaeval events, creation and fall, the flood and Babel; it discusses many themes of universal and abiding significance: the origins of the world, humanity, death and sin, culture and agriculture, and the proliferation of languages. The second tells the story of a single family and its growth from Abraham through successive generations, its relationships with the surrounding peoples, and its response (whether positive or negative) to the call of God. The final section tells, primarily through the story of Joseph, how the patriarchal family migrated to Egypt and settled there.

Although God plays his part throughout Genesis, in each section the manner of his activity is characteristically different. In the first section, apart from his initial creative act, he sometimes appears as a character among characters: he strolls in the Garden in the evening, and converses with its inhabitants (3.8-13); he converses with Cain (4.10-15); observes the wickedness of human beings on earth (6.5); and comes down to see the city and tower at Babel (11.5). Throughout the second section God appears, sometimes in dreams, at places which consequently are considered holy. At each appearance he offers guidance and reassurance to the patriarchs, and makes promises to them. In the last section, however, he is more a hidden influence, a providence detected and spoken of by Joseph, rather than a character who intrudes regularly to interact with the other characters. In this section, although dreams are numerous, with the exception of 46.2-5, he does not appear to the dreamers as he once did to the elder patriarchs.[1]

In spite of these and other differences of subject matter and presentation, readers have usually been able to detect a sense of purpose and progress running through the Genesis narratives sufficiently strong to deem the whole a more or less continuous story,[2] although the first 11 chapters are often treated as a sort of preface to the story which follows. In a recent study, D.J.A. Clines has raised the question whether a plot runs through Genesis, or whether 'this book as a whole is no plotted story, but merely a chronicle or merely some incoherent collection of episodes'.[3] Although I would not gainsay his contention that 'most readers. . . expect narratives to have plots', I am unhappy with the alternatives he posits to 'plotted story' and the way he states them. The terms 'merely' and 'incoherent' seem almost a throwback to the sort of excesses literary analysts and readerly readers often allege to have characterized the historical critical method. The kind of sustained storytelling which occurs in a book like Genesis, and the more so throughout a corpus so extensive as Genesis–2 Kings, may well amount to something other than plotted story without deserving to be damned by the terms 'merely' or 'incoherent'.

One might agree with Clines's agnosticism concerning the author or sources of Genesis,[4] while suspecting that the book has gained its

---

1.   Significantly, this vision is received by Jacob himself and after the manner in which he had formerly received God's promises at the outset of each of the great journeys of his life (cf. Gen. 28.12-15 and 31.3). It is associated with Beersheba, where both Abraham (Gen. 21.33) and Isaac (Gen. 26.25) had worshipped, and where Yahweh had appeared to Isaac to make certain promises to him (Gen. 26.24).

2.   Although critics identified the sources J, E and P, it was usually alleged that a similarly continuous story had once existed within each strand, even if considerable portions were no longer extant. Form criticism sought to reconstruct the putative original form of individual stories and the like, but, except perhaps in the most extreme instances, also had some concern for the later deployment of the individual stories to form a continuous narrative, while redaction criticism was concerned with the mechanics of how such continuity was achieved.

3.   D.J.A. Clines, *What Does Eve Do to Help? and Other Readerly Questions to the Old Testament* (JSOTS, 94; Sheffield: JSOT Press, 1990), pp. 49-66. Clines argues that 'Genesis looks like a narrative book, with events being told in roughly chronological order and characters remaining reasonably recognizable throughout their appearances', and that it is therefore proper to ask 'What happens in this narrative?'

4.   *Eve*, p. 49.

present form out of so complex a process that the reader may be hard-pressed to discover evidence of a coherent plot in every passage. Indeed, a thoroughgoing readerly criticism must be open to the possibility that the ancient writer(s) might not have been possessed by the same sense of plot as the modern reader. The sheer extent of Genesis–2 Kings, and the presence of genealogies and law collections side by side with narratives at so many points in the corpus, ought to make the reader doubly sensitive to this possibility.

It is no surprise that Clines does not find plotted story, either in Genesis itself, or in the longer narrative corpus. Perhaps his search is too parallel to the earlier quest of biblical scholarship for the theology of the biblical writer(s), or even for authorial intention, to promise success. With the benefit of hindsight, it may now be possible to see that the author's intention has proved elusive precisely because it is so difficult (perhaps even impossible) to detect plotted story, either among the putative sources or in the final form of the text, whether that text is understood as a single book or as a corpus comprising a number of books.

I wish to explore the possibility that something akin to literary coherence may consist in features of the biblical writings other than plot, and that the sympathetic reader should attempt to apprehend the narrative on its own terms rather than the sort of plot expectation of which Clines speaks. One such feature may be the patterning of story which occurs on a number of levels throughout Genesis and to some varying degree throughout Genesis–2 Kings. In this study, I shall confine my attention to story patterns which occur in Genesis,[1] and I shall begin by commenting on the deployment of narrative throughout the book before examining some examples more closely.

The Deployment of Narrative in Genesis

In Genesis, material which is not entirely germane to the progress of the story is often inserted towards the beginning or the end of the section in which it occurs; after the introduction or before the conclusion. For example, the Jacob cycle begins at 25.21-34 with the story of his birth and his purchase of Esau's birthright. The following

---

1. I refer to 'pattern' and 'patterning' rather than repetition because my concern is often with less precise parallels than the latter term might indicate.

chapter (26.1-33), however, tells the story of Isaac and Abimelech before reverting to Jacob (26.34-35). In much the same way as the Isaac story is inserted towards the beginning of the Jacob cycle (25.21–35.29),[1] the Judah–Tamar story is inserted following the introduction to the Joseph narrative (37.1-36). Moreover, the similarly anomalous story of the rape of Dinah is inserted towards the end of the Jacob cycle (34.1-31), and seems to provide a degree of balance with the Isaac story,[2] while the poetic blessing of Jacob is positioned just before the end of the Joseph narrative.[3]

This positioning of material suggests that the Genesis story is not completely unilinear, although the great majority of narratives deal with more or less sequential events. The recurrent positioning of such anomalous material towards the beginning and end of major sections suggests a convention for transmitting episodes which would not otherwise fit easily into the narrative. In many respects these episodes function something like flashbacks or previews, but it would be wrong to fault the biblical authors if their technique in incorporating such features was not so seamless as might be expected in the work of a modern author.

Genesis 1–11 includes several modes of repetition. Here are two stories of creation (1.1–2.4a and 2.4b-25); two accounts of human fallenness (3.1-24 and 4.1-16), three genealogical passages (5.1-32, 10.1-32 and 11.10-32), and two passages in which the human race is expelled from its place by a jealous God (3.22-24 and 11.5-9). The final form of the flood story seems to derive from more than a single hand, whether as the conflation of doublets or the rewriting and expansion of an original story. In addition, a story pattern which

1.   The Jacob cycle begins with Isaac's prayer for his barren wife (25.21), and ends with his death (35.29).

2.   Cf. M. Fishbane, *Text and Texture* (New York: Schocken Books, 1979), pp. 46-48, for a number of observations on the way Gen. 26 and 34 balance each other. However, Fishbane's emphasis on the rôle of Gen. 26 as an 'interlude' between Gen. 25 and 27 seems less helpful. The narrative clearly has considerable value in its own right; cf. my 'Studies in the Interpretation of Genesis 26.1-33' (unpublished DPhil thesis, Oxford, 1987).

3.   These examples all derive from the second half of Genesis (Jacob and Joseph). In the first half (Primaeval History and Abraham), the story of the quest for a bride for Isaac which occurs prior to the conclusion of the Abraham story may provide another example.

occurs in this section is repeated elsewhere in the Genesis narrative. I shall examine both this pattern and the two expulsion stories more fully below.

The Promise Theme

The promise theme recurs throughout Genesis 12–36, and many valuable studies have appeared on this subject, largely from a traditio-critical point of view.[1] My present concern is confined to the deployment of the promise materials throughout the narratives, and the extent to which that deployment imposes a pattern upon Genesis.

At the beginning of his story, Abraham is commanded by Yahweh to go 'to a country that I will show you', and promised that he will become a 'great nation' (12.1-2).[2] The promise is expanded in vv. 2-3, and includes the promise of a blessing for himself and others. Abraham then journeys from Haran to Canaan where he receives the promise of land for himself and his descendants (12.7). He nevertheless presses south into Egypt and perceives a danger which causes him to misrepresent his wife Sarah as his sister, thus bringing the promise under threat. In Genesis 13, the motif of strife between kinsmen occurs, and Abraham and Lot separate so that possession of the land falls to Abraham at his kinsman's whim! The promise of land is repeated at 13.15, 17, and is followed, in Genesis 14, by the story of the battle with the so-called eastern kings. Although this battle may not directly threaten the promise of land (Abraham's purpose is to rescue Lot),[3] a concern for the land again emerges when Abraham

---

1. J. Hoftijzer, *Die Verheißungen an die drei Erzväter* (Leiden: Brill, 1956); C. Westermann, *Die Verheißungen an die Väter* (FRLANT, 116; Göttingen: Vandenhoeck & Ruprecht, 1976) (ET *The Promises to the Fathers* [Philadelphia: Fortress Press, 1980]).

2. The promise of a 'great name' may also be noted; cf. A.K. Jenkins, 'A Great Name: Genesis 12:2 and the Editing of the Pentateuch', *JSOT* 10 (1978), pp. 41-57.

3. It is probable that Gen. 14 was inserted into the Patriarchal Narrative after the pattern of promise–threat was complete. Cf. J. Van Seters, *Abraham in History and Tradition* (New Haven: Yale University Press, 1975), pp. 296-308; M.C. Astour, 'Political and Cosmic Symbolism in Genesis 14 and its Babylonian Sources', in A. Altmann (ed.), *Biblical Motifs: Origins and Transformations* (Cambridge, MA: Harvard University Press, 1966), pp. 65-112. For a different view, see J.A. Emerton, 'Some False Clues in the Study of Genesis XIV', *VT* 21 (1971), pp. 24-27; *idem*, 'The Riddle of Genesis XIV', *VT* 21 (1971), pp. 403-39.

receives the benediction of Melchizedek, king of Salem—a veiled reference to Jerusalem and the land of promise.[1]

Given all his adventures, it is not surprising that when the promise of land is repeated at 15.7, Abraham responds doubtfully, 'Yahweh God, how can I be sure that I shall occupy it?' (v. 8).[2] The justice of his question is underlined when the deity tells Abraham that his descendants 'will be aliens living in a land that is not their own; they will be enslaved and held in oppression for four hundred years' (15.13). Nevertheless, at the end of this chapter, the land promise is repeated in terms of a covenant (ברית) set up unilaterally by Yahweh with Abraham, and promising the land belonging to a number of named nations to his descendants.

The promise of progeny is threatened by the recurrent emphasis on the matriarch's barrenness and, after the birth of Isaac, by the deity's strange demand that the long-awaited son should be sacrificed on Mt Moriah (22.1-19).[3] This bizarre episode, which recounts a threat more fundamental than any supposed threat to the ancestress, is followed by a repetition of the promise of numerous progeny (22.17). The promise of blessing for the nations (12.3; 18.18; 22.18) is also jeopardized in the experience of Abraham (12.10-20; 20.2-18; 21.25-34), as well as by the expulsion of Hagar (Genesis 16 and 21).

Like Abraham, Isaac receives the divine promise both at the begin-

---

1. U. Cassuto ('Jerusalem in the Pentateuch', in *Biblical and Critical Studies*, I [Jerusalem: Magnes, 1973], pp. 71-78) argues that the passage refers not only to Jerusalem, but also to the establishment of tithing for the benefit of the Jerusalem priesthood.

2. Biblical quotations are taken from the Revised English Bible, 1989, with the substitution of the divine name Yahweh for 'the LORD' where appropriate.

3. The statement, 'Some time later God put Abraham to the test' (v. 1), is often thought to mitigate the command which follows. However, these words contain no reason to suppose that the testing of Abraham must stop short of Isaac's death. Our knowledge of the ending of the story gives us an advantage over Abraham, as well as the first-time reader: neither he nor they can know that he will be pulled back from the brink of plunging the knife into his son's body. In the meantime he must plumb every horror which might be associated with the slaying of one's own child. I am not sure how a reader's knowledge of the outcome mitigates what is done to Abraham, or what this passage says about the God who needs to impose such a test on his servant. Perhaps it is only in (biblical) story that a character can emerge from such a 'test' with sanity intact.

ning of his story (26.3-5) and later (26.24). Yahweh promises to be
with him and bless him, and the promise is expanded in terms of land
and great progeny, a repetition of the promise of land, and the
promise of blessing for the nations. In the narrative which follows,
however, Isaac's behaviour jeopardizes the outcome of the promise.
As Abraham had done, he pretends that his wife is his sister (vv. 7-
11), his successful husbandry provokes Philistine envy (vv. 12-16)
and leads to his expulsion from the environs of Gerar, his servants
quarrel with the local herdsmen in the valley of Gerar (vv. 17-21) so
that he has to surrender to them possession of two wells. He gains
undisputed possession of a third well at Rehoboth where at last he
confesses the influence of Yahweh in his good fortune (v. 22) before
receiving a renewal of the divine promise at Beersheba. Finally, when
he comes to him at Beersheba, Abimelech confesses that Isaac has been
blessed by Yahweh and the two conclude a peace treaty.

Promise is also an important element in the Jacob material. When
Jacob was at Bethel, making good his escape from Esau and beginning
his quest for a suitable bride, Yahweh appeared to him by night and
promised him land, progeny and protection (28.13-15). This promise
is made as Jacob departs from the land which is promised to him, and
is followed by the story of his greatly protracted wooing of Rachel.
The promise that he will possess the land is threatened by his departure from it; and the promise of progeny is postponed if not directly
threatened by the time it takes him to win his brides.

As for Jacob's relationship with Rachel, his difficulty in winning
her, her theft of Laban's household gods (תרפים), and her prolonged
barrenness, are all matters which limit the fulfilment of the promise,
or subject it to serious delays. Then, when Jacob feels Laban's
oppression most keenly, Yahweh is said to have reappeared to him,
instructing him to return to the land of his fathers,[1] and repeating the
promise of 'being with' (31.3). Again the promise is threatened, first
by Laban's pursuit in search of his household idols (when Jacob, quite

---

1. There is a subtle change of emphasis here. Abraham had precluded Isaac's
marriage to one of the 'Canaanites among whom I am living', and had sent his
servant 'to my own country and my own kindred' in search of a wife for his son
(24.3). Isaac likewise precluded Jacob's marriage to 'a Canaanite woman', and had
sent him 'to the home of Bethuel, your mother's father, in Paddan-aram' to find a
wife (28.1-2).

unwittingly, endangers Rachel, the wife he loves best),[1] secondly by the mysterious (demonic or divine?) assailant at the brook Jabbok, and thirdly by the prospect of meeting again with the brother he had usurped.

The promise of progeny is repeated at 35.9-12, but is followed by the death of Rachel in childbirth (35.16-19) and Reuben's seduction of Bilhah, his father's concubine (35.22).[2] Outside of the Jacob narrative proper, the promise is repeated at 46.2-4 before the patriarchal family go down to Egypt.[3] There, however, the story will issue in the enslavement and attempted genocide of the nation. Indeed, the promise of land which stands towards the beginning of the Jacob narrative (28.13), is repeated elsewhere, and has been partially fulfilled by ch. 46, is again brought into question by this divine encouragement to migrate to Egypt.

The patriarchal narratives are therefore punctuated regularly by the divine promises, usually associated with a theophany, although sometimes with visionary experience. This punctuation forms one thread which provides a sense of continuity; perhaps the most obvious, but certainly not the only one. The foregoing shows that the significance of the promises lies not merely in their renewal in varied circumstances at every stage in the narrative, but that they are repeated in spite of patriarchal activities and attitudes—and even divine commands—which seem all but designed to bring them to nothing. There is a remarkable tension between the terms of the divine promises and the narratives among which they are set. The conjunction in these narratives of divine promise with a wide variety of events which bring the fulfilment of the promise into question provides the narratives with a powerful and compelling impetus. The fact that those fulfilments which take place are only partial and/or temporary prevents the story from ever reaching the sort of fulfilment which would signal its conclusion.

---

1. A comparison is drawn below with the episode where the life of Benjamin is similarly threatened (Gen. 44.9).

2. Reuben's relationship with Bilhah probably precluded further sexual intercourse between Jacob and his concubine; cf. G.G. Nicol, 'Genesis XXIX.32 and XXXV.22a: Reuben's Reversal', *JTS* ns 31 (1980), pp. 536-39.

3. In contrast to the command to Isaac not to go down to Egypt (26.2).

.

The Doublet Stories

Another form of story-patterning is encountered in the so-called doublet stories, a phenomenon which has given rise to considerable debate. Best known, perhaps, are the doublets where one of the patriarchs travelling abroad pretends that his wife is his sister, thereby coming into conflict (whether actual or potential) with the ruler of the land in which he finds himself (12.10-20; 20; 26.7-11), the stories which tell of the meeting of a traveller with a woman beside a well (24.10-14; 29.1-14 and Exod. 2.15-21), and the stories concerning the expulsion of Hagar (16 and 21.8-21).[1]

A reading which has regard to the sequence in which events are narrated and is both literary and critical must, through criticism, suspend prior knowledge of the text, including the ordering of events, their recurrence, and their outcome.[2] All too commonly scholars treat the stories which comprise each set of doublets as if they told the same story,[3] yet, at the very least, each version of each doublet occurs in a different context which contributes to the different effect which it achieves. Further, even if the same motifs, stock characters and the

---

1.   My concern here is with doublets which occur in Genesis. R.C. Culley (*Studies in the Structure of Hebrew Narrative* [Philadelphia: Fortress Press; Missoula, MT: Scholars Press, 1976], pp. 33-68) examines several sets of doublets which occur throughout the Hebrew Bible.

2.   P. Ricoeur has recognized the critics' difficulty that knowledge of the text precludes of the first pre-critical naivety of the reader who does not already know the text. He argues therefore that one should attempt to move to a second, post-critical, naivety, in and through criticism. Cf. *The Symbolism of Evil* (New York: Harper & Row, 1967), p. 250. See also, *idem*, 'From Existentialism to the Philosophy of Language', *Philosophy Today* 17 (1973), pp. 88-96. This points to a reading that, notwithstanding prior knowledge of events which will be related subsequently, refuses to allow such knowledge to interfere with interpretation.

3.   As a result, in the commentaries, the Isaac version of the 'wife–sister doublet' incidents often receives less attention than the Abraham version(s); e.g. E.A. Speiser, *Genesis* (Garden City, NY: Doubleday, 1964), p. 203. Several others do little more than draw out some comparisons with the Abraham stories; cf. J. Skinner, *Genesis* (Edinburgh: T. & T. Clark, 2nd edn, 1930), pp. 264-65; G. von Rad, *Das erste Buch Mose, Genesis* (Göttingen: Vandenhoeck & Ruprecht, 10th edn, 1976), pp. 217-18 (ET *Genesis* [London: SCM Press, 3rd edn, 1972], p. 271); B. Vawter, *On Genesis* (Garden City, NY: Doubleday, 1977), pp. 292-93; J. Chaine, *Le livre de la Genèse* (Paris: Cerf, 1948), pp. 301ff.

like are used, usually they are deployed differently. Each occurrence of the episode is therefore different, and the reader is invited to reflect on discrimination and difference as well as repetition and similarity.

When Genesis is read from the beginning, the first time any theme, motif, plot, stock character or the like is encountered, it occurs without analogy in the story. At its second or subsequent occurrence, the reader 'remembers' that such a feature has been encountered already and may be invited to reflect upon the earlier occurrence(s) as an element of narrative context. For example, when Abraham represents Sarah to Pharaoh as his sister in ch. 12, there is no precedent and the narrative represents a unique event; but when he practises the same deception upon Abimelech a precedent demands that the event should be apprehended differently. The first version has a bearing upon the interpretation of the second which the second does not have upon the first. Further, the effect is cumulative so that when Isaac represents Rebekah as his sister to the inhabitants of Gerar there are two narrative precedents to be considered.[1]

The existence or otherwise of narrative precedent is only one aspect of context, although an important one. The fact that Genesis may be read as an ongoing story implies that context may regularly provide clues which enrich the reading of any specific episode. The reading of 12.10-20 finds its context in the divine command to Abraham to make a new beginning, leaving behind his country, kinsmen and immediate family. Abraham is promised guidance to 'a country that I will show you', that he will found a great nation, be blessed, receive a great name, and that 'all the families on earth' will be blessed according to their relationship with him. Abraham responds immediately, yet he takes his nephew Lot with him so that his obedient response is complicated by a certain disobedience.[2] At Shechem Yahweh again appears to

1. This distinguishes my approach from that of R. Alter ('A Literary Approach to the Bible', *Commentary* 60 [1975], pp. 70-77) who notes 'the repeated use of narrative analogy' as a feature of biblical Hebrew narrative, and from those who have raised the term 'narrative analogy' almost to the status of method, e.g., P.D. Miscall, 'The Jacob and Joseph Stories as Analogies', *JSOT* 6 (1978), pp. 28-40, and R.P. Gordon, 'David's Rise and Saul's Demise: Narrative Analogy in 1 Samuel 24–26', *TynBul* 31 (1980), pp. 37-64.

2. *Contra* L.A. Turner, 'Lot as Jekyll and Hyde', in D.J.A. Clines, S.E. Fowl and S.E. Porter (eds.), *The Bible in Three Dimensions* (JSOTS, 87; Sheffield: JSOT

Abraham to promise 'this land' to his descendants. After building an altar there (12.7), Abraham journeys by stages into the Negeb, and finally, under the pressure of famine, down to Egypt.[1]

There is a tension between the account of Abraham's sojourn in Egypt and the material of vv. 1-9, for in going there he moves outside the area promised in 12.7. Through Abraham's lie (12.13), Sarah is taken into Pharaoh's harem and he receives great wealth in exchange for her. Yahweh inflicts a plague on Pharaoh's household, however, so that she is returned to Abraham and they are given a military escort from Egypt. Neither Lot nor the wealth Abraham had accumulated in Haran (cf. 12.5) are mentioned in vv. 10-20, although Lot is reintroduced abruptly at 13.1.

The sudden reintroduction of Lot hardly reflects on the question whether or not he was present with Abraham in Egypt. Clearly he is absent from the narrative at 12.10-20, and his presence is invoked now in order to remind the reader that Abraham had brought him on the journey out of Haran, and in anticipation of the incident concerned with the separation of Abraham and Lot (13.5-13).[2]

It is not possible in this study to trace the development of the story through subsequent chapters. It is sufficient to note that the promise of a son is debated by Abraham with Yahweh (15.1-5), and dealt with again in chs. 17 and 18. Lot reappears for a last time in ch. 19, before Abraham again perpetrates the deception that Sarah is his sister (20.1-18), jeopardizing at the very last moment the promise that she will bear his son. This time his victim is Abimelech, king of Gerar, but again the deception fails. Afterwards Abimelech invites Abraham to settle (שב) wherever he wishes in his land. So far as Abraham does not

---

Press, 1990), pp. 85-101, and D.J.A. Clines, 'The Ancestor in Danger; But not the Same Danger', in *Eve*, pp. 67-84, who argue that throughout the narratives where he appears Lot is represented as Abraham's only legitimate descendant.

1. On his journey, Abraham builds another altar between Bethel and Ai, so that altar-building appears to be a characteristic activity punctuating the itinerary contained in 12.1-9, 13.1-4, 14-17.

2. N. Sarna ('The Anticipatory Use of Information as a Literary Feature of the Genesis Narratives', in R.E. Friedman [ed.], *The Creation of Sacred Literature* [Near Eastern Studies, 22; Berkeley: University of California Press, 1981], pp. 76-82) notes several remarks embedded in the text which seem to have no immediate significance but which anticipate later developments in the story.

move on before Isaac's birth, that event is associated with Gerar
(גרר).[1]

The association of Isaac's birth with Gerar it is not without
significance for his return there to assume the status of a resident alien
(גר, 26.1). There he attempts to perpetrate the same deception as his
father in the same town and against the same king. Yet the story is
different, not only because it occurs in a different context and now has
two narrative precedents (12.10-20; 20), but because the motifs which
comprise the story are deployed differently and to different effect.
Isaac's ruse fails because Abimelech chances to see him caressing
Rebekah, who is never endangered, and he becomes immensely rich,
not by deception but successful husbandry and Yahweh's blessing.
Here the wealth motif is divorced from the wife–sister episode.

The foregoing discussion, confined to a single set of episodes, only
sketches the evidence for my contention that the so-called doublets are
used to tell different stories each time they are employed, and that the
difference consists largely in terms of context, deployment of motifs,
and emphases. Discussion of the other doublets, however, would yield
similar results.

The Jealous God (Genesis 3 and 11)

Another form of patterning occurs where stories are structured similarly through the deployment of a chain of themes or motifs, although
the surface narration may be completely different.

The story of the Garden ends with the expulsion of the first man
and woman, but first Yahweh Elohim makes the following comment:

> The man has become like one of us, knowing good and evil; what if he
> now reaches out and takes fruit from the tree of life also, and eats it and
> lives for ever?

The deity's reaction to man's taking possession of 'the knowledge of
good and evil' is thoroughly antagonistic. There is certainly nothing in

---

1.   Although the notice of Isaac's birth (Gen. 21.1-3) is not tied to a specific
location, from a purely literary point of view its position in the final form of the
narrative, immediately after Abimelech's offer to Abraham (20.15), suggests he was
born at or near Gerar. By Gen. 21.22-34, however, when Abraham and Abimelech
make a covenant at Beersheba, it appears that Abraham had been there for some time.
There is no great interest in itinerary in these later chapters of the Abraham story, and
Isaac's place of birth is not stated accurately.

the preceding narrative to suggest that the possession of such knowledge is anything other than thoroughly desirable, and the prohibition
against eating the fruit of that particular tree shows Yahweh Elohim
as one who jealousy guards the maturity which knowledge brings as
his own prerogative. Indeed, one might question the motives of the
one who inflicts such enticement upon his creature without providing
him with the moral equipment necessary to resist such enticement.[1]

The similarity of the divine reaction to the building of the city and
tower (11.1-9) is observed by Vawter:[2]

> In vss. 5-7 Yahweh reacts to the building of the city and the tower in the
> same manner that he reacted to man's gaining of 'knowledge' in 3:22-24.
> He reacts, moreover, in a way which marks him quite the same Yahweh
> of the earlier story. Again, almost with a start of surprise, he observes
> what man has done in his absence. Again he muses on the consequences
> which may befall man's deed. And again, finally, he resolves in confer-
> ence—*let us then go down*—on a course of action which will frustrate
> man's plan and restore the proper order of things intended from the
> beginning.

The major problem with Vawter's reading of these verses is his
assumption that Yahweh's purpose in frustrating man's plan is to
'restore the proper order of things intended from the beginning'. The
priestly account of creation is punctuated by the refrain 'And God saw
that it was good'. That goodness may well imply a proper order, but it
does not lay down what that proper order was, nor are the succeeding
chapters any more explicit on this matter. Rather, it seems, they all
too often portray the deity reacting strongly—perhaps over-strenu-
ously—sometimes to human initiatives (as in chs. 3 and 11) and sometimes to the human condition (6.1-8).

Although there is a considerable dissimilarity between the stories of
Garden and tower, particularly on the surface level of narration, and
each contains a number of features which is absent in the other,

1. At 1 Sam. 13.1-14, Saul is caught in a similar trap; after waiting long for
Samuel to appear and officiate at the proposed sacrifice, he finally takes matters into
hand himself, only for Samuel to appear as soon as the deed is done. He too is
punished for accepting the proffered enticement.
2. Vawter, *On Genesis*, pp. 157-58.

important structural similarities can be observed at a rather more abstract level.

In the first story, eating fruit from the forbidden tree causes the man and the woman to recognize their nakedness. This recognition leads to an industrious act, the sewing of fig leaves into aprons. Eventually Yahweh Elohim learns of the human discovery, not by observing that the two are now rudely clothed, but by the human admission of fear brought about by awareness of nakedness. Following divine interrogation and human attempts to avoid blame (vv. 9-14), a series of curses, and two brief notices (vv. 20-21) which strike the one hopeful note in this present context, Yahweh Elohim utters a speech replete with divine jealousy (v. 22). The story ends with the expulsion of the man and woman from the Garden.

In the second story, a brief introduction tells how at a time when all men spoke the same language, they migrated from the east and settled at Shinar (vv. 1-2). There they committed themselves to an act of great industry, the building of a city and tower (v. 4). Once again the deity visits the site of human endeavour and in a speech, which provides an ironic echo of the human consultation which initiated the building project,[1] he betrays the same divine insecurity as did the justification for the expulsion from the Garden.[2] Finally, he scatters mankind around the earth and confuses human language.

In spite of patent differences, there is a level at which both stories have much in common; both relate:

    a.   human industry;
    b.   an observation by the deity of this industry;
    c.   a speech betraying divine jealousy;
    d.   an expulsion scene.

This analysis exposes something which is essential to the two stories. Out of the naïve expression of narrative events arises the spectre of a jealous God who fears that he is threatened by successful human endeavour and whose judgment is aimed not at the morality of that

---

1.   To the builders' 'Come, let us make bricks. . . (Come) let us build ourselves a city and a tower', Yahweh responds, 'Come, let us go down there and confuse their language'.

2.   Gen. 11.6b, 'from now on nothing they have a mind to do will be beyond their reach'; cf. 3.22b 'what if he now reaches out and takes fruit from the tree of life . . . and lives for ever'.

endeavour, but against its success; the awakening of modesty on the one hand and of human co-operation on the other. It is surely not that the divine decision in 9.6-7 as in 3.22-24 'calls for preventative action against further abuse', as Coats would have it,[1] but that Yahweh protects the integrity of his divinity against human encroachment. Here is the jealous God setting strict boundaries which his creation must not transgress—a dark reflection of the one who gives dominion over creation as well as a partner to the first man.

Angels, Destruction and Shame (Genesis 6–9; 19)

A comparison of the flood complex with the story of the destruction of Sodom and its aftermath reveals that there is a sequencing of events in each case so that the destruction is preceded by a visitation of heavenly creatures which is associated with lust and followed by the degradation through alcohol of the hero and his involvement in some sort of sexual irregularity.

Gen. 6.1-4 involves intercourse between 'the sons of God and the daughters of men'. Whatever the point of these difficult verses (perhaps the death-bringing verdict of v. 3 echoes the expulsion from the Garden), intercourse is said to have taken place between divine and human beings (v. 4). Even if the initiative of the divine beings (vv. 2, 4) sits oddly with the verdict against man in v. 5, there is little reason to consider the verdict any more odd than the divine verdict against mankind in either the Garden or the Babel story. At any rate, these 'marriages' appear to provide the rationale for the decision to destroy mankind.

The story of the destruction of the earth and its creatures—apart from those in the ark—follows, as does the optimistic sequel in which Yahweh blesses Noah and his sons, and makes a covenant with them and all living creatures never again to destroy the earth. That sequel, however, is followed by a darker and much more mysterious conclusion in which Noah, the first vintner, lies drunk and naked in his tent, providing occasion for some sort of impropriety by his son Ham.

Genesis 19 follows a broadly similar sequence of events. The inhabitants of Sodom demand that Lot should surrender his angelic

---

1. G.W. Coats, *Genesis, with an Introduction to Narrative Literature* (FOTL, 1; Grand Rapids: Eerdmans, 1983), p. 95.

visitors to their sexual abuse. Although they are repulsed (by the strangers' magic rather than Lot's offer of his virgin daughters) again the sequence begins with a meeting of earthly and heavenly beings which is associated with the lust of the one for the other, although this time by the earthly for the heavenly

The central section tells of the destruction of the cities of the plain, by fire rather than water, and the destruction of an extensive locality rather than universal destruction. Again this is followed by a short episode which tells of the drunkenness of the hero who has escaped destruction. Lot is given wine by his daughters who seduce him in his stupor so that he fathers the Moabites and the Ammonites.

Within this broadly similar sequence of events, there is some reversal of detail. In the one, divine beings have intercourse with human women; in the other, men desire homosexual intercourse with divine messengers (although they apparently do not recognize the divinity of the strangers). In the one, the earth is subjected to universal destruction by water; in the other the cities of the plain are destroyed by fire. And in the one, the drunken father is offended against sexually by a son,[1] while in the other the father was seduced by his daughters. Nevertheless, the sequence is clear so that the two destruction stories of Genesis occur among the coalescing in identical order of a group of motifs.[2]

Rachel and Benjamin; Rebekah and Rachel

A striking example of the repetition of a single motif occurs where a patriarchal figure innocently endangers the life of someone who is highly valued because he does not possess all relevant facts. When Laban pursues him in order to repossess the stolen *teraphim*, Jacob declares that whoever is found in possession of Laban's god shall be put to death (31.32) because he does not know that the theft had been

---

1.   This is true no matter what was the nature of Ham's offence; whether it was simply that he subjected his father's naked form to verbal abuse, abused him physically, or committed incest with his father's wife.

2.   S. Gevirtz ('A Father's Curse', *Mosaic* 2 [1968], pp. 56-61) notes that the pattern of sexual violation followed by a curse on the offender or his offspring occurs both in the Noah story and later with respect to Reuben's seduction of his father's concubine. Although in this latter case the incident (35.22) is separated by many chapters from the curse (49.4), the curse cites the offence.

committed by his favourite wife Rachel. As a result, she has to save herself by means of her own quick-witted action.[1]

Similarly in the Joseph story when the brothers persuade their father to permit Benjamin, their youngest brother and (like Joseph) the son of his favourite wife Rachel, to go with them to Egypt. As they return home, the brothers are stopped by Joseph's agents, and accused of stealing Joseph's cup. With a single voice the brothers—not knowing that the cup had been hidden in Benjamin's sack on Joseph's instruction—declare that any of them who is found with the goblet shall be put to death.

The two stories employ the motif differently. Both tell of a pursuit and an accusation of theft,[2] and both tell of a character (or group of characters) unwittingly endangering the life of another. Yet in the first story the one who is endangered has in fact committed the theft while in the second he has not; and in the first the stolen goods are not recovered while in the second they are.

Other narratives provide several parallels between Rebekah and Rachel, the wives of Isaac and Jacob. Rebekah was a sister of Laban, while Rachel, Jacob's favourite wife (like Leah, the wife he does not love so well) is a daughter of the same Laban. Abraham's servant, sent by the aged patriarch to Aram-naharaim to find a wife suitable for Isaac (Jacob's father), had found Rebekah (Jacob's mother) at a well (24.11-15). In similar fashion, Jacob, in quest of a wife, first met Rachel at a well (29.1-14), and like Abraham's servant before him was taken by the woman into the house of Laban.

Laban tricked Jacob into marriage with Leah, his elder daughter. The parallel between Leah with her weak eyes and the dull eyes of the father he had deceived has been noted by Bland.[3] Just as clearly, he must have been reminded of his mother by Rachel whom he loved so

---

1. In narrating how Rachel prevented the discovery of the *teraphim*, the author indulges in harsh polemic against idols. Rachel excuses herself for not rising from the saddle-bag which covers the idol with the claim that she is menstruating.

2. In both stories too the pursuer is a kinsman (Laban and Joseph's agents).

3. K.P. Bland, 'The Rabbinic Method and Literary Criticism', in K.R.R. Gros Louis *et al.*, *Literary Interpretations of Biblical Narratives* (Nashville: Abingdon Press, 1974), pp. 16-23; cf. p. 19. Bland also notes that just as Jacob deceived his father with Esau's clothes (27.15, 27), much later his sons deceive him with Joseph's robe (37.31-35).

passionately, for the two are described in the passages where they are introduced as remarkably beautiful women.[1]

Concluding Remarks

This brief review of parallels, story patterns and repeated motifs shows that time and again these features cross the boundaries from one group of stories in Genesis to another. Although the book may be divided into three major sections,[2] and although differences of subject matter and presentation occur from one section to another, this varied patterning of story proves a powerful cohesive force in the structure of Genesis.

Clines's question of whether a plot runs through Genesis might therefore be judged inappropriate, or at best untimely. Biblical narrative is so extensive and comprises such disparate materials as narratives, genealogies, law collections, poetic fragments and short poems that the quest for plot in raw terms of 'what happens in this story?' may detract from its essential nature. So far as Genesis or the primary history (Genesis–2 Kings) might be said to possess plot it has to be understood as rolling plot. That is to say, there are critical junctures in the narrative up to which a particular statement of plot might make satisfactory sense, but following which the narrative takes a somewhat different direction and gives way to an amended plot. One such juncture arises at the end of Genesis, and another at the rise of the monarchy; but there may be others reflecting for example the entry into the land, the period of the Judges and, so far as the story always remains open to revision, when Jehoiachin receives his Babylonian pension (2 Kgs 25.27-30).

1.   Just as Rebekah is described as very beautiful (24.16), Rachel is graceful and beautiful (29.17); the parallel between mother and wife is first intimated by the introduction of Rachel as 'the daughter of Laban his mother's brother' (29.10). Other prominent recurring motifs include the barren matriarch (Sarah, Rebekah, Rachel and Tamar), and the making of border covenants as a means of establishing peaceful relationships (Abraham [21.22-34] and Isaac [26.26-31] with Abimelech at Beersheba, and Jacob [31.43-54] with Laban at Galed), although in every case the motif is utilized quite differently.

2.   Or four if the Abraham, Isaac, Jacob material is divided into an Abraham cycle (Gen. 21.1–25.18) and a Jacob cycle (Gen. 25.19–35.29).

Clines is unimpressed by the fulfilment the divine promise (12.1-2) receives in the Genesis narratives,[1] and argues,[2]

> The only progress that has been made by the end of Genesis towards establishing a great nation is that there are seventy persons of the house of Jacob in 46.26, admittedly not including Jacob's son's wives. . .

Nevertheless, this slow, at times negative, progress towards fulfilment enables the narrative to maintain our interest. The much-discussed outline story recorded at Deut. 26.5b-9 reduces the Patriarchal Narrative to the barest terms, stripping away every detail and complication: 'My father was a homeless Aramaean who went down to Egypt. . . with a small band of people. . . ' The Exodus texts might describe the existence of the Hebrew slaves otherwise, but the same outline story glosses all that with the phrase 'it becomes a great, powerful, and large nation'. We have to meet the story on its own terms, and if those terms preclude plot in the conventional sense, that preclusion no doubt becomes an element of the encounter. I submit that there is indeed a sense of direction in the narratives, and sufficient cohesion may be found in the varied patterning of story, a feature which spans the major sections of the book, to permit us still to be impressed by the literary achievement which is the book of Genesis.

It is with great pleasure that I dedicate this study to Robert Davidson whose lively teaching first kindled my interest in the Old Testament, and whose great enthusiasm and ability to make his subject live has placed both Church and University in his debt over many years. Like so many of his students, I shall always be grateful for his kindness and patience.

---

1. 'What Happens in Genesis', pp. 55-59.
2. 'What Happens in Genesis', p. 58.

THE READER IN PAIN: JOB AS TEXT AND PRETEXT

Hugh Pyper

Muriel Spark's *The Only Problem*[1] is a long-considered novel which takes the book of Job as its pretext. In it, she offers a reading of Job on two levels. Her hero, Harvey Gotham, is a wealthy recluse who is writing a monograph on Job in an effort to come to terms with 'the only problem' of the title: the problem of human suffering in a world created by a good and all-powerful God. Through his reflections and conversations as he wrestles with his reading of Job, Spark is able to engage directly with the critical and exegetical problems of the biblical text. At the same time, the plot of the novel brings events more or less analogous to those recorded in Job into Harvey's life. The play of harmony and dissonance between Harvey's critical reflections and his response to the events in the world around him gives the novel its characteristically deft and provocative irony.

On the back cover of the paperback edition of the novel the following quotation from a criticism in *The Guardian* appears. It picks up a

---

1. First published by The Bodley Head (London, 1984); paperback edition by Triad Grafton Books (London, 1985). Page references are to the latter edition. The novel is the culmination of a long fascination with Job. Peter Kemp (*Muriel Spark* [London: Paul Elek, 1974], p. 17) quotes an interview from 1953 which implies that she was then at work on a book on Job. The title of her first novel, *The Comforters*, published in 1957, is an allusion to Job's comforters. In it the heroine becomes aware that she is a character in a novel; her 'comforters' try to persuade her otherwise. This has interesting links with Job's situation. The reader is aware that Job is the subject of a divine experiment. Job has an inkling of this which his comforters try to argue away. He is aware of an 'author' in his life. Spark and Job raise the huge question of the freedom of the character and the author. On the face of it, the character is entirely at the author's mercy. However, authors can also find that the character takes over and demands that the plot follow a particular course. Such analogies between world and text are central to her interest in Job as expressed in *The Only Problem*, and in this article.

sentence from Harvey's reflections on his work:

> 'To study, to think, is to live and suffer painfully.' To read, though, is
> another matter, especially when the craft is as flawless as Muriel
> Spark's.[1]

The Guardian critic's remark raises some intriguing questions. Is
the quotation from the novel which it picks up to be read as Muriel
Spark's own view, or the view of a character in her novel? If the
latter, is she endorsing or satirizing that view? Is it a view which can
be defended? Leaving these questions aside, how valid is the critic's
extension of the quotation to exclude reading from the experience of
suffering? Is it, indeed, as complimentary as might at first appear?
Not if we are to take seriously the advice which Franz Kafka gave in a
letter to his friend Oskar Pollak:

> I think we ought only to read the kind of books that wound and stab us. If
> the book we are reading doesn't wake us up with a blow on the head, then
> what are we reading it for? So that it will make us happy, as you write?
> Good Lord, we would be happy precisely if we had no books, and the
> kind of books that make us happy are the kind we could write ourselves if
> we had to. But we need the books that affect us like a disaster, that grieve
> us deeply, like the death of someone we loved more than ourselves, like
> being banished into forests far from everyone, like a suicide. A book must
> be the axe for the frozen sea within us.[2]

For Kafka, reading is nothing if it is not a painful experience. But
in what sense does the reader feel pain? Certainly there is a commonly
attested experience of finding something 'too painful to read'. Most of
us find reading accounts of torture, for instance, deeply distressing.
But how does this distress relate to the physical anguish of the victim?
Is it merely a vicarious experience with a tendency to lapse into
voyeurism? Is there a valid pain for the reader?

Human beings can be distressed by the inability to find an interpretation of the world that will enable them to make consistent predic-
tions within it.[3] That world can be the world evoked by a text.

1.   The quotation on the book cover is unattributed. It derives from a review of the
novel by Carol Rumens in *The Guardian*, 13 September 1984.

2.   Franz Kafka, *Letters to Friends, Family and Editors* (trans. R. and C. Winston;
New York: Schocken Books, 1977), pp. 15-16; Letter to Oskar Pollak, 27 January
1904.

3.   Another indication that there is a kind of suffering of the reader can be seen in
the phenomenon of experimental neurosis. A classic experiment by Pavlov illustrates

Reading is a process of inference, and a text may not provide sufficient clues, or provide ambiguous clues, and thus defer a coherent interpretation. Up to a certain point, this can be stimulating and enjoyable. The popularity of crossword puzzles and detective novels is evidence of this. Above that level, it becomes frustrating; the unpopularity of some modern verse arises from its resistance to inferential processes. This either leads to boredom and an abandonment of the effort at interpretation, or else to frustration and anger. The reaction will depend on the perceived rewards of deciphering the text. If the reader is merely seeking entertainment, he will quickly seek it elsewhere. If, however, the text encodes the only way of escape from a

---

this (see I. Pavlov, *Conditioned Reflexes* [Oxford, 1927], pp. 290-91). He trained dogs to discriminate between a circle and a flat ellipse by offering them food consistently with the display of the circle and withholding food when the flat ellipse was displayed. By monitoring the saliva flow of the dogs, it could be demonstrated that a consistent link between the sign and the dogs' expectations had been established. The dogs were then shown shapes intermediate between the flat ellipse and the circle. They displayed a profound change in behaviour, becoming wild and snapping angrily, straining to get free. At the same time, they lost the ability to discriminate between clear signs which they had previously demonstrated. If the experiment was continued, the dogs evinced an abnormal listlessness and ceased to react to any signs whatever.

This is a well-attested phenomenon in many experimental animals. It only occurs when the animal is in a situation where it can perceive both that a problem exists and that it is being offered a potential solution. Frustration builds up when the animal is capable of seeing the potential results of solving the problem and yet is thwarted in its attempts to discern a replicable pattern in the results of its response to stimuli. For further discussion, see M. Polanyi, *Personal Knowledge* (London: Routledge & Kegan Paul, 1962), pp. 367ff.

It would be possible to draw a parallel here with Job's situation. He is unable to correlate his experience of suffering with his expectation of blessing, but he is beset by the tantalizing conviction that he should be able to make sense of this contradiction. He is bombarded with contradictory stimuli, both in the tragedies which beset him and the arguments to which he is subjected. The final straw is the overwhelming assault of the divine speeches to which Job responds in a way very reminiscent of the dogs in Pavlov's experiment. After the snapping and straining of his complaints in the dialogues, he is reduced to an abject and listless silence.

That may be stretching the point, but the fact remains that even dogs can feel this frustration of the failed attempt to make coherent sense of conflicting signs to the extent of exhibiting physical symptoms of distress.

perilous situation, then the reader will persist to the point of extreme rage and despair.

The idea that a text can by its difficulty of form produce emotional states in the reader which lead him to share the frustration of the protagonist is put forward by Longinus in his *On Sublimity*. He praises the use of *hyperbaton*, the distortion of the sequence of words and thoughts, in Demosthenes:

> His transpositions produce not only a great sense of urgency but the appearance of extemporization, as he drags his hearers with him into the hazards of his long hyperbata. He often holds in suspense the meaning which he set out to convey, and introducing one extraneous item after another in an alien and unusual place before getting to the main point, throws the hearer into a panic lest the sentence collapse altogether, and forces him in his excitement to share the speaker's peril, before, at long last and beyond all expectation, appositely paying off at the end the long due conclusion. . . [1]

Thus the emotional excitement of the incident is conveyed to the reader through his distress at the possibility that he will not be able to salvage a coherent reading from the text. Although Longinus is here concentrating on the syntax of a sentence, such an effect can be prolonged, so that the text as a whole may induce this 'panic' that it will in the end prove unresolvable.

I would argue that the suffering of the reader is a central issue in Muriel Spark's novel. Using the book of Job as her pretext, she composes a work which plays upon the processes by which readers try to evade, assuage or endure the pain of reading. Her method is mimetic, not diegetic, in keeping with the techniques of the book of Job itself. The biblical Job is a man unable to read his world and who suffers from that inability. It is not his physical plight which is the cause of his greatest anguish but his need to make sense of his situation. He is caught in the contradiction between his expectations and his experience, and offered authoritative readings of his situation which only add to his sufferings. Muriel Spark's hero, Harvey Gotham, is also a man who cannot make sense of the contradiction between his belief in a loving God and the obvious suffering of the world. But he is also

---

1. 'Longinus' [the ascription is suspect], *On Sublimity* 22.3-4, in *Classical Literary Criticism* (ed. D.A. Russell and M. Winterbottom; Oxford: Oxford University Press, 1989), pp. 167-68.

caught up in the difficulties of making sense of the contradictions of the book of Job. The parallels between Job's attempts to argue his way to an understanding of his plight and the modern reader's attempt to come to grips with the strangeness of the book of Job coalesce as themes in Spark's novel. Both are metonyms for the wider problems of the attempt to wrest meaning from world or work.[1]

It was arguably Spark's own pain as a reader, not of Job but of its commentators, which goaded her into writing on the book in the first place. In 1955 she wrote an article for the *Church of England Newspaper* on 'The Mystery of Job's Suffering'[2] in which she responds to the recently published interpretation of the biblical book in C.G. Jung's *Answer to Job*.[3] She castigates Jung for his disregard for the so-called epilogue to the book, which, however, she admits is the 'stumbling-block for most intelligent readers of Job'.[4]

Jung overcomes this problem by ignoring the epilogue completely. He even praises the author of Job for his 'masterly discretion' in drawing the book to a close at the point where Job is prostrate before God, blithely disregarding the fact that the book does not close with this scene. Jung's truncation of Job spurred Muriel Spark to write her article in which she insists on the importance of the epilogue to the understanding of the book. The issue of the reading of the book's epilogue also resonates throughout *The Only Problem*. Reading Jung's interpretation has pained her sufficiently to evoke a cry of protest.

This epilogue, Job 42.7-17, has been a bone of contention in the

1. In his essay 'The Book of Job in its Time and in the Twentieth Century' (The Le Baron Russell Briggs Prize Honors Essay in English 1971; Cambridge, MA: Harvard University Press, 1972), Jon D. Levenson reviews several modern English adaptations of the story of Job, concluding that a successful re-creation must await a time when 'the tension that informs the Book of Job is again real in the lives of most people'. By making her hero not simply a Job figure, but a reader of Job, Spark is able to circumvent the modern lack of engagement with God that Levenson sees as a problem for the contemporary recasting of the story. The problem Job has with God, Harvey Gotham and the modern reader have with the biblical text.

2. 'The Mystery of Job's Suffering: Jung's New Interpretation Examined', *The Church of England Newspaper*, 15 April 1955, p. 7.

3. C.G. Jung's *Antwort auf Hiob* (Zurich: Rascher, 1952) was published in an English translation in 1954 (*Answer to Job* [trans. R.P.C. Hull; London: Routledge & Kegan Paul]). It is this translation to which Muriel Spark refers in her article, which appeared in the following year.

4. 'Mystery', col. 3.

history of interpretation of the book, as Spark's description of its indicates. In the words of David Clines, it has been a source of 'discomfort'[1] to many of the book's modern interpreters. After the sublime poetry of the dialogues between Job and his friends and the awesome picture of a universe completely beyond human grasp which God reveals in his climactic speech, we have the banality of the restoration to Job of his livestock, his social standing and, most disconcertingly, of a surrogate family. 'And the Lord blessed the latter days of Job more than the former', as we read in Job 42.12. Not only does this ending seem to trivialize Job's sufferings, but it seems to vindicate the very theology of retribution and reward which Job so vehemently rejects in the dialogues. Job is apparently rewarded for his righteous refusal to link righteousness and reward. In Job the resolution of the conflict for the reader is so long delayed that the 'panic' which the epilogue of the book must allay is intense. No wonder it is the subject of the reader's wrath when it is felt to fail in this task.

The common response from biblical critics is to regard the epilogue as the product of a different and by implication inferior strand of material. Usually the epilogue is taken to be the remnant of an earlier folk tale which the author of the dialogues used as the basis for his poetic masterpiece, perhaps to expose the crudity of its retributive theology.[2] Alternatively, it is seen as the work of a pious later editor who is concerned to tone down the radical theodicy of the poetic dia-

---

1. D.J.A. Clines, 'Deconstructing the Book of Job', in *The Bible as Rhetoric: Studies in Biblical Persuasion and Credibility* (ed. M. Warner; London: Routledge & Kegan Paul, 1990), p. 70 and pp. 70-71 *passim*. Clines accounts for this as follows: 'I suspect that the discomfort is the psychological registration of the deconstruction that is in progress, though until recently we did not have this name for the process, and so did not perhaps properly appreciate its character' (p. 70).

2. For a concise summary of the historical critical debate on Job, see S. Terrien, 'Introduction to Job', in *The Interpreters' Bible*, III (New York: Abingdon Press, 1954), pp. 884-88. In the fifth century, Theodore of Mopsuestia regarded Job as an ancient story blasphemously distorted by a person of literary pretensions (discussed in W. Urbrock, 'Job as Drama: Tragedy or Comedy?', *Currents in Theology and Mission* 8 [1981], pp. 35-40). The modern 'folk-tale' theory derives from Wellhausen (*Jahrbücher für deutsche Theologie* 16 [1871], pp. 55-58) and Budde (*Beiträge zur Kritik des Buches Hiob* [Bonn: A. Marcus, 1876], pp. 27-62). G. Fohrer (*Introduction to the Old Testament* [Nashville: Abingdon Press, 1958], p. 325) speaks of 'almost universal acceptance' of the theory which sees the framework of Job as an independent and earlier narrative.

logues by giving Job his just deserts.[1] Both these solutions dissect the work into text and pretext. A later author has used a pretext whose theodicy demands a refutation, and produced a text which undermines the theology of its precursor. The discomfort which the reader feels is alleviated by an act of violence on the text, dismembering it into earlier and later portions. In either case, as David Clines points out, these historico-critical solutions betray:

> a curious but commonly entertained assumption that to understand the origin of a discrepancy is somehow to *deal with* the discrepancy, to bring about a new state of affairs in which the discrepancy does not exist.[2]

We are still left with a biblical book which presents us with a painful clash of interpretation of Job's predicament. If this is not the inept result of some editor's attempts to unite different traditions under some kind of constraint which prevented him from harmonizing the components of the book, what solution can we offer? How does Muriel Spark suggest we cope with the discomfort these clashes cause?

When in her 1955 article Spark reproves Jung for his textually indefensible disregard for the epilogue, especially in view of the interpretative weight he gives to the transactions between God and Satan, she writes, 'If Dr Jung wants the prologue (and his whole theory hangs upon it), he must have the epilogue. . . ' And she adds this very suggestive phrase: '. . . no less than his hero Job had apparently to *suffer his reward* [my emphasis]'.[3] Earlier in the same article she asks, 'Can we really imagine our hero enjoying his actual reward?'[4] For Spark, the ending of Job is 'not merely a conventional happy ending'. It transforms the ironic clash between the prologue and the dialogues into what she calls 'that type of anagogical humour

---

1. This position is argued for by R.H. Pfeiffer, *Introduction to the Old Testament* (London: A. & C. Black, 1952), pp. 668-71, who traces it to A. Schultens in 1737. Pfeiffer sees the folk tale as a later addition by a Jewish redactor to an Edomite poem, drawing on a Judaean version of the traditional material which is also behind the poem. See also K. Fullerton, 'The Original Conclusion to the Book of Job', *ZAW* 42 (1924), pp. 116-36, who writes, 'From my point of view this closing restoration ruins the book artistically' (p. 126).

2. Clines, 'Deconstructing', p. 70.

3. 'Mystery', col. 4.

4. 'Mystery', col. 3.

which transcends irony and which is infinitely mysterious'.[1]

Is Spark then aligning herself with those who argue that Job is formally a comedy? It certainly ends with restoration and reconciliation, but with a question mark over the status of Job himself. Northrop Frye, who does consider that Job should technically be classed as a comedy, nevertheless remarks of the epilogue:

> In its conventional comic form of renewal, this kind of conclusion is seldom very convincing: people who lose their daughters are not really consoled by new daughters; conditions that cause suffering can be changed but the scars of suffering remain. . . Perhaps if we were to see Job in his restored state we should see, not beautiful daughters or sixteen thousand sheep, but only a man who has seen something that we have not seen, and knows something that we do not know.[2]

Something of this quality is perhaps what Muriel Spark meant by the 'anagogical humour' of the ending, a sense in which even the balance of justice in the universe, which Job so desperately seeks to maintain for his sake, and for the sake of God's honour, comes to seem, not petty, not unimportant, but incongruous in the way that can give rise to a self-deprecating smile once we realize that we have totally misread the scale and implications of our concern.[3]

---

1. 'Mystery', col. 4.

2. Northrop Frye, *The Great Code: The Bible and Literature* (London: Ark Paperback, 1983), p. 197. See also J.W. Whedbee, 'The Comedy of Job', *Semeia* 7 (1977), pp. 1-39. Whedbee sees Job's suffering as leading to a sharpened sense of comic awareness. Job's 'happy ending' demonstrates the irony of the book by leaving its incongruities unresolved.

3. There is an affinity here with another disputed epilogue, the epilogue to Shakespeare's *The Tempest*. At the end of the play, Prospero has had his kingdom restored to him, yet the last scene and epilogue to the play do not depict a man overjoyed at regaining what is rightfully his and his triumph over his enemies. What he has suffered, and what he has learnt about his own nature and the nature of those around him both exhaust him and leave him with a profound sense of the unimportance of his triumph. Compare, too, the Oedipus of Sophocles' *Oedipus at Colonnus*. Oedipus in this play bears some resemblance to Job: a figure who sees himself as set apart from the rest of humanity by the cruel interventions of the gods, yet fundamentally innocent. The appalling crimes which he committed were done in ignorance, he protests. Oedipus now achieves a death unlike that of any other mortal, a mysterious translation to the world of the shades. The actual moment and mode of his passing is hidden in the play, but it becomes a secret source of blessing to Athens. The strange interaction of blessing and curse in the experience of being singled out by the gods bears distinctly on our picture of Job.

If we then turn to *The Only Problem*, we find that the structure of the novel itself reflects the importance that Spark places on the epilogue in achieving a coherent reading of Job. It falls into three sections, the final part being much the shortest and forming an epilogue to the tale of Harvey's tribulations over his wife's escapades. Early in the novel we find a report of a conversation where Harvey and his brother-in-law discuss the ending of Job. Harvey decides that Job probably suffered more after his restoration than before it because suffering had become a habit for him. In the epilogue to the novel, Harvey, having completed his monograph, reflects once more on Job's final state:

> And Harvey wondered again if in real life Job would be satisfied with this plump reward, and doubted it. His tragedy was that of the happy ending.[1]

Muriel Spark, then, seeks to accommodate the epilogue in her reading of Job by seeing it as continuing the theme of the suffering of Job rather than introducing an incompatible restoration. She rejects the kind of textual emendation many critics advocate. As Harvey says when explaining the textual problems of Job to a friend:

> The scholars try to rationalise Job by rearranging the verses where there is obviously no sense in them. Sometimes of course, the textual evidence irresistibly calls for a passage to be moved from the traditional place to another. But moving passages about for no other reason that they are more logical is no good for the Book of Job. It doesn't make it come clear. The Book of Job will never come clear. It doesn't matter; it's a poem.[2]

So the discomfort that the text causes the reader by its seeming incoherence is part of its status as a poem. Spark reads it as a deliberate device, an example of Longinus's *hyperbaton*. There is, of course, a danger that this could be seen as arguing that any illogical text could be defended on the grounds that it was really a poem. Neither Harvey nor Spark make clear how we are to make the prior decision that the text is to be engaged with as a poem and thus is permitted such logical aberrations. There is no doubt, however, that the critic who decides to

---

1. *The Only Problem*, p. 186.
2. *The Only Problem*, p. 132. Spark italicizes Job when referring to the biblical book and reverts to Roman type for the name of the character. The very fact that in certain cases there is otherwise ambiguity over which is meant is suggestive.

dissect the text has already made judgments on the criteria of coherence which the text ought to but does not display. At least Spark's approach allows for the possibility that the text might expand the reader's categories rather than have to be pruned to fit them.

Spark does not merely leave us to face the stark contradictions of the text. She does offer a way of alleviating the reader's discomfort at Job's restoration, but at the price of prolonging Job's suffering. His happy ending is not so happy after all. The Job of the epilogue is still scarred by the events of the prologue and dialogues. If the reader is to be more comfortable, Job must be less so.[1]

Such a reading, though unusual, is not unique to Muriel Spark. Robert Carroll also points out forcibly the impossibility of any compensation for Job, and the continued suffering which this must mean:

> For Job whose eyes had dwelt on the past there can have been no thorough restoration but a terrible sense of loss and perhaps even of impotent rage against a power that had so casually discarded his life to settle a wager. . . Job was left to live out the next 140 years brooding on the injustice he had suffered. The epilogue neither suggests this nor rules it out.[2]

Is there, though, any justification for such a reading other than the need to integrate the text by establishing a continuity of pain between the Job of the various poetic and prose sections of the book? After all, there is no getting past the plain statement in the epilogue that 'God blessed the latter days of Job more than the former'. Once we begin to examine this more closely, however, we find that it is by no means so straightforward a statement after all.

There is a strange relationship in Job between blessing and its antonym 'cursing' which depends on the mechanism of euphemism.

---

1. G. Josipovici (*The Book of God: A Response to the Bible* [New Haven: Yale University Press, 1988], p. 290) praises Muriel Spark in this novel for her 'intuitive grasp' of what is at issue in Job. 'Muriel Spark has understood that the end of Job, like the beginning, is not a mere frame. It is the assertion of the fact that meaning will never be able to catch up with life.' Another appreciative reader of the novel is D. Jaspers (*The Study of Literature and Theology: An Introduction* [Basingstoke: Macmillan Press, 1989], pp. 132-35). He sees both Harvey and Job as receiving 'no answers but a brave and honest faith, in we know not what, and in spite of all' (p. 135).

2. R.P. Carroll, 'Postscript to Job', *The Modern Churchman* 19 (1976), pp. 161-66 (p. 165).

The Hebrew root *brk*, usually translated as 'bless', is used several times in the prologue in contexts where it is clear that it must be translated as 'curse'. This ambivalence must raise a question about the meaning of the word in other contexts in Job.

We can tabulate the nine uses of the root *brk* in Job as follows, paraphrasing the RSV's translation of the verses in which it appears:

1.5	Job sacrifices lest his sons have *cursed* God in their hearts.
1.10	Satan reminds God that he has *blessed* the work of Job's hands.
1.11	Satan alleges that if God touches Job's possessions, Job will *curse* him to his face.
1.21	Job *blesses* the name of the Lord.
2.5	Satan alleges that if God touches Job's person, Job will *curse* him to his face.
2.9	Job's wife urges him to *curse* God and die.
29.13	Job was *blessed* by those about to perish.
31.20	Job swears to his being *blessed* by the poor man's loins.
42.12	The Lord *blesses* the latter days of Job more than the former.

It is noticeable that six of the appearances of the root occur in the first two chapters of the book, which form its prologue. Although the connection between them is not uncontroversial, the prologue and epilogue are often seen as answering one another. Meir Weiss[1] argues that the root *brk* functions as a *Leitwort*. The epilogue provides the seventh instance of this root in the prose framework and the completion of this perfect number serves to bind together prologue and epilogue.

There is also a noticeable pattern in the translation of the root as either 'bless' or 'curse'. In every case where *brk* is translated as 'curse', the object of the verb is God. This euphemistic use of the root, which avoids the name 'God' having to appear as the object of the verb *qll* 'to curse', is known from other biblical passages and from rabbinic writings.[2] Once the root has been taken as conveying these

---

1. M. Weiss, *The Story of Job's Beginning; Job 1–2: A Literary Analysis* (Jerusalem: Magnes, 1983), p. 81.

2. For a discussion of the phenomenon of euphemism in biblical and rabbinic literature in general and particularly in relation to the root *brk*, see C. Wright, *The*

two antithetical meanings, albeit in defined contexts, there is obvious scope for playing on this ambiguity. One striking example is the way that the reversal of meaning makes it possible to read Job in 1.21 as fulfilling Satan's prediction in 1.11 literally, while interpreting his speech as vindicating God's faith in his integrity. Both God and Satan are correct in their prediction of Job's response, Satan literally and God functionally. This reversibility of meaning needs to be borne in mind as we look critically at the two occasions where God is represented as blessing Job.

In 1.10, it is Satan who raises what becomes the fundamental question of the prologue: 'Does Job fear for naught?' What is the relation between Job's righteousness and God's blessing? Is Job righteous because he is blessed by God? Or does God bless him because he is righteous? Or is there in fact no relation between Job's prosperity and his standing before God? Already in this verse we meet the paradox that it is God's blessing of Job which becomes the point at issue between God and Satan. If Job had not been saddled with this status, he would never have figured in the conversation in heaven. God's blessing is what lands Job in trouble. The point at which curse and blessing coincide is that the bearer of either is singled out, differentiated from the mass of humanity.[1] It is that singular status of God's blessing which fits Job for his role as the subject of the experiment which Satan carries out with God's permission.

If we then turn to the use of the root *brk* in the epilogue, we cannot simply read God's latter blessing of Job as an unmixed affirmation. All uses of the root *brk* carry with them a shadow-side of curse. Job has to live on in the epilogue after the experience of his utter humiliation before God. Before the divine speech, Job is secure in his right to challenge God and demand justice before him. Afterwards, he has to live knowing how utterly dependent he is on God's grace. His restored

meaning of BRK 'To Bless' in the Old Testament (Atlanta: Scholars Press, 1987), esp. p. 163, and also C. McCarthy, *The Tiqqune Sopherim and Other Theological Corrections in the Masoretic Text of the Old Testament* (OBO, 36; Göttingen: Vandenhoeck & Ruprecht, 1981), pp. 191-95.

1. This common element of isolation from the community under both curse and blessing is discussed with reference to Abraham in G.W. Coats, 'The Curse of God's Blessing: Gen 12:1-4a in the Structure and Theology of the Yahwist', in *Die Botschaft und die Boten: Festschrift für Hans Walter Wolff zum 70. Geburtstag* (ed. J. Jeremias and L. Perlitt; Neukirchen–Vluyn: Neukirchener Verlag, 1981), pp. 31-41.

prosperity can be no comfort as its precariousness has been made so abundantly clear to him. Wealth and position offered no security against disaster the first time round. The comfort of his friends and family must ring rather hollow given their earlier desertion of him when he actually needed their support.

His new children are a different matter. There is almost a fairy-tale unreality about them in their perfection and the whimsy of his daughters' names.[1] The fact that he makes the unique provision for his daughters to inherit a share of his property along with their brothers may reflect the way in which his material possessions have become in some way unreal to him. And he has to survive under these ambivalent circumstances for 140 years, twice a normal life-span. Even the words which end the book carry an ambiguity. He dies 'full of days'. Usually this is taken as expressing the satisfaction of having completed a rich and rewarding life surrounded by his descendants, but at least one commentator translates the phrase as 'weary of life'.[2] In what sense has Job been blessed by God's intervention?

The Only Problem picks up on this central ambiguity of cursing and blessing, albeit in a rather oblique fashion. We find this in the consideration of a remarkable painting which figures prominently in Harvey's researches into Job. In the novel, Harvey is living near Epinal in Central France in order to be near the picture by Georges De La Tour which was identified in 1935 as depicting *Job visited by his wife*. Harvey is struck by the contrast of the sweet and solicitous grace of the wife in the picture with the angry impatience of the biblical character who incites her husband to curse God (Job 2.9). Commentators have argued whether Job's wife in this verse is urging him to provoke God into striking him dead, thus ending his sufferings, or implying that as he is to die anyway, he might as well relieve his feelings. The serenity of the picture belies either interpretation. In the novel, Harvey's interpretation of this serenity is that De La Tour

---

1. Anthony and Miriam Hanson (*The Book of Job: Introduction and Commentary* [London: SCM Press, 1953], p. 118) make this point by translating Job's daughters' names as 'Swansdown, Lavender, and Mascara'. They describe the epilogue as *The Tempest* tacked on to *Lear*.

2. F. Delitzsch, *Biblical Commentary on the Book of Job*, II (trans. F. Bolton: Edinburgh: T. & T. Clark, 1869), p. 392.

is idealizing the deep love between Job and his wife.[1]

Frank Kermode interestingly pursues the ambivalence which Muriel Spark has noticed in De La Tour's painting.[2] He puts forward a speculation that De La Tour may have been influenced by the Vulgate translation of Job's wife's speech. Translating the Hebrew literally, St Jerome has her say *benedic Deo*—bless God. De La Tour may be illustrating this. The woman's expression of pity had often led to the painting being tentatively described as the visitation of an angel to some biblical character. He points out, however, that the standard work on the painter written after 1935 when the woman in the picture was identified as Job's wife speaks of the anger and cruelty of her expression. So interpretation reveals its circularity. Kermode sees as this an insoluble interpretative problem but he does at least offer the possibility that 'blessing' could be a workable interpretation even within the biblical text:

> the painter and his patron may really have read the words benedic Deo quite literally, and seen Job's wife as tender, however foolish she might be; she may be saying that death is the only way out of such misery and that he should seek it, and make a good end.[3]

Kermode makes allusion to Freud, among others, as having called attention to the widespread phenomenon of the antithetical meanings of primal words. He end his paper thus:

> So I think there is a peculiar truth in Job's wife when we cannot decide whether she is tender or cruel, blessing or cursing. . . We bring ourselves and our conflicts to words, to poems and pictures, as we bring them to the world; and thus we change the poems and pictures, or perhaps it is ourselves we change.[4]

The same truth lies behind the ambivalence of our reading of the epilogue to Job. Here, however, the ambivalence is not in the attitude of Job's wife, but in God's attitude to Job. The question that this reading circles round is 'What is it to be "blessed" by God?' It is remarkable that this ambivalence over the meaning which so profoundly affects the reading of the epilogue arises from the attempt

---

1. *The Only Problem*, p. 78.
2. F. Kermode, 'The Uses of Error', *Theology* 89 (1986), pp. 425-31.
3. 'Uses', p. 428.
4. 'Uses', p. 431.

to preserve God's holiness through the use of euphemism. Do we change the text of the book to dispel that uncanny ambiguity between blessing and cursing which contributes to making the epilogue so disturbing, or do we allow the book to change our notions of how God relates to human beings?[1]

It is this alternative of change in the text or change in the reader which the history of interpretation of Job illustrates. Whether as historical critics, commentators or novelists, we rewrite the texts. The mechanism of counterpoising text and pretext is one that can be used in different ways to accommodate the ambiguity. Either we see Job itself as a composite text and thus deal with the ambiguity in terms of conflicting layers of textuality, or, as Muriel Spark does, we take the book itself as a pretext and write out of the conflict of our experience of reading it.

The crucial question remaining is whether, in either case, we are seeking to avoid or to express the alteration the text can effect in us. Do we seek to alleviate the suffering of the reader or, as Kafka would urge, to embrace its potential to shock us awake? The critical method may be used to disarm the text, but it is also possible to see the text itself as much as its retinue of interpretations as the product of a history of deflections of its assaults upon us. The interpreter's role therefore becomes the stripping away of these accretions in order to restore the text's power to change us.

One such reader is René Girard.[2] His reading is in keeping with his theory of mimetic rivalry which leads to the unifying act of the victimization of a scapegoat. Girard's Job is the Job of the dialogues, the innocent victim of communal persecution who refuses to play the

---

1. Carmel McCarthy (*Sopherim*) discusses the unanswerable question as to whether the use of *brk* in Job is original to the text or a later euphemistic modification. Was the text changed to mask the possibility of cursing God, or does the text demand that the reader changes his or her reading by using *brk* in seemingly incongruous contexts? This is a parallel to the attempt to decide whether the epilogue is earlier or later than the dialogues.

2. R. Girard, *Job the Victim of his People* (trans. Y. Freccero; London: The Athlone Press, 1987) (first published as *La route antique des hommes pervers* [Paris: Editions Grasset et Fasquelle, 1985]). For a convenient summary of Girard's theories see J.G. Williams, 'The Innocent Victim: René Girard on Violence, Sacrifice and the Sacred', *RSR* 14 (1988), pp. 320-26.

game that his society demands. He will not be silent about his innocence. For Girard:

> All the additions to the Dialogues do violence to the original text; they are victorious acts of persecution in that they have succeeded, until now, in neutralizing the revelation of the scapegoat. . . the epilogue drowns the scapegoat in the puerile acts of revenge of a Hollywood success story.[1]

Yet even for Girard the prologue and epilogue are pragmatically indispensable in that they have concealed the implications of Job's protestations from the eyes of those readers who would have suppressed the book entirely if they had been aware of its subversive revelation of the underlying victimage mechanism:

> By concealing Job's subversive power, the mystifying additions have made the text accessible to ordinary devotion and at the same time prevented it from being rejected in horror, or so completely censored, changed and mutilated that its meaning would be lost for ever. By protecting the texts from too rough a contact with a hostile world and serving as shock-absorbers, these additions and commentaries that falsify have made possible the preservation of the texts that no one reads, since they are meaningless within the context given them. If the extent of their subversiveness had been more visible, they might never have survived for us.[2]

So this sugar-coating of prose has preserved the drastic and bitter medicine of the Joban revelation of the poetic unmasking of the scapegoat mechanism. Girard's metaphors of persecution and mutilation could, of course, be turned against his own reading. It is only by an act of violence, a dismemberment of the text as it has survived that he can wrest out the heart of its meaning. It is the text as survivor, however, which has such fascination as an enactment of its contents. Job survived, and the book of Job has survived. Girard wants to strip away the features which have led to the book's survival, and thus must deny Job his survival within the text by discarding the epilogue. The strength of the kind of reading we have been tracing in *The Only Problem* is that it depends on this ambivalent status of the survivor as both blessed and cursed, preserved from death to live a life of pain, outliving the beloved only to have to endure the knowledge of their absence.

Girard's account of the function of the scapegoat focuses entirely on

---

1. *Job*, pp. 143-44.
2. *Job*, p. 144.

the unifying effect of communal murder of a victim who is reviled and then sanctified to conceal the fact that the blessing of unity is based on innocent bloodshed. The biblical tradition, however, works with a double mechanism, perhaps most fully explored by Karl Barth in his *Church Dogmatics*.[1] In the ritual of atonement in Leviticus 16, the sins of Israel are actually borne not by the goat which is killed, but by the goat which survived to be driven out into the desert. Barth points out the strange relationship between the elect and the rejected in biblical text. The rejected, or the cursed, are often the ones who live out their lives under a special protection. Cain and Esau are paradigm examples. Contrary to the common perception, which sees length of life as the sign of God's favour in the Old Testament, there is a strand of the tradition which sees prolonged existence as something to be shunned.

One story that illustrates this very clearly is the story of the death of Abijah, the son of Jeroboam, in 1 Kings 14.[2] When his child falls ill, Jeroboam dispatches his wife in disguise to seek out the prophet Ahijah. The prophet tells her that her son will die 'because in him there is found something pleasing to the Lord, the God of Israel'. The child is to die, not as a sign of God's displeasure with him, but as a mark of divine favour. He alone of Jeroboam's house will be properly mourned and buried. Jeroboam's wife has to return to her husband bearing this message, knowing that the prophet has said that her son will die as her foot crosses the threshold of the palace, as indeed happens.

Can we not draw a parallel here with the experience of the reader? The reader approaches the end of the book with the same knowledge as Jeroboam's wife. As soon as we cross the threshold of the last word of the text, the world we participate in within the book will end. Like her, we have the option of flight. We can close the book and thereby in one sense prevent its ending. Yet for her to flee might be to abandon her child to an infinitely prolonged suffering. It would be to abandon her responsibilities as wife, as mother, and as the bearer of God's word.

1. K. Barth, *Church Dogmatics*, II.2 (ed. G.W. Bromiley and T.F. Torrance; Edinburgh: T. & T. Clark, 1957); Barth's exegesis of Leviticus 16 is given on pp. 357-65.
2. 1 Kgs 14.13 (RSV).

I can recall how as a child I would anxiously count the pages left in a book, torn between the desire to reach the end quickly in order to know how things turned out, and a desire to prolong the pleasure of life lived in the world of the book. Coupled with this was a real sense of bereavement with which I would part from the characters as I closed the last page of the book. A re-reading could never quite recapture the sense of discovery, of uncertainty, surprise, and growth in understanding which I and my 'paper friends' had shared. This parting was as painful as partings with real friends. As a reader I survived beyond the end of their story in a world which they could never enter even though the book they inhabited might well outlast me.

Job's anguish is that of the survivor. Even in the prologue to the book, God makes it clear that Job is entirely given over to Satan's power, except that he is to be kept alive. Of course, like any experimental animal or torture victim, Job must be maintained alive if there is to be any validity to the heavenly experiment to determine the ground of his loyalty. The theme of survival is reiterated in the grim comedy of the impossibly coincident disasters that befall his property and at last his children. Each one of the procession of messengers who bring the awful news ends his proclamation with the phrase, 'And I alone escaped to tell you'. Job is left to outlive his children and in 19.13-19 he bewails his total abandonment by his wife and relatives. Job himself is left alone to tell—whom? A God who Job knows must be intimately involved with him for his life to be sustained, and yet who abandons him to his suffering and solitude without a word of explanation or comfort. Job is left inextricably in the grasp of a God who has become absolutely alien to him.[1]

It is now a commonplace to trace the development of literary criticism through this century as a movement from the stress on the author as the guarantor of meaning to the autonomy of the text and then to a re-awakened interest in the reader as the site of the generation of meaning. Illuminating as the insights of reader-response criticism have been, there is a tendency to make the reader a stable centre, to make him or her the replacement of the author as the authoritative judge of meaning. This can lead us to miss the transactive nature of

---

1. For a profound examination of this aspect of Job's experience, see K. Barth, *Church Dogmatics*, IV.3 (ed. G.W. Bromiley and T.F. Torrance; Edinburgh: T. & T. Clark, 1961), pp. 400-404.

the act of reading, a process by which the reader undergoes change as a result of reading. Indeed, this is what is involved in describing the process involving author, text and reader as a communicative one; the whole point is to achieve a change in the reader. Job creates us as readers as we seek to create a coherent reading of Job. We are left in the grip of a book which has made us its readers and yet refuses our demands that it lay bare its meaning. The book of Job makes great demands on the resources which enable its readers to survive as readers. We can survive our reading of Job by denying its capacity to change us, or otherwise defending ourselves against the possibility of being changed by it. If, however, we decide to open ourselves to it, we will be left bearing wounds.

Harvey Gotham does survive his engagement with Job and the loss of his wife, but he is not unchanged by the end of Spark's novel. Spark is reticent about his reactions, but she does explicitly mention his sadness at coming to the end of his monograph. Obliquely we infer from his doubt over Job's happiness that he does not end the book contentedly. He has suffered as a reader and in his daily existence. Yet how real is this suffering? Is it not to say the least tasteless to suggest that the suffering of the reader is in any way comparable to that of the victims of disease, misfortune and human evil?

This problem is also at the heart of Muriel Spark's choice of a reader of Job as the protagonist of her novel. Granted that there is a sense in which we can suffer as reader, is this not just a retreat from the real suffering of the world? Is the attempt to justify it as anything more serious not just the illusion which the academic has to believe or at least promote?

Harvey's assertion of the reality of the suffering of thought and study which prompts the quotation from *The Guardian* is part of his musings as he waits in a police station for news of his wife, Effie, who has been accused of terrorist crimes. He becomes fleetingly aware of a man whom he surmises to be a Balkan immigrant:

> Patience, pallor and deep anxiety: there goes suffering, Harvey reflected.
> And I found him interesting. Is it only by recognising how flat would be
> the world without the sufferings of others that we know how desperately
> becalmed our own lives would be without suffering? Do I suffer on
> Effie's account? Yet, and perhaps I can live by that experience. We all
> need something to suffer about. But Job, my work on Job, all interrupted
> and neglected, probed into and interfered with: that is experience too; real

experience, not vicarious, as is often assumed. To study, to think, is to live and suffer painfully.[1]

Are we to read this as a valid self-justification by Harvey or as an ironic revelation of the self-absorption which allows him to treat suffering as an intellectual problem? Harvey's response to the world's suffering is to wrestle with the theology of an ancient and obscure text. If, as Alan Bold suggests,[2] Spark is here satirizing Harvey's intellectual detachment, characterizing him as a virtual solipsist, what are we to make of Spark herself, writing a novel based on this problem, or ourselves as readers either of Job or *The Only Problem*, or indeed a paper such as this? But is Spark here being as one-sidedly satirical as Bold would have it? In its turn, his wife Effie's very different response of involvement in terrorist activity is certainly ironized in the novel as a childish but murderous revolt. The only result of her attempts to redress the sufferings of the world's oppressed is the death of a French policemen, the suffering of whose family is graphically depicted by Spark in a speech given to Harvey's police interrogator.

Elsewhere in the novel, Spark gives ambivalent signals about the reality of Harvey's suffering. She speaks of Harvey as being 'tormented' by his belief in God which leads him to have to confront the problem of undeserved suffering. His brother-in-law Edward, not always a reliable observer in the novel, notes undeniable anxiety and suffering in his face. But towards the end of the novel, Harvey writes in a letter to his brother-in-law:

> 'no one pities men who cling wilfully to their sufferings' (*Philoctetes—* speech of Neoptolemus). I'm not even sure that I suffer, I only endure distress. But why should I analyse myself? I am analysing the God of Job.[3]

Earlier in the novel, Harvey uses the opportunity of a press conference eager to know of his involvement with his wife's illicit actions to deliver a lecture on the meaning of Job. In a subsequent attempt to

1. *The Only Problem*, p. 153.
2. See A. Bold, *Muriel Spark* (London: Methuen, 1986), pp. 115-19. For a different response, which understands the end of *The Only Problem* as 'calm acceptance and commitment to social responsibility', see V.B. Richmond, *Muriel Spark* (New York: Ungar, 1984), pp. 166-76.
3. *The Only Problem*, p. 180.

placate his aunt who is outraged by his reported blasphemies, Harvey
says:

> Auntie Pet, you've got to understand that I said nothing whatsoever about
> God, I mean our Creator. What I was talking about was a fictional charac-
> ter in the book of Job, called God.[1]

Harvey's distinction between the God he sees at work in the world
around him and the fictional character represented in the text of Job
reveals the kind of distantiation which allows him to consider suffering dispassionately. Even the etymology of the word 'dispassionate'
shows the problem of the discussion of suffering. Those who suffer do
not have the luxury of enquiring into their experience as a problem.
Job is not at all interested in the question of evil in general. He does
not want to know 'Why is there suffering?' He cries out 'Why *me*?
Why am I singled out?' Job does not know he is a character in Job.
Harvey exemplifies the problem of those to whom this question
presents itself as 'Why *him*?' In its turn this question can reflect back
on the questioner in the form 'Why *not* me?' This is the question
every survivor asks. However appalling the events which readers
bring into being as they attempt to synthesize the world of the text,
they will walk away from them physically unscathed. Psychologically,
they may find it harder to shake off the effects. What we read, we
read as survivors.

It is the survivor who feels pain, the body's outraged cry at the
assault of death upon it. Even without physical injury, to survive can
lead to a kind of suffering, the phenomenon of 'survival guilt' testified
to among those seemingly privileged to live after an accident and seen
in a peculiarly intense form among many survivors of the Nazi
concentration camps.[2] The blessing which survival seems to represent
may turn into a life sentence of physical and mental anguish, both as a
legacy of the appalling experiences the survivor has undergone, but
also through the feeling of unworthiness at being singled out when so

---

1. *The Only Problem*, p. 135.
2. For discussion of the phenomenon of survivor guilt, see A. Gill, *The Journey
Back from Hell* (London: Grafton Books, 1989), pp. 95, 223-24; B. Bettelheim,
Surviving and Other Essays (London: Thames and Hudson, 1979), p. 26.
Bettelheim makes the point that the survivors of the holocaust were left having to live
through psychological traumas unimaginable to those who had not shared their experience. Surviving one set of horrors in itself laid them open to others.

many other people with as much or more claim to life perished miserably. To write a monograph like Harvey's or a novel like *The Only Problem*, or indeed this paper, argues a level of privilege, of freedom from the causes of suffering which may prompt the question 'Why *not* me?' Perhaps like Harvey we have to persuade ourselves that suffering the guilt of privilege is sufficient to give us some inkling of what it might be like to be without that privilege of protection. Part of the pain of the reader is the knowledge of the vicarious nature of the reader's pain.

TOWARDS A BIBLICAL THEOLOGY: VON BALTHASAR'S
THE GLORY OF THE LORD[1]

John K. Riches

In the preface to his Latin writings, published in 1545,[2] Luther describes the painful route by which he came to know God, no longer as a terrifying and avenging God, but as a God of mercy and grace. The stages along that route are marked out by his own lectures on different books of the Bible, first the Psalms, and then Galatians and Romans. As is well known, he records how it was the verse 'In it the righteousness of God is revealed' (Rom. 1.17) which caused him great anguish, for he understood it, as he had been taught by the schoolmen, to refer to the formal or active righteousness of God, that is to say righteousness considered as a characteristic of God himself and his actions *ad extra*. On such a view, the gospel merely added to the terror which the law of the Old Testament already struck into his heart. Was it not enough that the law should bring home to sinful men and women the enormity of their failings and the inevitability of God's wrath which they occasioned, without the Gospel reinforcing this by publishing again the righteous nature of God? But Luther did not abandon the struggle. If he hated the God which such an interpretation of Paul presented him with, he was the more determined to discover what it was that the apostle had intended by those words, specifically by his use of the genitive *theou*. It was in attending to the context of those words that illumination came. It was Paul's reference to Habakkuk, 'He who through faith is righteous shall live', that showed him that Paul was using the genitive to refer, not to the

1. Hans Urs von Balthasar, *The Glory of the Lord. VI. Theology: The Old Covenant*; VII. *Theology: The New Covenant* (Edinburgh: T. & T. Clark, 1990).
2. In J. Dillenberger (ed.), *Martin Luther: Selections from his Writings* (New York: Doubleday, 1961), pp. 3-12.

righteousness by which God himself is righteous, but rather to the 'righteousness with which merciful God justifies us by faith', the gift of righteousness which he bestows out of his mercy. Now, that is to say, he understood the genitive as referring not to the formal or active righteousness of God, but, in the schoolmen's phraseology, the passive righteousness. It was this strictly grammatical insight which brought release and joy to Luther: it was for him 'the gates of paradise'. Immediately from memory he ran through the writings of Paul, re-construing the genitives: 'the work of God, that is, what God does in us, the power of God, with which he makes us strong, the wisdom of God, with which he makes us wise',[1] like indeed an explorer who at long last reaches his goal and runs delightedly about, simply savouring the strange, new world which he has at long last entered.

This account of the work of the biblical theologian, for that is what it is, has been enormously influential. It is not difficult to trace its reception in our century both by Barth and by Bultmann. But it is perhaps useful to draw out certain features of this account, which, whatever its historical accuracy, has informed the practice of biblical and exegetical theology.

For Luther, we have seen, it is the search for Paul's intention which ultimately governs his search for the 'plain meaning' of the text. The 'plain' meaning of the text is not something that is necessarily lightly won; it may be discovered, at least on occasion, only by stripping away inherited readings of the text which obscure the original intention of the author. Nevertheless, for Luther the 'original meaning', or, at least, the new reading which he wished to offer, was still something which emerged out of his own vigorous debates with traditional, received understandings of the text. However much he may wish to set aside mediaeval readings of the text, he is also eager to show his continuity with Augustine. Nevertheless it is clear that for Luther, the struggle for Paul's intended sense was conducted with the full resources of humanist philology. The central religious experience of the Protestant Reformation was a 'grammatical' experience, and this has been reflected in the extraordinary treasury of biblical scholarship which the Lutheran tradition has given to the world. (This is by way of corrective to the currently modish attacks on 'Lutheran interpretations of everything'.) But it is important to notice that Luther's

1. *Selections*, p. 11.

wrestling with the sense of Rom. 1.17 is not an isolated phenomenon; it is part of his sustained attempt to read the Scriptures, of which his work on the Psalms, and importantly here, his understanding of Paul's use of the Old Testament, are integral parts. He is a biblical theologian, interested in the meaning of the Bible (singular!) for all his focus on the original intention of particular writers. This will set up a tension between the sense of particular utterances in particular books and the sense of the whole, a tension which Luther will tackle in his own vigorous way, but which will leave a difficult legacy for those who follow him.

Of course this picture of the work of the biblical scholar is only one among many, however influential it has been. It presents us above all with the story of the achievement of a major shift in cultural perspective. It marked the birth of a new world. But if Luther had opened the gates of paradise, he was arguably less effective in describing the territory which lay within. Indeed the metaphor is misleading; Luther did not so much discover a new world simply for the entering and enjoying. Rather, he discovered new concepts which would enable him and those who worked with him on the biblical texts to create new worlds, some of which would seem strange even to Luther himself. The work of other Reformers, notably of John Calvin, would then lie more in elaborating the ground rules of this new world, than in describing what Luther had discovered. But, and this is of the greatest significance, this was not how they or indeed others after them would see it. They saw themselves precisely as discovering the kind of world that God had—always—intended and indeed had communicated effectively through the biblical writings. (Hence for Luther the importance of the 'plain' meaning of Scripture and his insistence on 'what stands written'.) This explains both the Reformers' passionate attachment to the original intention of the author and the bitter conflicts which arose between rival Reformation groups as they discovered how different were the worlds which they severally delineated. How could paradise be divided?

I

I raise all this by way of introduction to a discussion of an interestingly different kind of biblical theology which has appeared recently for the first time in English, Hans Urs von Balthasar's concluding two volumes of *The Glory of the Lord*. Appearing in German first at the end of the sixties,[1] it has so far made little impression on the scholarly world, despite the glaringly obvious lack of any serious successors to Bultmann's *New Testament Theology*[2] of 1948. Nevertheless, there are, I believe, ways in which this most idiosyncratic of biblical theologians may contribute to the present revival of interest in the enterprise of biblical theology and these are related partly to his determination to reinstate aesthetics in theology, partly to his willingness to see biblical theology as an enterprise which is necessarily engaged in dialogue with the theological tradition. As his work is far from familiar, even to those with an interest in theology and aesthetics, let me begin with a brief introduction to the present two volumes.

It is von Balthasar's contention that theology, both Protestant and Catholic, has, since the Reformation, steadily turned away from aesthetics, conceiving God, that is to say, principally as good and true, only secondarily and infrequently as beautiful, the fulfilment of human desires.[3] In so doing, it has turned its back on central aspects of the Bible and the tradition: the sense of beauty and glory which pervades the Psalms, the prophets and the patriarchal narratives; the confession of the strange and wholly unprecedented glory of the crucified and risen Lord, which is to be found in measure at least in Paul and the Synoptics, and most clearly in the theological vision of the Fourth Gospel. Such a sense of beauty did indeed find a place in the great works of the theological tradition, as von Balthasar has impressively shown in the first volume of his *Studies in Theological Style*.[4] But in the later stages of theological history, it is the lay theologians, the poets, philosophers and playwrights who have kept the vision alive: Dante, Pascal, Hopkins, Solovyev, Peguy and others. Among modern theologians of stature it is only Karl Barth who has devoted time and attention to it, and it is, among his contemporaries, from Karl Barth that von Balthasar has learnt most.[5]

1. *Herrlichkeit: Eine theologische Ästhetik*. III.2. *Theologie*. I. *Alter Bund* (Einsiedeln: Johannes Verlag, 1967); II. *Neuer Bund* (Einsiedeln: Johannes Verlag, 1969).
2. English edition, London: SCM Press, 1955.
3. See, e.g., *Glory of the Lord*, I (1982), *passim*.
4. *Glory of the Lord*, II (1984).
5. Cf. above all his *Karl Barth: Deutung und Darstellung seiner Theologie* (Cologne: Hegner, 1951).

To speak of the aesthetic dimension is to focus on the manner in which an object appears and, correspondingly, on the manner in which it is sighted. Beauty,[1] so von Balthasar says, is intimately related to form. The artist's vision of beauty cannot be separated from the figure in and through which it is expressed. There are no external criteria which can be brought to judge the beauty of a work of art: the work must have its own *Evidenz* (evidential force), confronting the beholder, as it does, with its sheer otherness, its irreducibility. But, paradoxically, such radiance will only be grasped by those who have eyes to see, who have been to school with the works of the great artists and learnt to read the figure, the *Gestalt* of a work of art, its measure and proportions. The 'truth', that is to say, of a work of art lies in its rightness, the fact that the *Jupiter Symphony* could not be otherwise, is perfect as it is; and it is in this that its power to delight and restore lies. But such truth is not for all; it is only those who have been caught by such beauty, have had their eyes opened, have 'the eyes of faith' who in fact see, who are fulfilled.

Such talk of beauty and form may indeed seem a far cry from modern theology. To many it will sound strangely frivolous, diverting attention alike from the pressing moral issues of world poverty and injustice and the intellectual challenges which have been forced on Christian theology by the development of the sciences. But it is precisely von Balthasar's contention that beauty is one of the fundamental determinations of Being, that the aesthetic vision is a vision of reality, of the way things are. It is not therefore an optional aspect of theology; it is essential if we are not to lose sight of Being altogether. Without it, theology may degenerate into a chilly, overserious moralism; while metaphysics, divorced from its fundamental sense of wonder, will cease to command attention at all. Being is in risk of being forgotten altogether. And in his two volumes on *The Realm of Metaphysics*,[2] he has attempted to show, with enormous erudition, how the myth-makers and poets and philosophers have caught sight of Being, have themselves been possessed by a vision of the terrible beauty of the gods, of ultimate reality, which they have expressed in the rich treasury of antiquity and its modern mediations.

And it was at this point that von Balthasar had to meet the sharpest opposition from his mentor and friend, Karl Barth. If we press the

1.   The matter is most fully discussed in *Glory of the Lord*, I.
2.   *Glory of the Lord*, IV & V (1989, 1990).

analogy between the poetic, mythical vision of Being and the glory of God which is sighted in the Bible are we not in danger of reducing the revelation of the divine Word to a mode or variation of human apprehensions of reality, confusing the work of men and women with the work of God? Certainly it was this anxiety which had earlier led Karl Barth to claim that the doctrine of *analogia entis* was the work of the anti-Christ and the only serious reason for not becoming a Catholic.[1] Nor were von Balthasar's subsequent attempts to dissuade him by any means successful.[2]

Thus, in approaching von Balthasar's final two volumes of *The Glory of the Lord*, we must be at least aware of forces which pull at him in different directions. On the one hand his whole enterprise is concerned with re-instating aesthetics to its proper place within theology. And this means being alive to the analogies between expressions of the divine glory in the Bible and the works of the poets and mythmakers of ancient Greece and Rome, with all the attention which they gave to form and proportion. On the other hand, he has been put on his mettle to show that what is indeed perceived in the Bible is *totaliter aliter*, a vision where the dissimilarities to the visions of antiquity are always immeasurably greater than the similarities.

II

Von Balthasar is at some pains to insist that his study of glory in the Old and New Testaments is in no way an attempt at providing a complete biblical theology. In some ways indeed it is more like his earlier studies of theological styles, where he was attempting to show the place that aesthetics occupied in the tradition before its deposition, at least from the official schools. Thus, in the Old Testament volume, we are treated to a series of studies of the portrayal of the divine glory, from its almost physical manifestations in the patriarchal narratives through to the visions of future appearances in the apocalyptic seers. Such portrayals are properly called aesthetic, not least because they present the glory, the weight and majesty of God, as perceived through sight: whether it be the seeing of the physical events of the burning bush, Isaiah's vision in the temple, Ezekiel's vision of the

1. *Church Dogmatics*, I.1 (Edinburgh: T. & T. Clark, 1938), pp. x-xi.
2. Cf. von Balthasar's remarks in the preface to the second edition of *Karl Barth* (Cologne: Hegner, 1962) which Barth was by no means happy to accept.

chariot, or the apocalyptic seers' visions of the future appearing of the Almighty. There are elements in the Old Testament, constitutive elements indeed, whose similarities to the world of the Greek myths, of Homer and Pindar, or indeed to later Jewish traditions of Zohar mysticism are not to be denied, but which are fastidiously avoided by a Christianity purged of mysticism, where faith is schematized in terms of obedience to a prophetic word conceived of primarily in moral terms. Von Balthasar does not, for all that, overlook the powerfully moral dimension of the vision of God's *zedekah* in the Old Testament. Such visions spring out of the covenant between God and his people, a relationship which guides and governs the whole life of the people and is therefore in the deepest sense moral. And in this covenant there is seen something of that loving condescension by which God binds himself to his people, risking, as it were, his own glory by linking his name with a people who may betray and dishonour him. And yet the people of the covenant is intended precisely to show forth his glory to all the nations, to be holy as he is holy. And such holiness lies in faithfulness to the divine will and law.

But of course those who read the Old Testament from the viewpoint of the New conceive of it as only part of the story of the manifestation of God's glory. For von Balthasar the question of the relationship of the two covenants is posed in terms of form and fulfilment, as indeed is the case in the theology of Irenaeus. God's glory is perceived in and through the particular *Gestalt* which is constituted by the relationship of the two covenants. Already in the later books of the Old Testament the vision of God's glory becomes fragmented; there is a loss of the sense of the reality of the covenant, a looking to something which is yet to come. And this sense of fragmentedness, of the questionableness of existence in the face of death is brought even more sharply to expression in subsequent apocalyptic literature. So the fulfilment is not achieved by a process of steady development to a final climax: rather there is a sharp break between the two covenants, a caesura which could in no sense have been anticipated. The Word of God himself enters history in order to restore the broken relationships between God and his people. And such a coming involves both judgment and restoration; the breaking of relationships and their refashioning, the emergence of a new covenant where the Son unites in himself the unconditional love of God and the response of restored humanity, the birth of a new world in which people can live anew in praise of his glory.

It is, then, this central event of the Word becoming flesh which holds the two covenants together, by way of on the one hand, anticipation and on the other, response and witness. This is reflected clearly in the design of von Balthasar's second volume. If the first volume presented an account of the developing—and fragmenting—vision of God's glory in the old covenant largely by following the order of the Old Testament writings, the second can no longer sustain the design. What is abandoned is not so much the salvation historical schema. The caesura must be marked, and marked in its due place. But it cannot be grasped simply in terms of the subsequent New Testament accounts of the glory of God in Christ: these are reserved for the second and third parts of the volume. Before them von Balthasar sets a section which he entitles indeed *Verbum Caro Factum*,[1] but which is in no sense a straight interpretation of Johannine theology. It is rather his own creative attempt to point to the central reality which, as it were, holds together the two covenants. It is the centre to which the old covenant almost unwittingly leads up; it is that which is reflected on, worked out, brought to expression (*ausgewortet*) in all subsequent biblical theologies, whether those of the New Testament itself, or in later theologies which continue the process begun in those writings.

Thus for von Balthasar the New Testament writings are not the ending of the Old Testament, which without them would be incomplete, lacking a fitting 'closure'; rather in the word-less death of the Word made flesh, the glory of the Old Testament is gathered up, recapitulated in such a way that it can then flow out in the fulfilment of the New. The New Testament is not the last chapter in the Old: it marks the beginning of the new world which springs from the divine kenosis of the Son. And the fullness which is imparted is not 'given by measure': it is the inexhaustible glory of the divine self-giving which is only properly reflected in the multiplicity of the New Testament witnesses and of subsequent biblical theologies.

III

The first part of the volume, in which von Balthasar addresses himself to the event of the incarnation is not, it has to be said, in any way easy

1. *Glory of the Lord*, VII, pp. 33-235.

to characterize. In one obvious sense he is attempting to describe theologically the coming of the Word. In this he starts by relating its coming to that which has gone before, to the 'fragments of the old covenant', to the figure of the Baptist.[1] This is followed after some illuminating theological reflection on the nature of biblical theology, to which we shall return, by a section entitled simply 'Word-Flesh'.[2] It is in effect a theological account of the life of Jesus which presents it under the three heads of claim (*Anspruch*), poverty and self-abandonment, portraying the progress of the authoritative Word into increasing powerlessness and abandonment. There follows again a more generally reflective section, this time on the theology of time and salvation history,[3] which contains surely one of the most original discussions of eschatology, drawing out with great sensitivity the implications of the different stances of Dodd, Bultmann, Cullmann and others. And then in a final section, entitled 'The Momentum of the Cross' (*Wucht des Kreuzes*[4]), the final confrontation with the godless-ness of the world is reached, and we are offered a concluding medita-tion on the kenosis of the eternal Son, his taking upon himself the 'concrete human destiny'[5] which leads him ultimately to enter the realm of death, that which is wholly opposed to God, to life, to the very nature of the Word himself. The Word becomes word-less; he who was eternally related to the Father enters the God-forsakeness of hell.[6]

Of course a mere sketch of the contents of this section can hardly indicate the way in which the outline is filled out. Reading von Balthasar is often like reading Thomas Mann at his most allusive, say in *Doktor Faustus*. He is a man so deeply engaged in dialogue with the metaphysical tradition, the theological tradition, recent biblical schol-arship, literature and drama, with those sympathetic to him and those whom he passionately opposes, that only the closest reading of his text will do justice to it. And that is the first point to notice. For him the biblical texts feed naturally into the theological tradition, are at least

---

1. *Glory of the Lord*, VII, pp. 33-76.
2. *Glory of the Lord*, VII, pp. 15-161.
3. *Glory of the Lord*, VII, pp. 162-201.
4. *Glory of the Lord*, VII, pp. 202-35.
5. *Glory of the Lord*, VII, p. 212.
6. *Glory of the Lord*, VII, pp. 228-35.

analogically related to the metaphysical tradition and the traditions of European letters in such a way that a dialogue between them is in principle possible and to be expected. And this distances his work immediately from so much that stems from the Protestant rejection of metaphysics (notably I suppose by Ritschl) and the consequent attempt to set biblical theology up as an alternative and epistemologically distinct mode of discourse about God, one where indeed the moral would have the primacy over the metaphysical and the aesthetic. For von Balthasar it is a fundamental assumption that the biblical texts do address themselves to the perennial questions of the mystery of the universe, of the existence of evil, error and suffering, of the root of evil within the human will and the manner of its overcoming, of justice, restitution, judgment and mercy, and that they can do so in a way that is at least analogous to that of the poets, the myth-makers and even the philosophers.

Belief in the possibility of such dialogue with the theological and metaphysical tradition also of course sharply separates him from those for whom the 'cultural gap' between our appropriations of the biblical traditions and the writings of the New Testament themselves is so great that a complete shedding of our own cultural skin would be necessary before we could adequately begin to apprehend their meaning. Not that von Balthasar seriously considers such objections; for him the validity of his own position must lie in the fruitfulness of his method, his ability to draw illumination from his continuing dialogue.

But what indeed of the content of this first part of the volume? Where indeed does it come from? How does it relate to other attempts at a biblical theology? The section 'Word-Flesh' has a particular interest. It draws on theses from (then) recent discussion of the historical Jesus (the so-called 'New Quest') and yet clearly weaves them into a schema of his own devising, for all that its elements are individually drawn from the Bible. Thus the section on Jesus' claim[1] draws freely on work by Bornkamm, Käsemann, Fuchs and Schweizer. The claims to authority which Jesus makes in the antitheses on the Sermon on the Mount and his ability to see into people's hearts are taken as at least indirect confirmation of the church's confession of him as eschatological Word and Judge. That is to say, like the theologians of the

1. *Glory of the Lord*, VII, pp. 115-29.

New Quest (and like more recently R. Morgan), von Balthasar is ready to allow faith's understanding of the Word to be filled out, deepened by historical critical enquiry into the biblical traditions. Like them too, he is unwilling to take his overall schema from such enquiries, arguing that proper understanding is only possible from the perspective of faith. Where, however, they differ is in the way that they would each explicate the phrase 'faith's understanding of the Word'. For Bornkamm, Käsemann and Fuchs, faith is to be understood primarily in (Lutheran) terms of obedience to the Word of the kerygma, that is to say the proclamation of the gospel. It is a willing acceptance of the call to decision, an abandonment of one's attempts to find a meaning for, to justify one's own life, and a thankful acceptance of the new life which flows from the gospel. Thus faith knows the Word primarily as 'address' (*Anrede*), that which judges, challenges human pretensions and restores men and women to a life lived out in trust in God. In this, of course, the mythological language of final judgment is abandoned in favour of an anthropological (existential) account of the effect of the Word on those who hear. Judgment is present now in the words of Jesus, as it is present in the proclamation of the church.

It would be easy to misunderstand what von Balthasar has to say at this point as simply a re-affirmation of traditional mythological eschatology over against the existential interpretation of Bultmann and his followers. It is undeniable that he wants to hold on to the eschatological language of future judgment but equally clear that he does not want to do so in any simple, literalist sense. He quotes with approval Marxsen's dictum that such 'implicit' Christology always expresses more than any so-called explicit Christology, 'because the momentum of this claim can never be equalled by any formulation of it in words'.[1] He wants to give due weight to both present and future eschatology and not to resolve that tension by reducing judgment to an event within the lives of believers. All this, as the later discussion of the momentum of time will make clearer, is because for him the coming of the Word is an event in history which gives meaning to history as a whole, which answers the fundamental mystery of the *world*'s ills, and which cannot therefore properly be reduced to particular historical events, however much it may have concrete

---

1. *Glory of the Lord*, VII, p. 121.

implications, and may bear fruit in the lives of believers. And for that reason too the 'story' of the coming of the Word cannot be exhausted by discussion of the claims which he makes but must press on to explore the paradox of the Word made flesh, of his being stripped of his power and freedom as he freely accepts his deliverance into the hands of wicked men, into the grip of the powers of darkness, that the divine will for the world may be done.

This brings us to the final section of the first part, 'The Momentum of the Cross'. Here most obviously, von Balthasar is in dialogue with the theological tradition. But again it might be said with some justice that it is a dialogue which is at the least idiosyncratic, choosing with whom he will engage, laying his emphases where he will. His Christology draws heavily on the quite recent tradition of kenotic Christology, and develops it in creative and imaginative ways. The final section without question is deeply indebted to Adrienne von Speyr's visions of the descent into hell which she received regularly on Holy Saturday and which have had a profound effect on von Balthasar's theology.[1] For it is in the descent into hell that von Balthasar sees revealed the mystery of the Trinity and in it too that he finds the only possible answer to the ultimate riddle of how a loving, sovereign God could allow the misery and suffering and evil which afflicts our world.

IV

All of this may indeed seem a very long way from sober exegesis of the biblical texts and is certainly quite without precedent in recent works of biblical theology. Is there anything that we can learn from it? It may help first to bring out some of the dissimilarities and perhaps surprising similarities between von Balthasar's work here and the kind of biblical theology which I described at the beginning of this essay. At the very simplest level both Luther and he are seeking a comprehensive understanding of Scripture which will enable them to renew the Christian tradition when it has become ossified and restrictive, even oppressive. (It is important to recall that von Balthasar's early work was the subject of much criticism, and that even though he

---

1. See von Balthasar's account in *First Glance at Adrienne von Speyr* (San Francisco: Ignatius Press, 1981).

may have come to be regarded as a conservative, the foundations for his major work were laid when he was active among those who were working to break down the defensive bastions of the church.) More, both men write with quite specific theological, moral problems in mind: Luther the terrible moral anguish which was caused by the Babylonian captivity of the church; von Balthasar deeply wounded by the breakdown of European civilization and the appalling atrocities with which that was accompanied, possessed almost by a sense of pervasive evil in the world.

There is no doubt of the ultimate seriousness of von Balthasar's writing at this point, nor of the way in which Adrienne's terrifying visions of hell inform his treatment of Christology and soteriology. But the comparison with Luther raises a key question. Luther's account focused on the interpretation of biblical statements about God's justice. His struggle to discover Paul's intended meaning in such passages provided him with a key which would successfully unlock a wide range of passages and show him Scripture in a new light. By contrast von Balthasar brings to the text a set of powerful religious experiences (Adrienne von Speyr's visions of Holy Saturday) and uses them as the key to the understanding of central passages about the incarnation and passion, indeed as a guide to that central mystery of the Word become flesh which the biblical texts themselves witness to and reflect on. Yet it can hardly be said that the *descensus* motif (unlike, arguably at least, Paul's treatment of justification) plays a central part in the New Testament, even if it might be said that it serves to point to a gap in the admittedly quite schematic Christian narrative of salvation, one which von Balthasar fills out with great virtuosity.

How illuminating is this contrast between a historical, grammatical search for Paul's intended sense and a virtuoso performance of the text by von Balthasar, redolent as it is of discussions which have developed within theological circles only since the publication of the present volumes? On the one hand it does I think represent quite accurately the sense in which von Balthasar sees himself doing biblical theology, namely as an extension of the reflection on the *verbum caro factum* of which the New Testament volumes are the font and also the prime exemplars.[1] In that sense his theology is indeed a performance

1. *Glory of the Lord*, VII, pp. 103-14: 'theology in the Bible can have no fundamentally different form from later theology in the Church: each is an

of those texts with their quite specific referents in the life, death and resurrection of Jesus, however elusive any account of that might be. On the other hand, to press the contrast between 'performance' and the search for the original meaning of the texts too far would be mistaken. For von Balthasar it is clearly vital that any reading that he offers should be guided by, certainly should not conflict with the central claims made by those texts, precisely because they do refer to a central mystery, are not simply meaningful in and of themselves. But, and this again distinguishes his position from much recent Protestant biblical theology, he would not claim that the biblical texts give either a uniform, or indeed any exhaustive account of that to which they refer. Central though their witness is, they are always to be seen as mediating, through their various 'theologies', the central, inexhaustible and always greater glory of the word-less Word. And that mediation comes precisely as those texts interact with the life of the various communities which accord them authority, a hearing. What indeed von Balthasar brings to their interpretation from Adrienne is not a purely extraneous set of theological ideas and visions, but ones which have grown immediately out of her extraordinarily intense meditations on the *Triduum Mortis* and which provide a link with the torn and bitter experience of the present century.

This may perhaps also help to pave the way out a dilemma to which I alluded in the introduction. Luther suggests that his discovery of Paul's meaning in Rom. 1.17 had unlocked the gates to paradise, giving him a key to the whole meaning of Scripture and therefore allowing him to discover the divine will and purposes. But of course the Reformers who followed him gave very diverse accounts of the new world whose gates Luther had unlocked. One way of describing what had happened here would be to say that what Luther had done was to grasp certain concepts which would become the basis for a new family of Christian communities, rather that for a single church. Such concepts, that is to say, function as means for constructing new social worlds. And clearly there is truth in such an account and it enables us to discern the unity and diversity between the different historical

interpretative act of standing and circling around a mid-point that can indeed be interpreted, but is always in need of interpretation and *has never been exhaustively interpreted*' (p. 103, my italics).

communities which have taken their lead from Protestant biblical scholarship.

On the other hand such a view may seem to give a rather minimal account of the unity of such bodies, and to fail indeed to deal adequately with the question of how far such common basic concepts, together with their diverse elaborations, *refer* to the divine will and purposes (which they were certainly held to do). What von Balthasar's emphasis on the inexhaustibility and transcendence of the *verbum caro factum* does is to point to the ground of the unity of such diversity *in the referent itself* to which our concepts and their elaborations can only ever approximate. In this sense, von Balthasar's biblical theology (sometimes, it has to be said, somewhat *malgré lui*) provides a fruitful basis for an ecumenical theology—one which arguably is more satisfactory than Luther's search for the 'plain' meaning.

One further point of comparison may be made and referred to contemporary debates. Luther's study of Paul was rooted in a wider search for the meaning of the whole of Scripture. At the same time his emphasis on the *pro me*, the sense in which scriptural terms and concepts were to be understood in the light of a specific experience of divine judgment and grace, became itself a critical instrument by which the Bible itself could be judged, and passages which were found wanting could be relegated to the margins or indeed dismissed from the canon altogether. Von Balthasar's theology allows for a far greater diversity in the biblical visions of God's glory, and allots such diversity, fragmentedness, a place within the overall *Gestalt*. Such an enterprise with its emphasis on the overall *Gestalt* might be thought, however, to be vulnerable to another charge, namely of imposing on the openness of the Hebrew Bible a closure which it precisely and characteristically lacks. Such charges have been made against the Christian Bible and indeed much recent exegesis by Gabriel Josipovici,[1] who argues strongly for the radical openness, the resistance to any schema of fulfilment, of the Hebrew Bible, specifically of its narratives.

Perhaps enough has been said to show how far von Balthasar's theology might be thought to be vulnerable to such a charge. Clearly there is a sense in which he claims that the revelation of the Word made flesh is a final revelation of God's glory which therefore

1. *The Book of God* (New Haven: Yale University Press, 1988).

surpasses all other manifestations. But he is first at great pains not to suggest that there is a simple relationship of promise and fulfilment between Old and New Testaments. The manner in which the Word made flesh fulfils the visions of God's glory in the Old Covenant is wholly unexpected, outstripping all that might have been imagined. Above all it occurs in an event which is word-less, and which only subsequently liberates the images of the Old Testament to give expression to what is achieved in that event: the overcoming of death, the bounds of mortality:

> That which is Christian is anthropologically significant (in relation, that is, to what is already given in Israel), or it is nothing at all. It solves the unbearable contradiction that runs right through the very form of man: that he, knowing and touching what is immortal, yet dies; if it does not solve this, then it solves nothing at all. Therefore its truth does not lie primarily on the level of an invisible collision of the absolute weight of God with what is other, with that which has nothing in common with God. Only when this inconceivable event takes place, is the world of images liberated—what the old covenant still owes us, is possible only on the basis of what is unimaginable, so that the images. . . which surrounded the unconstructible midpoint, and which could not bring themselves together to make a credible whole form, suddenly crystallise and become thereby comprehensible both in themselves (as images of the Old Testament) and in their transcendence to the New Testament unity that gives them meaning.[1]

The figure of the crucified, dead Christ is a wholly strange figure of glory which—precisely as word-less—defies exhaustive interpretation. This is not closure in the sense of bringing the movement of the Old Testament to a term, giving it a rounded meaning in virtue of its conclusion in Christ. It is a radically new beginning which can nevertheless be seen to have its roots in the 'fragments' of the Old Testament as they are drawn together and 'handed over' in the figure of the Baptist. Moreover, the sense in which this vision of the glory of the Incarnate Word 'fulfils' is also resistant to the notion of closure, if by that is meant the setting of a limit to the possibilities of human existence and, indeed, knowledge. This is clear in von Balthasar's insistence on understanding fulfilment as something which inaugurates a new life of inexhaustible richness lived out of the contemplation of the divine glory: *in laudem gloriae*. It is also importantly to be seen in

1. *Glory of the Lord*, VII, p. 83.

his treatment of Christian universalism,[1] where he stressed the continuing struggle between God in Christ and men and women in an *Agonie* which is genuine only because of its open outcome.

V

It is unlikely that anyone will follow von Balthasar slavishly in the development of a biblical theology. Nor would he have wished it. What he has given us may, however, be a constant source of disturbance. He reminds us of the rootedness of the biblical texts in the deep and fundamental questions of human existence—and in the articulations of those questions in myth and philosophy. He reminds us of the centrality to the Christian Bible of an *event*, that which can only subsequently be expressed in words and which by its very nature as it crosses the boundaries between death and life can never be fully grasped in human language. He sets the task of biblical interpretation firmly back into the long tradition of biblical theology, asserting in his own way the predominance of 'literary' readings of the texts over purely historical-critical ones, and allowing those readings to be deeply informed both by the reader's own apprehensions of the human predicament and by the 'eyes of faith'. And he underlines the inexhaustibility of the glory and transcendence of God in the Old and New Covenants which holds out its own promise and spurns all attempts at systematization and reduction. It is an invitation to explore the 'strange new world of the Bible' which from the start encourages us to expect richness and variety, as the divine glory bears fruit in the lives of its beholders.

---

1. See 'Christlicher Universalismus', in *Verbum Caro* (Einsiedeln: Johannes Verlag, 1960), pp. 260-75, esp. 268-69.

SINS, DEBTS AND JUBILEE RELEASE

James A. Sanders

It has long been recognized that the Lukan account of the uninvited woman who shows extravagant love and devotion to Jesus, in Lk. 7.36-50, is considerably different from the accounts of a similar episode related in Mk 14.3-9, Mt. 26.6-13, and Jn 12.1-8.[1] Gospel synopses usually offer two titles for the same accounts, 'The Anointing at Bethany' when the synopsis follows the other three accounts, but 'The Woman Who Was a Sinner' or 'The Woman with the Ointment' when the synopsis focuses on Luke.[2] Raymond Brown seems to lean, with Pierre Benoit, toward there having been two historical but similar episodes lying behind the differences.[3] Fitzmyer thinks of one tradition taking various forms in an early oral stage, a point Brown also allows.[4]

A third option needs to be kept open; Luke might possibly reflect primary contours of the episode which was interpreted by the others in terms of the beginnings of the Passion account.[5] At least two points

1.   See Raymond Brown's very helpful summary comparison of the four accounts in *The Gospel according to John I–XII* (AB, 29; Garden City: Doubleday, 1966), pp. 450-52. See also Joseph Fitzmyer's comparative comments in *The Gospel according to Luke I–IX* (AB, 28; Garden City: Doubleday, 1981), pp. 684-86; and C.S. Mann's *Mark* (AB, 27; Garden City: Doubleday, 1986), p. 555.

2.   See K. Aland's *Synopsis Quattuor Evangeliorum* (Stuttgart: Bibelanstalt, 1964), pp. 160-63, 361-63, 426-28; and A. Huck and H. Greeven, *Synopsis of the First Three Gospels* (Tübingen: Mohr, 1981), pp. 79-80, 232-34.

3.   A. Legault, 'An Application of the Form-Critique Method to the Anointings in Galilee and Bethany', *CBQ* 16 (1954), pp. 131-45.

4.   Brown, *John*, pp. 450-51; see Fitzmyer, *Luke*, p. 686.

5.   Robert Holst has argued that more rigorous form-critical method shows that Luke reflects the most primitive version; see 'The One Anointing Jesus: Another Application of the Form-Critical Method', *JBL* 95 (1976), pp. 443, 446.

in favor of entertaining this possibility are (1) slippage from anointing of the feet to anointing of the head is easier to explain than the reverse;[1] and (2) the abuse of the paraphrase of Deut. 15.11 in Mark, Matthew and John. The manner in which the latter is used to support the woman's anointing of Jesus (head in Mark and Matthew, feet in John) is totally divorced from its function in understanding the jubilee theme and does nothing to advance the Markan point about Jesus' acceptance of his anointing by the woman in preparation for his Passion; by contrast, the theme of jubilee release of debts/sins is integral to the Lukan account, which lacks the paraphrase.

If Luke knew Mark, or the others, he does not let knowledge of Mark's totally different points affect the power of meaning of jubilee for Jesus' ministry and teaching.[2] It is, of course, possible that Luke knew an early account similar to Mark's, and was encouraged by the paraphrase of Deut. 15.11 to pursue his jubilee interpretation of events reported and transmitted about Jesus, giving this episode its distinctive jubilee cast and thus taking it completely out of the Passion context of anointing. The two objections noted above are strong enough, however, to cause one to think rather that the traditioning movement was from a spontaneous act of adoration, cleansing Jesus' feet with tears and anointing them with oil, toward anointing his head with valuable oil made of pure nard in anticipation of his Passion, with the jubilee cast of the whole reduced, in misunderstanding, to Jesus' patently proof-text defense of the woman's act by paraphrase of Deut. 15.11.

Comparison of the four accounts shows that, in Luke, the woman's extravagance is expressed not in terms of the market value of the ointment but in terms of her spontaneous actions. In Luke there is no indignation shown on the part of others toward the woman's extravagance but rather toward Jesus' acceptance of her devotion.

Jesus' act of acceptance causes his host to question his authority as a prophet, a point Luke has carefully established by crowd and audience

---

1. See Holst, 'One Anointing', pp. 435-46; Brown supports the point (*John*, p. 451)

2. See my 'From Isaiah 61 to Luke 4', in *Christianity, Judaism and Other Greco-Roman Cults: Studies for Morton Smith at Sixty* (Leiden: Brill, 1975), Part 1, pp. 75-106. See also S.H. Ringe, *Jesus, Liberation, and the Biblical Jubilee* (Philadelphia: Fortress Press, 1985).

reactions to his teachings and miracles (4.32, 36, 37, 41, 44; 5.1, 15, 25, 26; 7.3, 6, 16, 17; cf. 8.1, 4, 34, 35, 39-40, 42; 9.43).[1] Jesus' quotation of the proverb, 'No prophet is acceptable in his own country', in the Nazareth sermon (4.24), however, anticipates the negative reactions to this point by Pharisees and other leaders (4.28-29; 5.21-22; 6.7-8). As in our story the doubts harbored by scribes and Pharisees, in contrast to the Nazareth congregation, have not yet been voiced; they are perceived by Jesus, however (5.22; 6.8; 7.39, 49), thus underscoring for the reader/hearer Jesus' prophetic power and authority.[2] The question of the Baptist concerning Jesus' identity (7.20) contrasts with the certainty of the demons' knowledge of Jesus' identity (4.34, 41) and contributes to the atmosphere of doubt created by the silent questioning of the leaders.

The narrational ploy of interjecting the leaders' doubts into the unfolding story of Jesus' perceived popularity permits Luke to underscore for the hearer/reader Jesus' prophetic powers of knowing their unexpressed thoughts; it is intensified in our story by the host's doubts about Jesus' knowledge of the identity of the woman, when it is he who doubts Jesus' identity. Indeed, Jesus shows no interest in convincing Simon of his own identity, in contrast to his later concern about the lack of faith by the questioning disciples (8.25). If he did so, he might simply have to admonish Simon not to tell, in the same manner in which he had rebuked the demons; and that would not advance the flow of the narrative at all. In fact, the host is probably to be understood as included in 'those seated together', in 7.49, who do not move from doubt to belief, but rather from doubt to offense taken at Jesus' expression of authority to forgive the woman's sins. This beautifully anticipates the very same move on the part of the leaders

1. See Robert Tannehill's insightful literary-redactional analysis of Jesus' quite different relations in the Lukan narrative to the oppressed, the crowds, the authorities and the disciples, *The Narrative Unity of Luke–Acts*. I. *The Gospel according to Luke* (Philadelphia: Fortress Press, 1986), pp. 101-274.

2. A point also stressed by D.A.S. Ravens in 'The Setting of Luke's Account of the Anointing: Luke 7.2–8.3', *NTS* 34 (1988), pp. 282-92. I agree with Ravens, against others, that our story is well placed in the flow of the Lukan narrative, but for more reasons than he offers; he is certainly right, however, that part of Luke's thesis in this crucial section of the Gospel before the journey to Jerusalem begins is that Jesus was the prophet expected and promised in Deut. 18.15, 18. This latter point is stressed convincingly by D. Moessner, *The Lord of the Banquet* (Minneapolis, MN: Fortress Press, 1989), pp. 45-79, 259-88.

generally as one moves through the central section into the Passion account.[1]

A marked difference between Luke's account of this episode and that of the other evangelists is the abuse of Deut. 15.11 in the latter, its total absence in Luke, but in its place a parable about what a truly charitable creditor might do when the jubilee year came around. The narrative of the episode of the uninvited woman, as Luke recounts it, hinges on the story within the story (7.40-43). The remarkable thing which the creditor did is not even mentioned in the story. Verse 42 might have read at some early point in the traditioning process: 'Since they could not repay, the creditor, instead of seeking a prosbul, graciously remitted both (debts)'. It is easily understood that as the traditioning of the story moved into more distinctly Gentile settings the technical detail of Jewish halachah would easily be omitted since it would probably raise unnecessary legal questions and detract from the point understood in any cultural setting, the creditors' release of the debts. It is also possible that in the same process, reference to Deut. 15.11 would be dropped, since its appearance in Mark, and perhaps his sources, was seen as impertinent and abusive of the jubilee legislation, and since the statement that the two debtors did not have the money to repay made the point about poor people still being around in a truly pertinent way.

The verb used twice in the inner story is *echarisato* from *charizomai* meaning freely remit or graciously grant. Luke had just used the verb (Mt. 11.2-6) in 7.21 in narrative preparation of Jesus' response to the question of the Baptist about Jesus' identity: 'and to many blind folk he granted sight'. Here Luke's Jesus says that the creditor 'graciously granted or remitted to both (debtors)', 'their debts' being understood. These are the three times Luke uses the verb in the Gospel. The other evangelists do not use it. He will use it four times in Acts, each time having the basic denotation of 'remit' or 'grant'. In Acts 3.14 he uses it in reference to the remittance or release of Barabbas.

charizomai does not appear in the Septuagint except in late texts; it undoubtedly came to be used in the place of the Septuagint's *aphiemi* which occurs with the noun *aphesis* five times in the jubilee legislation

---

1.   One of the marks of Luke's literary style is that of 'anticipation'; see Fitzmyer, *Luke*, pp. 207, 445, 518, 538, 632, *et passim*.

in Leviticus 25. *aphiemi* is used in the LXX to translate both **shamaṭ* and its derivatives in Deuteronomy 15, and **darar* and its derivatives in Leviticus 25, the two passages establishing jubilee legislation. Whether it was also used in the early traditioning stages of the story in Lk. 7.40-42 is difficult to say; but *charizomai* is a beautiful synonym for *aphiemi* in these contexts and apparently came to be used for forgiveness of debts as well as sins.[1] Luke uses *aphiemi* and derivatives four times in our passage but only in vv. 47-49 in terms relating to the forgiveness of sins—its most common usage in the New Testament.

Paraphrase of Scripture throughout Early Jewish literature was very common, and *charizomai* in 7.40-42 is an appropriate synonym for *aphiemi* in vv. 47-49, which in the New Testament most often pertains to remission, release or forgiveness of sins. The importance of jubilee themes to Luke's view of Jesus' mission and ministry was already signalled by Jesus' mixed citation of both Isa. 61.1 and 58.6 in Lk. 4.18.[2]

The legislation in Deuteronomy 15 includes exhortations to creditors to be generous toward fellow Israelites even and especially when the jubilee year approaches. While in 15.3-4 there is a promise that faithful remission of debts in the jubilee years would bring such divine blessings that there would be 'no poor among you', considerably more space is given to the exhortation not to be mean to a poor brother when the jubilee year draws near (Deut. 15.7-11). Within the parenesis is the statement that there would always be the poor in the land (v. 11); this is in contrast to the promise in v. 4 that faithful obedience to the jubilee legislation about remission of debts would bring divine blessing 'in the land which the Lord your God gives you by inheritance'. Leviticus 25 includes considerably more exhortation than Deuteronomy concerning generosity to the poor and obedience to the principles and stipulations of the jubilee.

When Jewish society moved into the more complex Hellenistic situations of an increasingly urban culture, loans became an intricate part of day-to-day commerce and not merely charitable sharing. Hillel is attributed with instigation of the institution of the prosbul (Hebrew

---

1. See Josephus, *Ant.* 6.7.4, 144, and the helpful note by Fitzmyer, *Luke*, p. 690.
2. Again see my 'From Isaiah 61 to Luke 4'.

prozbul, Greek *prosbole*), a sort of waiver, signed before a judge, in which a creditor could reserve the right to call in his loan regardless of the jubilee legislation.[1] Nearly every creditor would take advantage of the provision. Not to do so would have surely been rare indeed; but it could happen. Our inner story tells of a creditor who was generous and charitable enough to forgive two debts and hence not secure a prosbul.

Luke casts the story of the forgiveness of the sinful woman's many (*pollai*) sins in the light of the jubilee provision for the forgiveness of debts.[2] The woman did not have human creditors; at least we are told of none. On the contrary, she had means enough apparently to bring the myrrh with which she anointed Jesus' feet. Luke does not mention the market value of the ointment, but it is left to one's imagination about how she might have earned the money by which she might have bought it herself—a point lacking in the other Gospels where the woman's reputation is unmentioned. Possibly from one or more of the *synanakeimenoi* about the table?

Be that as it may, Jesus states that she loved *polu*. There has been a great deal of discussion trying to understand the force of Our Lord's description of the woman's activity. The force of Jesus' question to Simon after he had told the jubilee parable was to affirm that a heavy debtor would love the forgiving creditor more than one who had owed less (vv. 42-43); so Simon answered and so Jesus agreed. Commentators have puzzled, then, over Jesus' statement about how much the woman (had) loved. The exchange with Simon about the debtors would indicate that it was the woman's many 'loves' indicated by *polu*; but it surely also refers to the love and devotion she has on the scene shown toward Jesus. All three of the verbs for 'love' in the story are from *agapao*, which in koiné Greek had taken on many shades of meaning. It seems to be purposefully ambiguous in the received text, however it might have been in the early traditioning process. One aspect of the multivalency might be that 'little love' could refer to Simon's attitude or to the attitude of any of Jesus' antagonists in the fuller narrative Luke crafts.[3] Luke more than the

1. See *Shebi'it* 10.1-2, 3-4, 8-9.
2. The terms 'sin' and 'debt' are found in synonymous juxtaposition in 4QMess$_{ar}$; see Fitzmyer, *Luke*, pp. 223-24.
3. See Fitzmyer's comments, *Luke*, p. 692.

other evangelists stresses Jesus' offensive behavior, with just such
people as the uninvited woman, to the 'righteous', in contrast to his
great popularity and attraction for sinners and outcasts in society. He
indeed has just made a point of contrasting his behavior with that of
the Baptist's (7.31-35); the woman in that sense was indeed one of
Wisdom's children.[1]

The second suggestion of silent controversy, or offense taken by
those at the table, comes in v. 49: 'And those reclining at table began
to say among (to?) themselves, "Who is this who even forgives
(*aphiesin*) sins?"'. In contrast to Jesus' seeming acceptance by the
crowds, the religious leaders, the tradents of all the traditions about
God's grace, are the ones who must ask, 'Who is this that speaks blasphemies? Who can forgive sins but God only?' (5.21). God alone
forgives sins, but others are not infrequently commissioned by God to
announce divine forgiveness, such as members of the heavenly council
(MT Isa. 40.2), or priests (LXX Isa. 40.2), a herald (Isa. 61.1-2), John
the Baptist (Lk. 3.3), and others.[2] Jesus' pronouncement of forgiveness in 7.48 is simply, 'Your sins are forgiven (*apheontai*)'.[3]

The manner in which Jesus is presented as offending leaders elsewhere in the Gospel leads the reader/hearer to understand that Jesus
here is viewed as something more than simply herald. The cultural
and social history in which the persona of the sender is viewed as
incarnate in the one sent is too extensive and well known to document
here; this is especially the case where the one sent does not, with
socially acceptable signs of humility, make the distinction clear. Luke
leaves the whole scene pregnant with multivalency; he could not do

1. Moessner, *Lord*, p. 109.
2. See E.P. Sanders, *Jesus and Judaism* (London: SCM Press, 1985), p. 273.
Ravens ('Setting') citing Sanders, mistakenly assumes with LXX Isa. 40.6 that
40.2-5 refers to the prophet. The MT of Isa. 40.1-11 is a report of a meeting of the
heavenly council, including God's commission to its members to pronounce
forgiveness and salvation. The LXX resignified the whole scene to include priests
(40.2) and the prophet (40.6) as herald of the good news.
3. Undoubtedly a theological passive, 'forgiven' by God. See Fitzmyer's discussion of the frequency of such theocentric expressions in Luke, *Luke*, pp. 143-
258. See also the study in depth of passive forms in the Synoptic Gospels in
D.S. Deer, *Les constructions à sens passif dans le grec des évangiles synoptiques*
(Université des sciences humaines de Strasbourg, Faculté de théologie protestante,
1973).

otherwise, given the total story he has to tell. There is in the multi-valency, then, room for sympathy for the sensibilities of the fellow guests: 'Who is this fellow? He is popular as a teacher and healer. But does he think he is also God's herald?' The answer is yes; that role was established already at Nazareth in ch. 4, before the teaching and the healing started.

What Luke wanted to establish for the reader/hearer is that Jesus was indeed the one who was to come (7.20), the herald of the arrival of God's jubilee, God's acceptable year (Isa. 61.2a; Lk. 4.19) of release of sins. This was not simply a jubilee year indicated by the calendar; this was the introduction of God's jubilee, indeed God's kingdom of love, faith, salvation, peace and forgiveness (7.50). Responsible religious leaders of any society would have to be cautious about and skeptical of whoever presented himself on his own authority (4.21, 32, 36) as herald of God's jubilee, the long-awaited eschaton. Even modern religious leaders, academic or cleric, must in all honesty appreciate the multivalency of the passage, and find some reflection of their own humanity in the thoughts of Simon and his *synanakeimenoi*.

Like the prophets of old, whose role Luke insists Jesus assumed in his day with his people, Jesus went about challenging powerful sinners, the leaders with social and institutional responsibility. But in all the Gospels, and Luke's especially, Jesus is portrayed in addition as going about forgiving powerless sinners, like this marked woman. The one role got the prophets into trouble enough with the authorities of their day; but this added role of herald of the release of all debts to God, pronouncer of the forgiveness of sins and the introduction of a whole new order, had to be a serious threat to those who had given their lives to being responsible to the established order, even when it included the promises of hope that the new order would bring. Jesus presents a double offense precisely to those who have tried most to be responsible. Like the prophets of old, he forces responsible folk to identify with those in the past whom Nathan, Isaiah, Jeremiah, Ezekiel, Hosea, Amos and the others had addressed. That would be bad enough, but he also makes the same responsible folk face up to what divine grace really means, the strangeness of it, and the threat it harbors to established institutions in society, and to familiar modes of piety and practice.[1] The word Luke used to express the cancelation of

1.   See my 'The Strangeness of the Bible', *USQR* 42 (1988), pp. 33-37.

the two debts in 7.42-43 is based on the same root as the word 'grace', *charis*. Their debts were pronounced released, indeed graced out, and forgiven by the creditor. In like manner the sins of the uninvited woman Jesus pronounced released and forgiven by God. God's jubilee had arrived. 'Go in (to) peace.'[1]

It does not require great imagination to perceive how meaningful this story on its simplest level might have been to Luke's congregation. One possible question it might have answered would have been whether there was anyone back then when Jesus was alive who loved him the way they obviously loved him. To remain in The Way, and not to revert to Mithraism, the imperial cult, or even Judaism, particularly after the fall of Jerusalem in 70 CE, the apparent failure of the parousia, and the increasing persecution and rejection on all sides, meant that the little Christian remnant of Luke's day must indeed themselves have experienced a depth of faith that was undeniable and irrepressible. They would have many questions for a teacher like Luke. And one of those questions would surely have been something like the following. 'Teacher, was there anyone back then who loved him the way we would like to? Do you know of anyone who expressed directly to him what we ourselves feel? Was it one of the disciples? Was it a religious leader of the time?' No, Luke would have had to respond. None of those. But there was one, also rejected and misunderstood in normal society, who loved him quite extravagantly because she had found in him true release.

---

1. Most manuscripts read *eis eirēnēn* which was idiomatic and common enough; but D reads *en eirēnē*, which brings to mind the possibility that the other prepositional accusative expression bore with it the connotation of entering into peace, God's peace, not just into a momentary clear conscience, which might soon again be sullied. A good bit of Luke's Gospel from this point on depends on the reader/hearer clearly understanding that Luke believed that in Christ's coming, God's jubilee, or kingdom, had been introduced. Because of this, a new hermeneutic had been introduced in Jesus' teaching whereby to re-read and re-signify familiar Scripture passages and traditions; see, e.g., my 'The Ethic of Election in Luke's Great Banquet Parable', in *Essays in Old Testament Ethics (J. Philip Hyatt, in memoriam)* (ed. J.L. Crenshaw and J.T. Willis; New York: Ktav, 1974), pp. 245-71.

A 'FARCED EPISTOL' TO A SINKING SUN OF DAVID.
ECCLESIASTES AND *FINNEGANS WAKE*: THE SINOPTIC VIEW

Douglas A. Templeton

Dear Robert,

end of the making of many articles there is none, but Qoheleth you say, is a 'cuckoo' (1983: 196). (That is not all you say there, but it's all I'm saying here.)

'Vility of vilities', says Joyce (1975: 354), '. . . allasvitally. . . '

As Tertullian says (*de vel. virg.* 1), there is 'a time to everything'.

There is a time to 'escape otherwise than by death the last humiliation of an aged scholar, when his juniors conspire to print a volume of essays and offer it to him as a sign that they now consider him senile' (Collingwood 1938: 119).

There is a time (for you) to escape and a time (for me) to ensure the refraining from escaping. And there is a time for the senescent to make it clear that they are not senile. And for the senile to make it unclear that they are.

There is also a time to speak of Sheshonk of Libya (Gordis 1968: 9), but this is neither the time nor the place.

Consider the work of God:
For who can make that straight, which She hath made crooked?
Consider the nature of God:
For who is a crook, but She that hath made crooked?

Better is a dish of herbs where love is
than a stalled ox and BSE therewith.
A wise man's heart is at his right hand;
but the doctor's heart is on his left.
The sluggard says, 'There is a lion outside!
I shall be slain in the streets!'
The lion says, 'I have a sluggard inside!
For he came outside.'

A fool's voice comes with many words,
    and a scholar's voice with weariness of the flesh.

Remember now your Destroyer in the days of your age
        when the good days have past, and the good years have gone,
        when you said that you had pleasure in them.
Remember now your pit in the days of your age.

'Winter is icummen in,
Ludhe sing Goddam. . . ' (Pound, *cit*. Macdonald 1964: 330)

But were we to walk in the steppes of St Paul and the subjection (in Romans 8) of all things to vanity, then, yes, for 'corpse' (via 'hocus-pocus') becomes 'cropse' (Joyce), the
    Yours and hers,

P.S. 1. 'Please froggive my t'Emeritus and any inconvince that may have been caused by this litter' (Dixon V., in Beckett 1972: 194).
    2. There are disciplines within which problems occur and a discipline, or indiscipline, which is itself a problem. May I also have the 't'Emeritus' to say that it is the very great merit of *The Courage to Doubt* (Davidson 1983) that its concentration on problems has the further implication (is this fair?) that the context, the discipline, within which the problems arise is itself problematic. For how is the mind to manage, when it is called on to deal with 'the unmanageable' (*das Unverfügbare*)?
    This has the implication that any attempt to solve problems in this area may be such as to invite mirth. In 7.17-18, Job, you say (181), 'bursts forth into a bitter parody' of Psalm 8.4. What the psalmist asks is:

what is man that thou art mindful of him,
    and the son of man that thou dost care for him?

What the psalmist answers is:

thou hast made him little less than God,
    and dost crown him with glory and honour.

Job asks much the same question:

What is man that thou makest much of him
    and turnest thy thoughts towards him,

and goes on, to be sure, to speak of 'crowning', but of 'crowning' not in the psalmist's sense, but in the sense in which modern governments 'target' (I use their term [and Job's ('he set me up as his target' [16.12])]) the needy:

> only to punish him morning by morning
>   or to test him for every hour of the day?

Thus the Governor of the Universe is aligned with government; He/She 'sins', *sc.* 'misses the mark':

> 'I am like William Tell,' says the Lord. . .

> 'I am like William Tell's son,' says Job,
>   'but Abba cannot shoot straight any more.'

S/he has perhaps an aversion from apples.

A similar result is reached by the collocation of Psalm 139 as pretext with Job 23 as text:

> 'If I ascend to heaven, thou art there!' (Ps. 139.8).
> 'If I go forward, he is not there. . . ' (Job 23.8).

And then to 'forward', Job, for good measure, adds 'backward' and, not to be outdone, 'left' and 'right'. If this collocation is not eristic, it is perhaps dialectical: *simul revelatus et absconditus* (the latter with a vengeance).

Much theology richly invites, and indifferently, mirth or mourning, or both together; what Joyce would call the 'jocoserious'. And if Scripture parodies Scripture, does that not give Writing a licence (or license) to do the same? There are songs, of course, that give rise antiphonally to 'the song alongside the song' (the *Beigesang*), but also songs that evoke 'the song against the song' (the *Gegengesang*). And man being plural, with a legionary soul, both functions, singing alongside and against, can be fulfilled simultaneously and ambiguously. To which a third may be added: a song sung against itself, a text written against itself (and every other), a literary critical text that is also critical of the criticism; in a word, *self*-parody.

Parody can, it is true, be a crude weapon, can 'crown' an author not in the psalmist's sense, but in Job's; in the hands, say, of an Aristophanes, for 'when one is trying to make thousands of people laugh and applaud there is a limit to judiciousness' (Dover 1972: 186). But what of the poet at the breakfast table or the supper table? What would Aristophanes have said then? The fact that Aristophanes could be injudicious on the stage does not prove that he was not judicious off it. And *Northanger Abbey* crude? And *Tristram Shandy*?

And if an author is very wicked, the parody of that author may be no less than our duty, Qoheleth, say. There is no commentator on *The Preacher* who is not profoundly in the debt of the limpid and sardonic *aperçus* of Renan, for whom 'one reads badly when one reads on one's knees' (1882: 67), and if Renan is right, first, in saying that, when 'the haranguer' (Renan's word [1882: 10]) speaks of 'the sacrifice of fools' (Eccl. 5.1) and of the 'fool's voice (that) is known by multitude of words' (Eccl. 5.3), he is speaking of 'those madmen of the kingdom of God whose madness was to win the world' (Renan 1882: 61-62) and, second, in saying of the author that he was 'perhaps some great-grand-father of Annas or of Caiaphas', then short of defenestrating (if that is the *mot juste*) the cuckoo from the nest, the fate usually of the other fledglings, but believing rather with the rabbis, that 'both these and the others are the words of the Living God' (*b. Erub.* 13b and parallels, *cit.* Gordis 1968: 87), or, to moderate this rabbinic enthusiasm, that both *some* of these and *some* of the others are the words of the Living God, we are perhaps in honour bound, or at least transcendently free, to drive the odious aspects of the Preacher from their place in the sun and put them under a cloud, which is not at all the same thing as saying that the Preacher does not have some good lines: 'Go thy way, eat thy bread with joy, and drink thy wine with a merry heart; for God now accepteth thy works' (9.7). But some texts, some aspects of some texts offer a sure and certain pretext for parody, for a counter-song, for cachinnation.

But, as song-alongside, parody is a mode of appropriation of texts, a mode of literary criticism. All ancient texts deserve to be parodied, for all ancient texts have an ancient location, are composed according to curious conventions. If art, if theology is *mimesis*, their conventions are local; local and temporal, not to say temporary. The old register changes, giving place to new. And if these conventions are to be understood, they may need to be transposed into a different key. The arms of Molly Bloom differ (though not *totaliter aliter*) from the arms of Penelope. The fall of Finnegan, the 'foenix culprit', the *felix culpa* in Phoenix Park, the fall of Humphrey Chimpden Earwicker (= HCE = Here Comes Everybody = Everyman = Adam) is narrated differently from Genesis, or rather guenesis (for the living have their beginning in guinness, as the dead in whisky).

It is arguable that parody, as a species of the genus comedy, replicates no less successfully than tragedy the essence of Christianity. Qoheleth is happy to recommend the enjoyment of wine, women (or a woman, if you can find one) and the wearing of white. He seems less happy to recommend the parameters within which wine, women and white clothes occur: 'that which befalleth the sons of men befalleth beasts' (3.19). Paul of Tarsus is not much celebrated as a comic writer, but his turning of a handful of dust into 'the glorious liberty of the children of God' (Rom. 8.21) is a move in the right direction. Similarly, the ending of *Ulysses* with a word no less affirmative than 'Yes' and of *Finnegans Wake* with a word no less definite than the article, 'the', unless the Viconian circle, the *ricorso* from Theocratic age through Heroic to Human and back again (Beckett 1972: 4), is vicious, implies that in our end is our beginning, something more perhaps than that *Finnegans Wake*, steeped in intellection as it is, may not be fully intelligible the first time through. 'Wake' is not only noun; like Jesus it is verb; or one has a licence to go on talking (for other reasons and) in praise of the 'redeeming fish' (Tindall 1959: 252), the 'brontoichthyan' (Tindall 1959: 266), though I dare say that we should remember that Joyce turned down a project for work in South Africa on the grounds of the prevalence there of thunder. But, all that said, we may learn, with Agathon in the *Symposium*, that the tasks of tragedian and comedian converge. There are non-negligible senses in which Ecclesiastes tells the truth.

Not one word of the Bible is usable as such. To be used a word must be appropriated. If a pretext is to become a text, if someone else's text is to become my text, it must, at least in some sense (what sense?), be re-written. Or is to say so much no more than a cavalier and irresponsible admission? But a cavalier is a knight. Why not be one? And it is hardly irresponsible to claim that a text that somehow arrived onto paper must somehow arrive off it. Commentary and parody are twin aids to enable this parousia.

But this is not to say that there are not two distinguishable, though I think inseparable, questions: (1) What are you responding to? And (2) what is your response? Then, further, why is your response what it is? To what degree is your response more than the mere replication of the text to which you are responding? And does this 'more than', this excess, assist in clarifying the text responded to? Or is this 'more than' a new text? If a new text, does it relate in any way to the old one?

Ecclesiastes, itself a text, is a response to earlier texts (Davidson 1983), of which it offers a critique. These earlier texts give him a pretext for offering his own views. When he comes to the government, he seems overly inclined to the prudential: 'Curse not the king, no not in thy thought. . . For a bird of the air shall carry the voice. . . ' But on the whole the comments of 'this Sadducean' (Renan 1882: 25) are not without a certain validity. By speaking of being 'distracted from distraction by distraction' (*perispasm* is the Septuagint's word for it, Qoheleth's estimate of academic life under the conditions then prevailing [*per impossibile*, one might think]), he fastens on an authentic moment of a complex whole which would not be exhaustively described without it, however inexhaustively that complex would be described with only it and no more moments at all. Man cannot live by Ecclesiastes alone, but by every book that has ever been written—Ernst Käsemann, much given to them himself, would call this a daring thesis (*eine gewagte These*), but the doctrine of the *logos* has, I think, as one of its correlates, the inability to stop talking. A *corpus*, the Hebrew Bible, without this component, Ecclesiastes, would be as halt as a commentary on it without *Vanity Fair* would be claudicant: 'As the Manager of the Performance sits before the curtain on the boards, and looks into the Fair, a feeling of profound melancholy comes over him in his survey of the bustling place' (Thackeray n.d.: 1). Beckett (1972: 4) may be right to insist that 'literary criticism is not book-keeping', but it may be right nevertheless to insist that the commentator should keep more books about him, even if 'a trouble is that something in which everything involves everything else demands notice of everything at once', a fine definition, or rather *in*finition, of theology—thus Tindall (1959: 237) on a demand 'to which Joyce' (*sc.* in *Finnegans Wake*) 'was equal'; his members ran in parallelism with his task. But what other course, or recourse, or *ricorso*, is open to the theologian, if God is 'the cipher or emblem of the undefined openness of our researches' (Jossua 1989: 7)?

Not one word of the Bible is usable as such? What Augustine read after his *sume, lege* ('not in rioting and drunkenness, not in chambering and wantonness. . . ' [Rom. 13.13-14]) might be thought to be an exception to this. Did not Augustine use his text directly? No, he did not. A text needs a context in the reader's mind as a seed needs a soil. There is no lotus without dung, as there is no brass without muck. The whole of the *Confessions* is, in a sense, what the French call *explication du texte*, but there is a great deal in them which is not in Rom. 13.13-14. In other words, that, as Ebeling somewhere claims, the history of the church is the history of the interpretation of Scripture is only true if the history of the church is the interpretation of a great many other things besides. And after these great many other things have been named, there remains, perhaps, the un-nameable element, the element of the *je ne sais quoi*, the element, indifferently, of wind (*ruach*) or mere vapour (*hebel*). The claim, one might as well say, is untrue. A churchman, a human being, is not a rower in a skull, but the coxswain of an eight. One does not face the future by looking backwards.

But my speech bewrayeth me, for a coxswain only gets forward, because he, or as we must nowadays say 'her', has eight good men, or persons, and true, who are looking backwards. And 'without a firm and solid grip on the past out of which we have come, there can be no order, no clear line, and thus no future' (Smith 1970: 28-29).

> As we there are where are we are we there from tomtittot to teetootom-totalitarian. Tea tea too oo.
>   Whom will comes over. Who to caps ever. And howelse do we hook our hike to find that pint of porter place? Am shot, says the big-guard.
>   Whence. Quick lunch by our left, wheel, to where. . . (Joyce 1975: 260).

To still the cry of the Ethiopian eunuch in his attempt to process the word (to Philip's 'Understandest thou what thou readest?' the eunuch replies: 'How can I, except some man should guide me?' [Acts 8.30-31]). Joyce has helpfully here the marginal comment (*inter alia* [*et obscuriora*]): UNDE ET UBI. None of the three 'ecstases of time' (Heidegger) may safely be ignored by the man of sense. My point here is rather to stress the importance of the present moment in the reading of texts (is the future, too, involved? How?) with the further claim that a parodic reading *is* a reading: 'My intention', writes Joyce (1957: 146-47, *cit.* Tindall 1959: 132), 'is to transpose the myth' (he means the *Odyssey*, for *Ulysses*) '*sub specie temporis nostri*', much as Aquinas transposes the Christian myth with the help of Aristotle, and Bultmann with the help of Heidegger, unless these two, Aquinas and Bultmann, were not interpreting an old one, but producing a new, if the distinction between interpretation and production makes any sense at all.

But there is a further reason why we should be given to mirth and parody, a reason less admirable than real. And this is because McAdamson, or Humphrey Chimpden Earwicker, combining in himself, camel, monkey and insect, is, we might say, much given to blasphemy, incest (or 'the loyal desire to keep sex in the family' [Burgess 1966: 7]) and eating apples, or more baldly speaking, to 'total depravity'. For if it is true on the one hand at any rate that he has been made little lower than the angels, it is true on the other that he has been made little higher than the devils. It is neither surprising that such a malicious creature should be given, where others are concerned, to the taunt-song nor that, where himself is concerned, he should wish to laugh because he does not wish to weep, though as both unacceptable and accepted, as pronounced innocent though guilty, he will, no doubt, be much given to both. Some like the lament; laughter loves others (we may compare: 'I didn't sneeze, it sneezed me' or Heidegger's *die Sprache spricht,* 'language talks'). For laughter is a transcendental, which comedians 'invent' (in the etymological sense of that word), they *find* it and *it* finds *them.*

But parody today has a more mysterious cause. It has something to do with the *Zeitgeist,* a mystery from the explanation of which Macdonald (1964: xv) resiles. But 'we are backward-looking explorers and parody is a central expression of our times' (Macdonald 1964: xv, *cit.* Hutcheon 1985: 1 [but *cit.* not quite accurately; she substitutes the definite for the indefinite article]). The 'incorporation and inversion' (Hutcheon 1985: 5) of *pre*-texts or prior texts is the game. It is 'reverberation' and 'reapplication' (the terms are Beckett's [1972: 5]) that does justice or makes love to the literature of the past, though the literature of the past, while it can be read *in* the present, can never be the literature *of* the present. Parody is *one* mode by which it may enter the present.

3. Having, however, 'dumptied (this) wholeborrow of rubbages on to soil here' ('Where the bus stops, there shop I' [Joyce, *cit.* Burgess 1966: 22]), it is time to summon 'Taciturn, our wrong-story shortener' (Joyce: 1975: 17). *Tacebo.*

4. 'Grant sleep in hour's time, O Loud!' (Joyce 1975: 259). *Tacui. Paene.*

5. στὸ καλὸ νὰ πᾶτε, go to the beautiful, ὥστε... ἀνεπι κωλύτως προκόπτειν τὴν πρὸς τὸ κυρίως καλὸν ἔφεσιν [ὑμῶν], 'so that your longing for what is properly speaking beautiful should

advance without let' (how Maximus the Confessor, and his friends [Lucà 1983: 3], would have loved that!)

BIBLIOGRAPHY

Beckett, S. *et al.*
1972   *Our Exagmination Round his Factification for Incamination of Work in Progress.* London: Faber & Faber.
Burgess, A.
1966   *A Shorter Finnegans Wake.* London: Faber & Faber.
Collingwood, R.G.
1938   *An Autobiography.* Oxford: Oxford University Press.
Davidson, R.
1983   *The Courage to Doubt.* London: SCM Press.
Dover, K.J.
1972   *Aristophanic Comedy.* London: Batsford.
Ellmann, R.
1959   *James Joyce.* New York: Oxford University Press.
1972   *Ulysses on the Liffey.* London: Faber & Faber.
Gilbert, S.
1952   *James Joyce's Ulysses.* London: Faber & Faber.
Gordis, R.
1968   *Qoheleth—The Man and his World.* New York: Schocken Books.
Hutcheon, L.
1985   *A Theory of Parody.* London: Methuen.
Jossua, J.-P.
1989   *Le Dieu de la foi chrétienne.* Paris: Cerf.
Joyce, J.
1957   *Letters,* I. Ed. S. Gilbert. London: Faber & Faber.
1975   *Finnegans Wake.* London: Faber & Faber.
Lucà, S.
1983   *Anonymi Auctoris 'Catenarum Trium Patrum' Opera.* Leuven: Leuven University Press, Brepols-Turnhout.
Macdonald, D.
1964   *Parodies.* London: Faber & Faber.
Renan, E.
1882   *L'Ecclésiaste.* Paris: Calmann Lévy.
Smith, R.G.
1970   *The Doctrine of God.* London: Collins.
Thackeray, W.M.
n.d.   *Vanity Fair.* Ed. G. Saintsbury. Oxford: Oxford University Press.
Tindall, W.Y.
1959   *A Reader's Guide to James Joyce.* London: Thames & Hudson.

BIBLIOGRAPHY OF ROBERT DAVIDSON

1957–1965

a. *Books*

The Service of God: Studies in Jeremiah (Edinburgh: St Andrew Press, 1957).

The Bible Speaks (London: Skeffington, 1959 [American edition: New York: T.Y. Crowell, 1959]).

This book was the American Religious Book Club choice in January 1960.

Le message de la bible (Paris: Editions Meddens, 1962 [French edition of *The Bible Speaks*]).

The Old Testament (London: Hodder & Stoughton, 1964 [American edition: Philadelphia: Lippincott, 1964]).

b. *Articles and Contributions to Books*

'The Religion of Israel', in *The Bible Companion* (ed. W. Neil; London: Skeffington, 1959), pp. 161-75.

'Some Aspects of the Old Testament Contribution to the Patterns of Christian Ethics', *SJT* 12 (1959), pp. 373-87.

'Universalism in Second Isaiah', *SJT* 16 (1963), pp. 166-85.

'Orthodoxy and the Prophetic Word: A Study in the Relationship between Jeremiah and Deuteronomy', *VT* 14 (1964), pp. 407-16.

'The Old Testament in the Roman Catholic Church', *Biblical Theology* 14 (1964), pp. 1-13.

'The Old Testament and the Christian Faith: The Contemporary Debate', *St Mary's College Bulletin* 7 (1965), pp. 10-16.

1966–1975

a. *Books*

Sacrifice and Service—Four Bible Studies (Ninth International Conference of the World Federation of Deaconess Associations; Edinburgh, 1966).

Biblical Criticism (Pelican Guide to Modern Theology, III; with A.R.C. Leaney; Harmondsworth: Penguin Books, 1970).

Genesis 1–11 (Cambridge Bible Commentaries; Cambridge: Cambridge University Press, 1973).

The Bible Speaks (Edinburgh: St Andrew Press, repr. 1974).

b. *Articles and Contributions to Books*

'The Interpretation of Isaiah II.6ff', *VT* 16 (1966), pp. 1-7.

'Faith and History in the Old Testament', *ExpTim* 77 (1966), pp. 100-103.

'Some Aspects of the Theological Significance of Doubt in the Old Testament', *Annual of the Swedish Theological Institute* 7 (1968–69), pp. 41-52.

'In the Beginning', 'The Patriarchs', and 'Moses', in *A Source Book of the Bible for*

Teachers (ed. R.C. Walton; London: SCM Press, 1970), pp. 96-113.
'The Old Testament and the Fourth R', *New College Bulletin* 6 (1971), pp. 16-26.

c. *Journalism*
'The Old Testament for Today'—A series of twelve articles for the Church of Scotland Journal, *Life and Work*, January–December, 1974.

1976–1985
a. *Books*
Genesis 12–50 (Cambridge Bible Commentaries; Cambridge: Cambridge University Press, 1979).
The Bible in Religious Education (Edinburgh: Handsel Press, 1979).
Constantin von Tischendorf and the Greek New Testament (with M. Black; Glasgow: Glasgow University Press, 1981).
Jeremiah I (1–20) (Daily Study Bible: Edinburgh: St Andrew Press, 1983).
The Courage to Doubt (London: SCM Press, 1983).

b. *Articles and Contributions to Books*
'The Old Testament—A Question of Theological Relevance', in *Biblical Studies in Honour of William Barclay* (ed. J.R. McKay and J.F. Miller; London: Collins, 1976), pp. 28-43.
'A Guide to Translations of the Bible', in *Resources* (Edinburgh: Church of Scotland Education Department, 1976), pp. 5-11.
'Biblical Classics: V. George Adam Smith: Preaching the OT', *ExpTim* 90 (1979), pp. 100-104.
'Theology in Prospect' (Aberdeenshire Theological Club Century Lecture), *Aberdeen Divinity Bulletin* 24 (1983), pp. 2-8.
'God—A Journey to Discovery', *The Furrow* (October 1984), pp. 616-21.
'What is Faith—An Old Testament Perspective', *Methodist Review* (October 1985).

c. *Journalism*
'The Old Testament for Today' (New Series), *Life and Work* (September 1976–February 1977).
'The Psalms and Worship', *Life and Work* (October 1980–February 1981).
'The World of the Old Testament', *Life and Work* (February–September 1985).

1986–1990
a. *Books*
Jeremiah II (21–52) and Lamentations (Daily Study Bible; Edinburgh: St Andrew Press, 1986).
Ecclesiastes and Song of Solomon (Daily Study Bible; Edinburgh: St Andrew Press, 1986).
Soseiki (trans. Y. Ohno; Tokyo: Shinkyo Shuppan-sha, 1986). (Japanese translation of Genesis 1–11 and 12–50.)
Christian Faith in a Nuclear Age (Edinburgh: Handsel Press, 1989).
The Courage to Doubt (American Edition) (Philadelphia: Trinity Press International, 1989).
Wisdom and Worship (London: SCM Press; Philadelphia: Trinity Press International, 1990).

c. *Journalism*
'How to Listen to the Bible', *Life and Work* (October 1987–July 1988).

INDEXES

INDEX OF REFERENCES

OLD TESTAMENT

PSEUDEPIGRAPHA

QUMRAN SCROLLS

RABBINIC WRITINGS

INDEX OF AUTHORS

JOURNAL FOR THE STUDY OF THE OLD TESTAMENT

Supplement Series

DATE DUE

FEB 07 1995			
APR 14 1995			
DEC 15 1999			
MAR 07 2002			